# THE STRUCTURE OF
# LOCAL GOVERNMENT IN
# ENGLAND AND WALES

# The Structure of
# Local Government in
# England and Wales

### W. ERIC JACKSON
*LL.B., Barrister-at-law*
*Assistant Clerk of the London County Council*

**GREENWOOD PRESS, PUBLISHERS**
WESTPORT, CONNECTICUT

**Library of Congress Cataloging in Publication Data**

Jackson, William Eric.
  The structure of local government in England and Wales.

  Reprint of the 4th ed. published by Longmans, London.
  Includes index.
  1. Local government--England. 2. Local government
--Wales. I. Title.
JS3111.J3 1976       352.042      74-29792
ISBN 0-8371-8001-5

*Fourth Edition © W. Eric Jackson 1960*
*First published 1949*
*Second Edition (with Addenda*
*to the end of 1953) 1954*
*Third Edition (with Addenda*
*to the end of 1956) 1957*
*Fourth Edition 1960*

The London County Council
accepts no responsibility for the
author's opinions and conclusions

This edition originally published in 1960 by Longmans, London

Reprinted with the permission of Longman Group Limited

Reprinted in 1976 by Greenwood Press,
a division of Williamhouse-Regency Inc.

Library of Congress Catalog Card Number 74-29792

ISBN 0-8371-8001-5

Printed in the United States of America

# Contents

# Author's Preface

LOCAL GOVERNMENT is in a state of flux. Like other human organizations it has, of course, never remained completely static, and has undergone continuous change since its inception as part of the national framework. Local government is largely concerned with the administration of public services, and as new needs, new methods and new ideas emerge and develop, the system must inevitably be adjusted to meet the changing conditions.

In the last hundred years or so, the alterations which have taken place in the local government system of this country have been very considerable. In the early part of the nineteenth century the administration of the local services which then existed was largely in the hands of the local justices of the peace, assisted by parish vestries and officers—surveyors, overseers and constables. Most of the main roads were maintained by bodies of turnpike trustees. Numerous small local bodies of commissioners attended to the paving of local streets and the management of sewers. The ancient boroughs were, so far as local services were concerned, largely inefficient and moribund.

From 1834 onwards tremendous changes and developments have taken place, many experiments have been tried, many reforms instituted, many ideas have been adopted and many abandoned. The public services undertaken in the field of local government have been increased in number and vastly enlarged in scope. Numerous Royal Commissions have been set up and have reported. Poor Law Commissioners, a Central Board of Health, a Local Government Board have been created and superseded. The administrative powers of the justices and of the vestries and local commissioners have been transferred to other newly created authorities, some of which in turn have themselves been displaced by others; the ancient boroughs have been reformed and many abolished and a number of new ones brought into being. The organization of poor relief has been successively transferred from parish vestries to Boards of Guardians and from them to county and county borough councils, and is now taken over by a national authority. Education and public health services have been greatly developed, and the administrative authorities for these services have been much varied. All this has occurred in not much more than a hundred years.

The tempo of these changes in a relatively short space of time makes a striking comparison with the other governmental institutions of this country. The central government organization of Crown, Lords and Commons seems, in comparison with the organization of local government, to have remained in its outward form, in a state of traditional stability. The relations between the Crown and Parliament have been more or less settled for the past two hundred years. The relations between the two Houses of Parliament have undergone important changes, a number of new departments have arisen, and the procedure of Parliament has been altered to suit changing needs and conditions, but there has not been any continued series of radical alterations in the parliamentary structure to compare with the numerous developments which have taken place in the sphere of local administration. Our present system of local government and the series of authorities operating it—county councils, county, non-county and metropolitan borough councils, urban and rural district councils and parish councils, together with the number of *ad hoc* bodies carrying out particular local services—are with few exceptions less than a hundred years old, and those among them that can claim ancient origin have been subject to a number of vital reforms.

Even so, a condition of stability has not yet been reached. New ideas are being canvassed. Local government areas are under review by Local Government Commissions. Adjustments of powers and duties are continually in prospect. The future for all classes of local authority is uncertain.

Why is this? Why has there been and why is there still this state of fluidity in the sphere of local government? It is due in the first place to the great changes which have occurred in our mode of life since the industrial revolution, with the growth of the towns, and the consequent need for proper sanitary services, housing, town-planning, and urban amenities.

It is due in the second place to the enlargement of the social conscience, to the demand for national efficiency and to the increasing concern of the state for the welfare of the people. Education, medical and hospital services, public transport and other utility services have thus become matters of governmental concern. It is due also to the fact that technical achievements have made possible an improved standard of living so that what were once regarded as luxuries (piped pure water, main drainage and well-surfaced roads, for example) are now regarded as necessities.

These causes have prompted an urge for change which has not come to an end. Presumably the urge will continue as human capacity enlarges and as ideologies develop. Social and economic adjustments of one kind or another will always be taking place. To meet them, alterations in the public services and in the mode of their administration will need to be made. The functions and processes of local government will continue to evolve, like a living organism, because its main concern is with living beings, with human mental and physical welfare.

The system of local government, concerned as it is with numerous matters of intimate effect on the lives, homes and work of the people, is always an appropriate subject of study. Such a study is even more in point at a time when the system is in process of intense and rapid development. An examination of what the system is, what it does, and of the way it does it, should serve to clarify its underlying principles and purposes.

The object of this book is accordingly to examine the existing forms of local government in England and Wales, and the various types of local authority, their purposes and operation, in the hope that this examination may assist towards an understanding of the various considerations which influence the development of the system.

# Preface to Fourth Edition

THE numerous and important changes in local government law, falling within the scope of this book, which have
taken place since the issue of the first edition (many of
which were in later editions mentioned in the form of
addenda) have now been dealt with in the main text.
Each chapter has been completely revised with a view to
bringing the present edition fully up to date (June 1960).

# Introduction

THE term 'local government' as applied to England and Wales is hardly capable of precise definition. The term has, of course, certain implications. Local government is concerned with localities and not with the country as a whole; it must for this reason be subordinate to the national government. The term further implies (as does any other form of government) some jurisdiction or activity of a public nature; it implies also the existence of authorities empowered to exercise that jurisdiction and activity.

A simple approach to the understanding of the term is obtained by a perusal of the two principal modern Acts of Parliament which deal with local government generally, the Local Government Act, 1933, and the London Government Act, 1939. These two Acts describe the constitution of several classes of public body concerned with local government.

The Act of 1933 starts off by stating that 'for the purpose of local government England and Wales (exclusive of London) shall be divided into administrative counties and county boroughs'. The term 'local government' is not defined in the Act. The Act goes on to say that the administrative counties shall be divided into county districts; these county districts are to be either 'non-county boroughs' (to distinguish them from the county boroughs), urban districts or rural districts. The Act further provides that county boroughs and county districts shall consist of one or more parishes.

Thus for England and Wales outside London there are laid down, for local government purposes, six types of area—the county borough, the administrative county, the non-county borough, the urban district, the rural district, and the parish.

The Act largely excludes London because London has a separate set of arrangements. These are described in the London Government Act, 1939. There is an administrative county of London, which is composed of the City of London and twenty-eight metropolitan boroughs.

These two Acts also provide for each administrative county

to have its county council, each borough (whether county, non-county or metropolitan) its borough council, each urban and rural district its urban district council or rural district council as the case may be, and for the establishment of parish councils for rural parishes. The City of London has its own special constitution which includes a 'Court of Common Council'.

All these local councils have two features in common. First of all, they are publicly elected periodically by the people of the area (county, borough, district or parish) which the council represents.

Second, they all depend to a large extent for their finances on the local taxes (known as rates) levied on occupiers of property in the area. The amount of the rates collected in each locality depends to a considerable degree on the expenditure of the local council. Great expenditure tends to put the rates up, low expenditure tends to keep the rates down. Since the rates are paid by the people in the area of the council, that is, by the people who have elected the council, there is local financial responsibility as between council and electors.

All these councils have concern in varying measure with local government. It is appropriate to use, in relation to them, the term 'local government authority' to distinguish them from other types of local authority.

The functions of local government can be broadly divided into two main groups, namely (i) functions of control over the activities of private citizens, and (ii) the provision of public services.

In the first main group—functions of control—is the power to make by-laws. All the local councils have this power. The extent of the power and the matters in relation to which it may be exercised vary considerably. By-laws are a form of local legislation and (like other laws) are designed to regulate the conduct of members of the public. Penalties may be imposed for non-compliance.

County councils and borough councils may, for instance, make by-laws for good rule and government. Disorderly behaviour, street noise, and the defacing of public notices are the type of subject dealt with. Those councils which manage public property, such as a park, a swimming-bath or a mortuary, may make by-laws to regulate the management of those places. By-laws may also be made to regulate the conduct of certain businesses, such as fried fish shops and various offensive trades. Another important subject on which by-laws are made is the stability of buildings, the manner of their construction and the strength of the materials to be used in them.

Another example of functions of control is the issue of certificates or licences without which certain activities are not allowed to be carried on. Establishments such as cinemas, music halls, nursing homes and lodging-houses, may not be carried on without the proper authorization of the appropriate local council; this authorization is not given unless the person in charge of the establishment complies with conditions laid down by the authorizing council as to the management and suitability of the premises.

Weights and measures used in trade are illegal unless duly tested and approved by the appropriate local council; certain local councils test the quality of the food and drugs supplied by local traders; the duty of inspecting shops to see if the hours of closing and the hours of work of shop assistants are duly observed is also a function of some local councils; and in these various cases the council concerned may take appropriate steps.

A great many local councils have power to deal with the suppression of nuisances which offend against public health, with dangerous structures, the clearance of slums, and the planning of towns.

All these are examples of the manner in which local councils may control what goes on in their areas. These functions represent their truly governmental duties and powers.

The provision of public services (the second main group of local government functions) is not strictly speaking a governmental function, that is, in so far as government is to be regarded as the regulation of the conduct of private citizens. Modern governments, however, do not restrict themselves to government in this limited sense. The governments of civilized countries make it their concern not only to restrain by guidance or control the activities of their subjects, but also to provide for the public welfare by the establishment of systems of education, of sanitation, of roads and other services.

With this aspect of government, local authorities have much to do. The practice in this country is for the central government to distribute among the local government authorities in varying measure a large share of the work of providing these public services; the expense is shared by the central government (out of national revenues) and by the local authorities concerned (out of the local rates or out of fees and charges collected for the service provided); the local councils have the duty of providing the service in their own locality and the necessary buildings, works, equipment, and staff, subject to a general supervision and influence from the central government. In this way there is an alliance between local interest and national policy. The local council contributes its knowledge of local wants and conditions, and bears its share of the responsibility for the cost; the central government contributes its stimulus or restraint with a view to ensuring a general overall standard of efficiency throughout the country, and for some purposes helps with a financial contribution.

In addition to the series of local councils, which have the common features of public election and dependence upon local rates, there are a number of other bodies operating in local areas throughout the country and having functions which are similar to or allied with the functions of those councils.

In the Metropolitan Police District the police service is administered by a Commissioner—an appointee of the Crown. The City of London has its own police force. Police services throughout the country outside these areas are organized on the basis of administrative counties and boroughs. In county boroughs the authority responsible locally for the administration of the borough police is a special watch committee of the borough council. In administrative counties the county police authority is a standing joint committee composed of representatives of the county council and of the county justices. The cost of the local police forces is borne out of local rates, with subventions from the central government.

The groups of justices of the peace for counties and boroughs have, in addition to the duty of dealing with offences against the law, certain non-judicial or administrative functions. In some parts of the country the local justices have the power to license premises for public music and dancing (a function which in other parts is performed by the local government authority). The justices also issue licences for the sale of intoxicating liquor. Local government authorities have an intimate concern in the work of the justices, in that the expense of providing courts and staff for the justices is borne out of county or borough funds. Moreover, it is usual for the clerk of a county council (outside London), and, in some boroughs, the clerk of the borough council (or town clerk) to be also the clerk of the peace in which capacity he acts as general secretary and adviser to the justices.

In some localities joint boards and joint committees have been set up, representing two or more local councils, to carry on, within the combined area of those councils, some particular public service which can more conveniently and economically be carried on in that way rather than by the individual councils acting separately. These joint authorities are not directly elected by the public; their membership is usually made up of representatives appointed by the constituent councils. Their finances may be derived from fees and charges for the service they provide, from contributions from the constituent local authorities, and in some cases, from the central government.

In addition to these joint bodies there are a number of special local authorities created for particular purposes such as the management of harbours and docks, the drainage of land and the protection and control of fisheries. The membership of this type of special local body is made up in various ways. Sometimes a number of the members are appointed by the central government, sometimes the body is elected by the persons receiving the benefit of the services provided by the authority, sometimes the local government authorities appoint the members. Sometimes these various methods of appointment are used in combination. It is to be noticed that, in every case, although the body is not directly elected by the general public, it does contain some representation of the general public interest or of the interests of the persons served or affected by the operations of the body. Thus a land drainage board is composed of representatives elected by the landowners in the area of the board's operations; a harbour authority may have members elected by the users of the port as well as members nominated by a government department. The finances of this type of special authority are generally derived from fees, charges, dues or contributions paid by the persons receiving the benefit of the service provided.

The pattern of local administration in England and Wales is further complicated by the fact that the sphere of operations of local authorities in providing for certain public needs coincides with or overlaps that of private enterprise, and is closely related also to that field of public enterprise which has become, by the nationalization of certain public services, reserved to the central government.

For example, housing and education may be provided both by local authorities and by private bodies or persons. And so may entertainments, restaurants, art galleries, games facilities, certain medical services and provision for the aged and afflicted.

The overlapping of the respective fields of local government and private enterprise is however, less than it formerly was, particularly in relation to the public utility services such as the supply of electricity, gas and piped water. These services, capable as they are of being run at a profit, were, in the early days of their development, provided largely by commercial companies who were given statutory powers to break open streets, lay mains, and do other things necessary for carrying on the service. When in due time the services gained greater acceptance and came to be regarded as 'essential services', local government authorities were empowered to provide them or take over the undertakings of the commercial enterprises. Thus both local authorities and commercial companies became 'statutory undertakers' each operating in their own defined areas with an exclusive right to provide the particular service, subject to limitations as regards prices and profits. The areas of operations for these particular services did not necessarily correspond with local government areas. Whether a particular service in any locality was run by a public authority or a commercial company depended on local circumstances. In some localities all these public utility services were provided entirely by the local government authority.

The Electricity Act, 1947, and the Gas Act, 1948, removed two of these services from the sphere of commercial and local government enterprise and placed them under national control. Local area boards are appointed to manage the services in areas defined for the purpose and which are by no means co-incident with the area of any one local government authority.

Water supply has not been nationalized, and this service is in some localities in the hands of public authorities and in other localities is provided by commercial undertakers.

Under the National Health Service Act, 1946, hospital services formerly provided by local authorities and private voluntary bodies have been transferred to the central government and are managed by Regional Boards, appointed by the Minister of Health. Certain local health services remain, however, with local government authorities. Nursing homes and certain ancillary activities related to medical care may be provided by private persons or charitable bodies.

The relief of the poor is now, by the National Assistance Act, 1948, a national responsibility. Relief in money or in kind is provided by the National Assistance Board, while institutional accommodation is provided by local government authorities. Private charitable bodies may still operate.

The domain of local government is accordingly not easily definable, for it merges into the realms of both private enterprise and government ownership. Local government forms only a part of the scheme of local arrangements for carrying out needed services.

The word 'government' when used in relation to local authorities takes on a peculiar character different from that which the word has when used in the phrase 'national government'.

The functions of government consist in the giving of directions and in seeing that they are carried out. The giving of directions is a legislative act. The carrying of them out may involve the organization of arrangements for the purpose (administrative functions) as well as their actual performance (executive functions).

Thus, the government of Great Britain is composed of a body of Ministers acting under the authority and direction of Parliament. Parliament is the legislative assembly. It makes laws, issues directions, confers duties, and sanctions the raising and spending of public money. But having authorized certain action it leaves to others the taking of that action. The functions of Parliament contain little that is executive. Members of Parliament, as such, do not personally engage in the management of the public services. Parliamentary time is not, however, taken up entirely by the making of legislation. Parliament concerns itself in administration by examining and discussing the state of the nation and the conduct of its affairs. Parliament is, none the less, eminently a legislative organ.

The administrative and executive functions of national government are exercised by the Ministers of State, or by the government departments under their direction. The organization and management of the armed forces and the postal services are performed in this way. Certain other branches of public work are carried on by special national bodies such as the Forestry Commission, the War Damage Commission, and the British Transport Commission. Each Ministry, Commission or other body is administrative in so far as it makes its own organizational arrangements and supervises them, and is executive in so far as it actually provides the service entrusted to it by Parliament.

The series of elected local government authorities have functions which are legislative, administrative and executive. The legislative functions are limited in scope. Such control as local authorities exercise by means of by-laws forms only a small part of their operations. Certain duties of a clearly executive nature are given them as, for instance, the collection of national licence duties on motor cars, but a great part of their work is administrative in character in that it is concerned with the management of their areas and the organization and supervision of various public services.

The method of carrying out public work by means of locally elected bodies financed out of local rates controllable by the authorities themselves has substantial advantages both in relieving the central government of administrative and executive functions, and in providing opportunity for the display of local anthusiasm, knowledge and experience whereby local provision can be matched to local needs, and a certain liberty of discretion be left to the local bodies in view of their financial and electoral responsibilities towards the inhabitants of the areas administered.

This brief sketch of the outlines of the system of local government in this country is intended to do no more than provide, in the place of a definition, a general idea of the subject. Succeeding chapters will attempt to provide necessary detail for a closer understanding of it.

# I

# The Areas of Local Government

SINCE local government is concerned with the exercise of particular functions in particular areas, the areas used for local government purposes are an important feature. In the English system, some of the areas are traditional, or, in other words, are areas adopted for historical reasons and not specially delimited for the functions for which they are now used. Other areas are functional, or specially defined for their present purposes. All the local government areas were functional to begin with, but the functions for which they were originally designed have altered with the passage of time.

The three principal traditional areas used to-day are the parish, the county and the borough. They originated in Norman and pre-Norman England for feudal purposes long before local government in the modern sense was thought of. They have been adopted, not without some alteration in number and boundaries, through the centuries for varying purposes as the local government system developed.

Among the functional areas may be classed the special areas laid down for water supply, land drainage, and other modern services. The delimiting of these areas is governed mainly by the technical requirements of the particular service.

### THE PARISH

The parish is one of the most ancient of the areas of local government. It was originally an area for ecclesiastical purposes, and as such was in existence long before the Norman conquest. This does not mean that the parishes which exist to-day are identical in number and size with those of early England; for by various statutes, schemes and other processes parishes have been amalgamated, divided, and absorbed, and their boundaries adjusted from time to time.

In early times the inhabitants of a parish held meetings in the vestry in order to consider questions relating to church affairs. Churchwardens were elected, and the parishioners would deal with such matters as the repair of the church and its furniture. To produce the necessary funds, the parishioners would agree as to a rate of contribution to be paid by each one of them. In other words, they levied upon themselves a church rate.

The parish in those days had little or nothing to do with matters of secular government. For governmental matters the local area of the vill (township) and of the manor were used. For purposes of public order the tithing, or group of ten free-men, and the hundred, or group of ten tithings, were adopted. These various units were not necessarily coincident, although it so happened that in a number of cases the area of the parish was similar to that of the vill and the manor, since church, vill and manor had at least one aim in common, namely the organization of human beings—the church for religious pur-poses, the vill for social and economic purposes, and the manor for agricultural purposes and the rendering of feudal dues and services.

As the feudal system decayed, the vill and the manor ceased to have any public status as areas of administration, but the parish as a church unit remained. When the monasteries were dissolved by Henry VIII a local government problem arose. The monasteries had performed the function of relieving the poor. Some alternative organization was necessary. The govern-ment of Elizabeth I adopted the parish. Each parish was made responsible for relieving its own poor. Overseers of the poor were appointed for each parish by the local justices, and rates (following the precedent of the church rates) were levied on the parishioners in order to meet the cost of poor relief.

Thus the parish emerged from the ecclesiastical sphere into the field of local government. The sixteenth-century central government also adopted the parish as the unit for highway administration. The parishioners were required to elect annu-ally two surveyors of highways to organize highway repair in the parish. Each parishioner was personally required to take part in the work or pay a penalty. Many preferred to pay the penalty. The assessment of these penalties upon the liable

2

parishioners developed in time into a system of highway rates. The parish for highway purposes was not always identical with the original ecclesiastical parish.

The history of the parish thus shows the origin and development of two of the main features of English local government —the local responsibility of the inhabitants for the carrying out of public services, and the system of meeting the cost of services out of rates.

In later centuries further minor duties were placed on the parishes. The parish authority was the 'vestry' consisting of either the whole of the parishioners, known as a common or 'open' vestry, or of an appointed committee of the parishioners, a select or 'closed' vestry. Vestries as local government authorities are now abolished.

The parish in urban districts and boroughs has ceased to be a unit of local government, but in rural districts the parish is an area for rating and is an administrative area with its own form of democratic local authority—the parish meeting or the parish council.

In former times the area of a parish did not necessarily fall completely within the area of a county or borough Under various statutory provisions, particularly the Local Government Act, 1929, the areas of parishes have been adjusted so that there are very few cases, if any, where the area of a parish overlaps that of a county or borough. A parish may be divided into wards for electoral purposes.

There were, in 1958, about 11,100 parishes in England and Wales. They consist of villages, or groups of hamlets, with the adjacent lands.

## THE COUNTY

The county as a local unit is probably more ancient than the parish. Counties, or as they were called in pre-Norman times shires, existed in Saxon days.

Originally each shire had an earl as the local governor. In those days, as later under the feudal system, land ownership and official responsibilities were to a great extent in the same hands. The earls acquired their areas of jurisdiction by various means—gift, conquest, marriage, purchase or inheritance. Like medieval kings each earl probably regarded his shire as to some extent his personal property. Certainly he had a great personal interest in it, and, if he acquired an addition to his estates, he considered the addition as part of his shire. This mixture of official jurisdiction with personal ownership and the various alterations, amalgamations and divisions of estates for various reasons in the course of the early centuries had due effect upon the administrative areas.

The medieval church, too, was a great landowner and had considerable jurisdiction over its estates. Every acquisition had to be fitted into the parish organization, and this probably had its effect upon the areas and groupings of parishes, and to some extent contributed towards the make-up of the counties.

It is possible in this way to account for the very irregular sizes and shapes of the ancient English counties. Up to 1930 there were a number of cases where a part of one county was embedded in the area of another county. Worcestershire is a famous example where 'detached portions' of the county were to be found in four neighbouring counties. These unusual irregularities in county areas have to a great extent been disposed of, and adjustments of county boundaries throughout the country have taken place from time to time particularly since the passing of the Local Government Act, 1929, but the counties of England and Wales have remained to a very great extent much as they were several hundred years ago.

By the time of Henry VIII the number of counties in England and Wales had become fixed at fifty-two. One new county, the county of London, was created in 1888.[1]

The county is not a unit for local government properly so called. It is an area for the administration of justice.

The judicial functions of a county have been conferred upon certain boroughs and towns by royal charter. There were, in 1947, nineteen places having the status of a county of a city or county of a town.[2]

The term 'county' in the judicial sense must not be confused with the term 'administrative county' which is an area for local government as opposed to judicial purposes. The

[1] See as to the county of London, p. 13.
[2] As to the judicial arrangements in these places see chapter 4.

4

area of an administrative county is controlled by a county council, and is in many cases quite different from that of a 'county'.[3]

## THE ADMINISTRATIVE COUNTY

The administrative county is an area designated for the carrying out of functions of administration, as opposed to judicial functions.

Previous to 1888 certain important functions of a non-judicial character were carried out in counties by the 'justices of the peace in quarter sessions assembled'. These non-judicial duties included the supervision of asylums, reformatories, and other county buildings, bridges and roads, and the issue of licences for public music and dancing.

In certain counties the justices were organized on the basis of areas less than the whole county at large. In some instances the county had, for convenience, been divided into divisions for which separate courts of quarter sessions were held; in other areas such as the Soke of Peterborough or the Isle of Ely, there were, by reasons of ancient privilege, separate judicial arrangements.[4]

Under the Local Government Act, 1888, two new forms of local government area were created—the county borough and the administrative county. The county boroughs were certain large towns, which were by the Act given their own local government organization. These county boroughs were made quite separate from the county in which geographically they lay.[5]

[3] As to other uses of the word 'county' see note 5 later.

[4] A 'soke' is an area in which special privileges in relation to the administration of justice and other local affairs have been conferred by Royal authority. The area was to some extent exempt from the Royal prerogative and from the jurisdiction of the county justices.

The term is substantially identical with a 'liberty'. For all the important local government purposes these special areas have either been virtually abolished, or merged in the counties at large, or formed into separate counties. The Isle of Ely is a 'liberty' which has, in common with the Soke of Peterborough, gained the full status of an administrative county.

[5] A county borough may still have a connection with a county for non-administrative purposes. Moreover, for postal and other purposes unconnected with local government the geographical relationship between county and county borough tends towards their being identified. A letter addressed to 'Brighton,

The Act provided that for every administrative county a county council should be established and be entrusted with the management of the administrative and financial business of that county. The non-judicial duties of the justices were thenceforth to be transferred to the new county councils.

To form the new administrative counties, the existing ancient counties at large, less the area of any county boroughs, were taken. Where an ancient county had been formed into divisions or other areas less than the whole county, as in the case of Yorkshire with its three Ridings, these lesser areas were used. Thus out of the fifty-two ancient counties were formed sixty-one administrative counties. Each Riding of Yorkshire (East, West and North) became a separate administrative county, as did each of the three divisions of Lincolnshire (Holland, Kesteven and Lindsey), the two divisions of Suffolk (East and West) and the two divisions of Sussex (East and West). In Cambridgeshire the Isle of Ely became one administrative county, and the rest of Cambridgeshire became another; and in Northamptonshire the Soke of Peterborough became one, and the residue of the county another. Certain parts of Middlesex, Surrey and Kent, formerly known as the 'Metropolis', were formed into the separate administrative county of London.

In 1889, under a special Act, the Isle of Wight was made an administrative county separate from the county of Southampton (or Hampshire).

There are thus sixty-two administrative counties in England and Wales, each with a county council. Each administrative county is divided into smaller local government areas.

There is great variety in the areas of administrative counties. The largest is Devonshire (2,583 sq.m., population in 1958—515,700), the smallest is the Soke of Peterborough (83 sq.m., population in 1957—68,270). The administrative county of London has the largest population (3,254,000 in 1958), but is one of the smallest in area (117 sq.m.).

Sussex' is not incorrect because it does not display the fact that Brighton is a county borough, or that Sussex is divided into two administrative counties.

To indicate a county in this popular and non-governmental sense the term 'geographical county' is sometimes used to denote what, in legal language, is meant by a 'county at large'. The phrase 'ancient county' or 'shire' is used also for a similar purpose.

6

## THE COUNTY BOROUGH

The Local Government Act, 1888, conferred upon certain boroughs in England and Wales the special status of 'county borough'. This status is in respect of non-judicial or administrative functions. A county borough does not form part of an administrative county.[6] For judicial purposes it may or may not be (according to each particular case) a separate county. But for non-judicial purposes every county borough is a self-contained unit and, unlike an administrative county, has no county districts or smaller local government units within its area.

The term borough has been long known to English history. As a unit of local administration it dates back to Saxon times. The inhabitants of a town, particularly of a medieval walled town, inevitably gain, by living in juxtaposition, a certain civic sense. They feel themselves to be different in their way of life and their social and commercial activities from the inhabitants of the rural areas outside the town. In former centuries these differences were much more definite than they are to-day. It accordingly became a practice from the earliest times for towns of any size to seek special protection and privileges. Charters were obtained from the Crown authorizing the townspeople to organize themselves under their own municipal government, and the privileges obtained in those charters included such items as power to hold local courts, power to control trading, licences to hold markets, exemption from taxation and interference by the King or overlord, power to appoint their own sheriffs, and the right to own land. The charter granted by the Crown conferred on the town a corporate status. The inhabitants, with their governing body of mayor and aldermen, were formed into a legal entity, a corporation, with the powers rights and obligations laid down in the charter. A town so incorporated is a 'borough'.

One of the privileges frequently given to a borough was the right to send a member or members to Parliament. A borough which had this privilege was a 'parliamentary borough'.

The grant of this privilege led to some unpleasant and dis-

[6] See note 5 above.

graceful episodes. During the reigns of Charles II and James II a number of borough charters were cancelled or declared forfeited and new ones issued in a form designed to secure the return to Parliament of members who were supporters of the Crown. The method used to obtain this result was to incorporate the borough as a 'close corporation', which meant that instead of all the inhabitants having a vote at the borough election for Parliament, only the members of the governing body (nominated or approved by the Crown) were able to vote. The attempt on the part of James II to interfere with the constitution of the boroughs was one of the main factors which led to his being deposed.

Nowadays a parliamentary borough is not always coincident with the area of a borough for local government purposes. There are three types of borough in the local government sense. There are county boroughs which include the largest towns and cities, and are self-contained administrative units. There are other boroughs, including the smaller towns and cities, known by the inelegant term 'non-county borough' and which are county districts forming part of an administrative county and not therefore entirely self-contained. Both these types of borough are sometimes referred to indiscriminately as 'municipal boroughs' to distinguish them from parliamentary boroughs.

There is a third form of borough peculiar to London and known as a metropolitan borough. These have no charter, but are created by statute.[7]

A borough of any class may obtain the title of 'City'. This is entirely a matter of ceremonial title, and is conferred by the Crown in the borough charter, or by letters patent. The status is not dependent (as is commonly supposed) on there being a cathedral within the city area. The title 'City' makes no difference to the local government functions and services.

The number of county boroughs in England and Wales in 1957 was eighty-three. Many of them are of great antiquity and have had a corporate existence for hundreds of years. They vary considerably in size. Birmingham has an area of about 80 square miles, and a population in 1957 of over one

[7] See later, p. 13.

million. Canterbury has an area of about 7½ square miles and a population of about 30,200.

The original sixty-one county boroughs mentioned in the Local Government Act, 1888, were boroughs which either had each a population of not less than 50,000 or were counties of themselves. In other words they were important either because of their size or by reason of their historical prestige. Most of them are, like Manchester, Southampton, Leicester or St. Helen's, large industrial centres or ports. Others are cathedral cities like Gloucester, Lincoln or Exeter, or seaside resorts of substantial size like Blackpool, Brighton and Southend-on-Sea.

New county boroughs may be created from time to time.[8] Since county boroughs form independent units for local government purposes, it follows that each county borough should have sufficient area, population and rate income to enable the borough authorities to run their own local government services.

Accordingly in 1926 it was enacted that no borough should be made a county borough unless it had a population of at least 75,000. To-day the minimum population is generally in the neighbourhood of 100,000.[8]

A county borough may, for electoral purposes, be divided into wards.

### THE COUNTY DISTRICTS

In the middle of the nineteenth century there arose, with the industrial revolution and the rapid growth of urbanization in many parts of the country, a realization of the need for new and improved public services.

The Poor Law Amendment Act, 1834, provided for the reform of poor-law administration by the grouping of parishes (the units for poor relief) into unions each under an elected Board of Guardians. Among the new services for which the greatest need was felt were those concerned with public health. Under the Public Health Act, 1848, local boards of health were set up as and when required in areas chosen as suitable for the needs of each particular case. For other services, such as street paving and lighting and water supply, there were

[8] See chapter 15.

9

bodies of commissioners set up from time to time in areas specially designated.

In 1872, the Public Health Act provided for the setting up, throughout the country, of a series of urban and rural sanitary authorities. For this purpose the existing boroughs and areas of commissioners were taken. The urban sanitary authority was, where the district coincided with that of a borough, the borough council, and in other cases was either a special body of Improvement Commissioners or a Local Board. The rural sanitary districts were, with certain local variations, conterminous with the areas administered by the Boards of Guardians of the Poor. The Guardians were made the rural sanitary authorities.

Thus in 1888, when the administrative counties were formed, there were in each county a number of these urban and rural sanitary districts. The pattern of areas was not quite so simple as that; for there were various other designated areas, for example, school districts and highway districts administered specially by separate education and highway boards. Moreover, there were the parishes. All these various areas did not necessarily coincide.

The Act of 1888, as has been seen, gave some boroughs the improved status of county boroughs and separated them from any administrative county. Certain small boroughs with populations of less than 10,000 had some of their powers transferred to the new county councils. The rest of the boroughs were practically unaffected by the Act, so far as their administrative functions were concerned.

Those urban sanitary districts which were not boroughs were, by the Local Government Act, 1894, re-named urban districts, and were placed under the jurisdiction of popularly elected urban district councils. By the same Act rural sanitary districts became rural districts each with an elected rural district council to which were transferred the sanitary duties of the Boards of Guardians.

With the turn of the nineteenth century the increasing trend of local government legislation was to reduce the number of local authorities by transference and adjustment of powers. By the time the Local Government Act, 1933, was passed, school boards and highway boards had been abolished, poor law functions had been transferred from the former Boards of Guardians to the county councils and county borough councils, and the general pattern of local areas was much less complex.

The Act of 1933 provided that, for the purposes of local government, England and Wales (exclusive of London) should be divided into administrative counties and county boroughs, and that every administrative county should be divided into county districts. These county districts should consist of either non-county boroughs, urban districts or rural districts.

The pattern of county areas for local government purposes is therefore simple. Each administrative county is composed of smaller units. These units, according to local circumstances, have varying status. The administrative county of Rutland, for instance, is divided into one urban district and three rural districts, and has no non-county boroughs. Middlesex has eighteen non-county boroughs, eight urban districts, and no rural districts. Most counties have an assortment of all types of county districts. Kent, for example, has twenty-three non-county boroughs, fifteen urban districts and eighteen rural districts.[9]

In addition to these minor areas, there are, of course, the parishes, which in rural districts are still minor units for local government purposes and are areas for electoral purposes.

*The Non-County Borough* is a county district which has not the independent status of a county borough but which none the less is sufficiently important for reasons of size or historical associations to have a charter of incorporation. There is, in the Local Government Act, 1933, a list of 273 non-county boroughs. They vary in size from about 5 to 13 square miles, and in population from about 1,000 to 180,000. Some have the title 'City'. They comprise for the most part pleasant typical country towns with many historical associations, although in many there is considerable commerce and industry. Some are pleasure resorts, others, in areas where there has been much urban expansion, have become part of a larger concentration and virtually suburban in character. New boroughs

---

[9] These figures relate to 1957, and are subject to any alterations in area or status of the county districts made from time to time. See chapter 15.

may be created from time to time.[10] The number of non-county boroughs in 1957 was 319. For electoral purposes a non-county borough may be divided into wards.

*Urban Districts* comprise the small towns or urban groupings or the suburban areas of the great cities. The area of an urban district is not necessarily entirely built up. The district has no charter and owes its existence and status to orders made under Acts of Parliament. It may be divided into wards for electoral purposes.

Urban districts vary greatly in size from a square mile or so to about 20 square miles. The population may range from about 200 to over 200,000. There were in 1957, 564 urban districts in England and Wales.

*Rural Districts* have one peculiarity which the other county districts do not have. They are divided into still smaller local government units—the parishes. In 1957 there were 473 rural districts in England and Wales. They are generally much larger than urban districts, are more sparsely populated and less compact in shape; some of them in fact have an urban district or a borough embedded within them, so that the rural district is roughly a ring-shaped area surrounding the urban centre, or, in some instances, consists of a number of detached parts separated by intervening borough or urban areas.

## LONDON

At the beginning of the nineteenth century the city of London and the surrounding districts were administered in somewhat the same way as comparable areas elsewhere. There was the ancient city with its corporate governing body set up under ancient charters. The city's influence had extended beyond the city walls into the associated 'liberties' and into the borough of Southwark. For vital statistics the association between the city and the districts around had long been recognized; London, Westminster and certain adjacent parishes became known as the 'Bills of Mortality', a term which found official recognition in a number of Acts of Parliament.

Outside the city, local government was in the hands of the county and parish authorities—the justices and the vestries.

[10] See chapter 15.

12

As urbanization proceeded, it was found necessary to set up under special local Acts of Parliament separate local bodies to carry out particular functions of paving, lighting and the like. By 1855 there were, in the area now known as the county of London, some 300 bodies of local commissioners of sewers, trustees for street management, and other small organizations of that type. Their operations were governed by some 250 Acts of Parliament. Each body had limited powers over a small area; most of them were publicly elected, and all had power to levy a rate for the services they rendered. Needless to say, there was little or no co-ordination.

By the Metropolis Management Act, 1855, the old parish vestries were supplanted by special administrative vestries for the larger parishes, and district boards for groups of the smaller parishes. Over the whole area, which was officially designated 'The Metropolis', was set up a Metropolitan Board of Works which was not directly elected by the people, but was composed of nominees of the City of London, of the vestries and of the district boards. The Board of Works and the minor authorities between them carried out the various duties of sewerage, paving, street lighting and other local government functions. The Metropolis remained within the counties of Middlesex, Surrey and Kent.

In 1888 the Metropolis was taken out of those counties, and formed into a new county. The London County Council was set up in place of the Metropolitan Board of Works. In 1899 the vestries and district boards were supplanted by metropolitan borough councils. All this left the City of London untouched.

The Administrative County of London is an area of about 117 square miles. It includes the City. The City is not a county borough, but it is a separate county for judicial purposes. The rest of the Administrative County (i.e. without the City) forms the County of London (for judicial or non-administrative purposes), and has its own lord lieutenant and sheriff.

There are twenty-eight metropolitan boroughs. These have not been created by charter, but owe their existence to Orders in Council made under the London Government Act, 1899.

The pattern of administration in London is, in form, similar to that of some other counties, with a county council and

13

twenty-nine minor authorities. The City of London is unique. The twenty-eight metropolitan boroughs are equal in legal status, although Westminster has the title of a City, and Kensington has the title of Royal Borough.

The whole of the administrative county is built up. The City of London, the commercial core, is almost entirely occupied by business premises. It is just over one square mile in area (677 acres). The resident population is about 5,000, but the day population coming into the City for business purposes approaches half a million.

Of the metropolitan boroughs, those in the east end are the most heavily industrialized, and include the dock areas. Westminster, Kensington and St. Marylebone include the West End shopping and entertainment centres, government offices and both high-class and (in the back streets) working-class residential development. The remainder of the boroughs are of mixed development, largely residential, and form, broadly speaking, the dormitory suburbs.

# 2

# Local Government Authorities

A COUNTY borough and a non-county borough have certain features in common. These boroughs are defined areas, as are any other local government units; what makes them different is that the inhabitants of the borough are formed into a corporate body. The title of the corporate body is, in the majority of cases, 'the Mayor, Aldermen and Burgesses of the Borough of ——'. Where a borough has the distinction of being a city, the title is 'the Mayor, Aldermen and Citizens of the City of ——'.[1]

The point to notice is that all the townspeople, or burgesses, are members of the corporation. This feature is not possessed by any other local authority. A person may be a resident or a ratepayer of a county, urban district or parish, but he is not part of the legal corporate body. Nor is this feature possessed by the metropolitan boroughs.[2]

*Freemen.* In earlier times the burgesses, or freemen of a borough, had certain definite privileges as laid down in the charter. The borough, as a corporate body, could own land and enjoy the profits. Local tolls and dues could be exacted from traders. The borough income could be dispensed in various ways—educational, charitable, or otherwise. The borough may have sent its own member to Parliament. The privileges conferred on the freemen or burgesses included exemption from tolls and dues, a vote at elections, and the right to participate in borough charities and amenities. The process of becoming a burgess or freeman depended on local cus-

[1] This distinction of title does not, of itself, affect the local government powers of the corporation. Where the mayor, as in the case of the more important cities, is called the Lord Mayor, the name of the corporation will be 'the Lord Mayor, Aldermen and Citizens of the City of ——'.
[2] See later in this chapter.

15

tom and the rules of each borough. The child, apprentice or wife of a freeman was often admitted. The names of those admitted were inscribed on the freeman's roll.

Nowadays the powers of a borough corporation are exercised by a borough council elected by all the local inhabitants over the age of twenty-one. For local services the borough council levies rates according to laws which do not take into account whether the ratepayer is a freeman or not.

The borough may, however, still have certain property and funds as the corporation's own private property (so to speak) which is available for charitable purposes, educational endowments, and similar uses, which freemen may enjoy. The Local Government Act, 1933, however, provides that all inhabitants of a borough, near relatives of and apprentices of freemen, and all persons who might have otherwise been admitted as freemen, shall be entitled to have similar benefits from the corporate property. Moreover, the Act provides that all receipts by the council of a borough, including the rents and profits of all corporate lands, shall be paid into the general rate fund of the borough and be therefore used to meet the general liabilities of the council. The distinction of being a freeman is therefore, in modern times, largely titular. The freeman's roll is still maintained, and must be kept by the town clerk. Freemen may not be admitted by gift or purchase. A borough may, however, confer honorary freedom on persons of distinction or who have rendered service to the borough.[3]

This right of conferment is often used as a compliment or mark of appreciation. A meeting of the council must be specially convened and a resolution of two-thirds of the members is necessary. The occasion is accompanied by appropriate ceremonial.

*Borough charters.* Both county boroughs and non-county boroughs have charters, conferred by the Crown by virtue of the royal prerogative. Other local authorities owe their existence to some act of the legislature, either a statute or some order made under statutory authority. The particular functions of the borough and therefore its status as a county borough or otherwise are defined by a legislative act and not by the exercise of the royal prerogative.

[3] Metropolitan boroughs also can confer honorary freedom.

The fact that a borough has a charter makes a certain difference to the powers which may be exercised on behalf of the corporation by the borough council. An authority set up by statute can only do what the statute allows. An authority which has a charter may do anything which a private individual may lawfully do, so long as the charter does not forbid it. Modern legislation has laid down certain limits on the matters which may be included in a charter, and there are, of course, a large number of statutes which confer powers on borough councils as local authorities. These statutes may affect the powers of the boroughs under their charters. The fact remains (and it is a point that borough authorities consider to be of importance) that a borough, whether county or non-county, is, by virtue of its charter, in a somewhat advantageous position as compared with other local authorities.

*Ceremonial apparatus.* The features hitherto referred to which distinguish a borough from other forms of local authority—the incorporation of the inhabitants and the creation by means of a charter—are, perhaps to the ordinary inhabitant of a borough, features which are rather academic and legalistic. What in the practical sense makes a borough different is the ceremonial apparatus. Only boroughs have mayors; only cities have Lord Mayors. Other authorities have a chairman. County councils have aldermen, but the county aldermen, like the chairman and councillors of other authorities which have not borough status, attend their official meetings in ordinary plain clothes. A mayor or Lord Mayor and alderman of a borough have for ceremonial occasions coloured medieval robes, often fur-lined, with cocked or beaver hats, badges and chains of office. The town clerk, by old custom, wears robes and a legal wig, and the whole assembly is graced by a mace-bearer, sword-bearer or other officers, suitably apparelled with their insignia. These ceremonial features are not enjoyed by any other type of local authority.

The dweller in an urban district may be proud of his town and take an interest in the doings of the local authority; the rural dweller may be devoted to his village and his fields; but the absence of any special colourful features in the councils of urban and rural districts makes it less easy for him to accept those authorities as an embodiment of the community sense.

In a borough, local government is combined with civic page-antry, and the carrying out of modern public services is linked with ancient traditions. The civic consciousness of the citizen will be stimulated by the traditional and historical elements in the make-up of his borough, its charter, insignia and cere-monies. In this respect the borough has an undoubted advant-age over other types of local government organization.

*The Borough Council.* Although doubtless the original purpose of creating a borough was to enable the town to organize itself for the better administration of the town affairs, a num-ber of the borough corporations degenerated into corruption and negligence. In many cases local services were hardly per-formed at all, and the corporate money was spent for the personal benefit and entertainment of the members of the governing body who were often not elected by the towns-people at all but were co-opted by the other members.

By the Municipal Corporations Act, 1835, 178 of the boroughs then existing were reformed. The governing bodies were to be henceforth elected by the people, their finances were subject to regulation, and they were given more up-to-date powers. By subsequent statutes many borough corpora-tions have been dissolved and the boroughs reduced in status accordingly.

The general position of a borough outside London is now dealt with in the Local Government Act, 1933. The powers of a borough corporation are exercised by a council[4] com-posed of a mayor (or Lord Mayor), aldermen and councillors. The councillors are elected by the inhabitants and occupiers of rateable property in the borough. The aldermen are equal in number to one-third of the councillors and are not elected by the people, but by the councillors. The mayor (or Lord Mayor)[5] is elected by the aldermen and councillors together.[6]

*Complex nature of a Borough Council.* The personnel of a borough council is to some extent open to change every year. The mayor is appointed annually. The aldermen serve for six years, and the councillors for three. The composition of the council

[4] The borough council is not itself a corporate body, and it has no common seal of its own. It is an organ and instrument of the corporation as a whole. Among its powers is the capacity to use the corporation's common seal.

[5] As to the general position of the mayor and deputy mayor see chapter 10.

[6] As to their election see chapter 9.

18

becomes complicated by the further requirements that half the aldermen retire every three years, while every year, one-third of the councillors retire.[7]

A borough council is therefore a continuously evolving organism. It suffers no violent change in its composition. At any one point of time there are always on the council members with different periods of service. There is never a complete landslide or sudden change-over in membership as may happen at a parliamentary election. The greatest change that can take place in borough council membership is at the end of the third year, when half the aldermen retire. For, besides these retiring aldermen, one-third of the councillors, as well as the mayor, go out of office. If none of them get re-elected, the new council will have changed over one-third of its total membership. In an ordinary year, when no aldermen retire, the council will change (subject to there being no re-elections) to the extent of a quarter or so.[8]

All this was intended to make for continuity. It certainly does, except in those cases where the membership of a council is made up of persons of strongly opposed political views. The local government system does not take political parties into account as does the organization of the national legislature, with its arrangement of Her Majesty's Government on the one side, and Her Majesty's Opposition on the other. In a borough council where there are opposing political parties, there may come a time when, at one of the annual changes of membership, the balance of political strength will change from one party to another. And this change may have a sudden and immediate effect on the policy of the council. The complex structure of a borough council does not, therefore, make violent and sudden change impossible, but it makes it more difficult to achieve, in that it reduces the number of seats to be vacated, and to be filled, at any one election. In the case

[7] i.e. those aldermen and councillors that have completed their full term of office. In metropolitan boroughs all the councillors retire together every three years. What is said in the text above is therefore not applicable in London.

[8] It should be remembered that the mayor need not have been a member of the council to begin with, in which case, when his year of office ends, he will cease to be a member of the council. If he is elected from within the council he may, after his year of office, still continue to be a member of the council, if he is not in his capacity of alderman or councillor otherwise due for retirement. See further chapter 10.

of some other local authorities, there are periodical general elections of all the councillors, and the council is exposed to the prospect of a complete change of membership. This may happen at every election as the political pendulum swings back and forth. Changes in political balance may indeed, and do, occur in borough councils outside London, but the total personnel can never be suddenly altered. There will always be, on a borough council, some remnant of the former membership.

*The County Borough Council*, composed of mayor, aldermen and councillors, has all the features above-mentioned. The powers which it exercises are wider than those of any other local government authority. It is possible that within the area of a county borough there may be some special body, an *ad hoc* authority or statutory undertaker, exercising functions. The county borough council may have agreed to form a joint board or joint committee with other authorities for the carrying out of certain operations, and it may be allied for certain judicial purposes with the county at large. The county borough is, however, not divided, as is the administrative county, into smaller units with councils, nor is there any other local government authority exercising functions within a county borough.

The result of this is that county boroughs have, broadly speaking, all the various local government services to perform. The county borough is from the administrative point of view self-contained.

Accordingly one may expect to find, in a county borough, all the usual local services being carried on by the corporation. The Manchester Corporation, for instance, provides water supply, education (primary, secondary and advanced), the fire brigade, midwifery and local health service, and is responsible for the care of children, for sewerage and sanitary services, allotments, parks, maintenance of streets, housing and planning, libraries, art galleries and museums, swimming-baths and cemeteries. The Corporation has numerous powers of control over building work, places of entertainment, food and drugs, and ships, deals with inspection of weights and measures, and the suppression of nuisances. Institutions are maintained for the aged and the poor and the welfare services for blind and disabled persons.

This is a typical example of the great range of undertakings for which a large county borough council may be responsible. The powers of all county boroughs are not the same; and the extent to which each county borough council exercises its powers varies with local needs.[9]

The police force in a county borough is managed by a special committee, the watch committee, which, although appointed by the borough council, has a semi-independent status.[10]

## COUNTY AUTHORITIES

*The Justices.* The county is an area for the administration of justice. There is no local government authority concerned with the area as such. To a certain extent, however, there is a connection between the judicial business of a county and the functions of a county council. Each county has a body of justices of the peace.[11]

Before 1888 these justices in quarter sessions had administrative functions which were by the Local Government Act of that year transferred to county councils. Among the powers transferred from them was the power of making county rates, and the control of the county fund. They were thus deprived of important sources of revenue. But since justice cannot be administered without expenditure on such matters as court houses, sessions houses, justices' rooms, lodgings for the judges of assize when they come on circuit, clerks of courts and other staff, in which matters the justices rightly have a say, the Act of 1888 provided that in each administrative county a standing joint committee should be set up composed of equal numbers of members of the county council and of justices of the peace appointed by the county quarter sessions.[12]

This standing joint committee decides what accommodation and staff shall be provided for the justices, for their judicial duties, and the county council meets the expense out of the county fund.

*Social connotations.* The county cannot, however, be regarded

[9] See chapter 5.      [10] See chapter 11.

[11] Justices have certain duties which are partly judicial and partly administrative, e.g. liquor licensing and the licensing of public music and dancing, as to which see chapter 4.

[12] This joint committee is also the authority for managing the police force in the administrative county. See chapter 3, p. 44.

as merely an area designated for the more or less limited purposes of organizing judicial arrangements. While it is true that the lives, work and well-being of the county inhabitants are affected in numerous directions by the operations of the local authority for the administrative county—the county council— and that the operations of a county council are more widespread and intimate in their effect on the public than are the operations of the justices, the concept of the county as a social unit is probably stronger in the popular mind than that of the administrative county.

The ancient county offices of sheriff and lord lieutenant have persisted into modern times and are filled by direct royal appointment for duties associated with the administration of justice.[13] These appointments, although shorn of their medieval significance, confer high prestige and social prominence upon their holders and have the effect of maintaining the continuity of the county's long history as a local unit.

Many famous regiments of the British Army bear the names of the ancient counties. The professional cricket clubs bear the ancient county names. Other county societies exist. All this serves to foster in the mind of the county dweller a sense of belonging to a social organization and it is probable that he (or she) looks to the county, rather than the administrative county in this regard, in spite of the fact that practically all those public services which make for civilized conditions of living are provided by the county councils and not by the authorities of the counties at large. County councils are, in the historical sense, new creations dating only from 1888. The areas they administer, being by no means coincident in every case with those of the ancient counties, are not always realized by the general public and lack the social and traditional significance of the ancient areas.

*The County Council.* The county council is the local government authority for an administrative county. Since each administrative county is divided into county districts, each with its own council, and rural districts are divided into parishes, the county council is not responsible for all the local services within the county. Some services are not its concern at all and are left to be carried on by each district (or non-county

[13] See chapter 4.

22

borough) council; some of the services are shared between the county council, the district councils and the parish authorities.

The county council administers those services appropriate to a large area, such as main roads, and bridges, the general planning of town and country, the fire brigade, the care of children, and services which require a specially qualified staff for which there would be insufficient work in a small area, such as the testing of weights and measures, and the inspection and licensing of places of entertainment.

The education service is administered by county councils, with a varying amount of local assistance from the district councils. County councils are local health authorities, but may delegate certain functions to district councils. For some services county councils and the district councils have similar powers. For instance, all the district councils and the county council may provide parks, have powers of food sampling and may provide libraries. Motor vehicle and driving licences are issued by county councils, nursing homes are registered, and institutions for the poor and aged are maintained. In the rural districts the county council is responsible for the licensing of petrol stations.

County councils have certain powers over the electoral arrangements in county districts; they may, in certain cases, act in default of a district council; they may exercise control over the establishment and activities of parish councils; and they have concern in the general county finances. The county council, and the district and parish authorities, form, therefore, an inter-related group in which the county council is not without influence.

A county council is composed of a chairman, aldermen and councillors. It is a corporate body, with a common seal, and has power to hold land. The usual size of a county council is about fifty or sixty members.

The chairman of a county council is elected annually. A vice-chairman must be appointed.

County aldermen are elected by the chairman and county councillors from among the councillors or persons qualified to be councillors. The aldermen are equal in number to one-third of the whole number of councillors.[14]

[14] Or, if that number is not divisible by three, the aldermen are to be one-third of the highest number below that number which is divisible by three.

County aldermen are, like borough aldermen, elected for six years. The county councillors are elected for three years. Every time there is a general election of county councillors (i.e. every third year), half the aldermen retire, so that, at each general county council election, half the aldermen stay in office and help to make up the new council.

County councillors are elected by the local government electors for the county in every third year. There is no annual retirement of one-third of the councillors as in the case of boroughs. The county councillors all go out of office together.

*The Non-County Borough Council* has a constitution similar to that of a county borough, with mayor, aldermen and councillors, and the same rules as to period of office and retirement apply. The usual size of a non-county borough council is between thirty and forty members. The council exercises the powers of the borough corporation.

A non-county borough council has the duty of lighting and maintaining the borough streets, and bridges, the local sewerage and drainage, refuse collection and other sanitary services; it may provide allotments, parks, public entertainments, libraries and swimming baths, has duties of control over building work, petrol stations and shops, various powers in relation to disease and public health, and has the important function of providing municipal housing. It may, by local scheme, exercise certain of the county council's powers in relation to education, welfare and health services. Many non-county boroughs provide water.

*Urban District Councils.* Every urban district has an urban district council composed of a chairman and councillors. The council is a body corporate and has a common seal.

The chairman is elected by the council from among the councillors or persons qualified to be councillors. A vice-chairman may be elected from among the councillors. The membership of an urban district council is about thirty in number.

Urban district councillors are elected for three years. The Local Government Act, 1933, provides that each year one-third of the councillors shall retire, in which case there is an annual election of councillors to fill the vacancies. If the urban district is divided into wards, then one-third of the councillors for each ward retire each year.

The urban district may, however, make a formal request to the county council to direct that all the councillors shall retire together every three years. A number of such orders have been made by county councils, with the result that some urban district councils have a general election every three years.

Where such an order is in operation, the county council may, on a formal request from the urban district council, rescind the order and restore for that urban district council the annual elections for a third of the councillors at a time.

Urban district councils are sometimes popularly referred to as 'town councils', the town being a more easily understood conception and the unit for social purposes. Many urban districts are, however, not complete towns. Many form parts of larger agglomerations; some consist of two or more small towns or large villages; some consist of a little town with its associated villages. Some are large enough in population, area and rateable value to qualify for borough status.

The powers of an urban district council are the same as those of a non-county borough council, allowing for the fact that the borough has a charter as mentioned earlier in this chapter. Urban district councils have responsibility for streets, housing, sewerage, refuse collection and sanitary services, baths, cemeteries, libraries, parks, the control of buildings, petrol stations and, in some cases, shops. Some have education, local health and welfare functions. Public entertainments and allotments may be provided. Some councils provide water supply.

*A Rural District Council* is provided for every rural district. The council is composed of a chairman and councillors. A vice-chairman may be appointed. Councillors are elected for three years, and one-third retire annually unless the county council has made an order directing the general retirement of all the councillors every third year.

The membership of a rural district council is usually larger than that of an urban district council, although in some cases the number may be much fewer.

Rural district councils have power to provide housing, to control building work and to suppress nuisances. They have duties in relation to disease, disinfection and food and drugs and the duties of providing sewerage and maintaining and lighting local roads. Refuse is collected and disposed of. They may provide public entertainments, parks and cemeteries.

The work of rural district councils has to be performed over comparatively wide and sparsely populated areas. Accordingly it has been found convenient for certain special arrangements to be made for the carrying out of the functions of the district councils in the various parts of the district. The rural district council may, for instance, appoint a parochial committee to carry out the council's duties in any particular parish or group of parishes; and may delegate functions to the local parish council.

Where there is no parish council for a particular parish, the councillors representing that parish form, together with the chairman of the parish meeting, a 'representative body' to act on behalf of the parish.

*Parish organization.* The Local Government Act, 1894, took away any existing powers of the former vestries in rural areas and conferred those powers with others on a new set of local authorities created by that Act—the parish meetings and the parish councils.

The general provisions relating to the constitution of these bodies is now laid down in the Local Government Act, 1933.

Every rural parish has a parish meeting, consisting of all the local government electors for the parish. If the parish has a population of 300 or more the county council must establish a parish council. If the population is between 200 and 300 the county council must appoint a parish council if the parish meeting so resolve. If the population is less than 200, the county council may at its discretion establish a parish council if the parish meeting so resolve. The county council may also make orders grouping or regrouping parishes under a common parish council.

Thus in a large number of parishes (over 7,000 in 1957) there is a parish council and a parish meeting. In the rest of the parishes (some 4,000 in 1957) there is only a parish meeting.

*The Parish Meeting* must be held annually between 1st March and 1st April inclusive and at other times as necessary. If there is no parish council the meeting must take place at least twice a year. The parish meeting (if there is no parish council) has the powers of a parish council in relation to public rights of way, and has opportunities of making complaints to the county council. The county council may on the request of the parish meeting confer upon the meeting any or all of the general powers of a parish council.

If there is a parish council, the parish meeting has a certain control over the acts and expenditure of the parish council; the consent of the meeting is required to the sale of parish land, and to any expenditure which will involve a loan or a rate exceeding 4d. in the £ for any financial year. If the population of the parish is less than 200 the parish meeting may by resolution ask the county council to dissolve the parish council (if there is one) and the county council may at its discretion comply with this request.

The formal acts of a parish meeting are signified under the hands (or if need by the seals) of the chairman of the meeting and two other local government electors present at the meeting.

The parish meeting is not a corporate body. For parishes where there is no parish council there is a 'representative body' composed of the chairman of the parish meeting and the rural district councillors for the parish. If there is only one rural district councillor for the parish, some additional councillor is appointed for the purpose by the district council.

This representative body is a body corporate and has power to hold land, and to act according to the instructions of the parish meeting. The representative body has no common seal, and its acts must accordingly be signified by the hands (and seals where necessary) of the individual members of the body.

*Parish Councils* consist of a chairman and councillors The councillors are elected by the local government electors for the parish. Councillors are elected for three years and all retire together. The number of councillors must be not less than five or more than twenty-one.

The chairman is elected annually by the councillors from among the councillors or from persons qualified to be councillors. A vice-chairman may be appointed from among the councillors.

It will be appreciated that since, in a rural parish, there are already two other local authorities carrying on local government functions—the county council and the rural district council—the share of functions left to the parish authorities is

comparatively small. Parish councils have powers of maintenance of field paths and rights of way, may provide recreation
grounds, village halls, allotments, maintain war memorials,
provide baths, wash-houses and swimming baths, burial places,
clocks, and street lighting, seats and shelters, may suppress
nuisances, and have certain rights of complaint and representation to the major local authorities.

For many years after their creation parish councils and
parish meetings were, as an experiment in local government,
regarded as a failure. The creation of these authorities was
doubtless due to some extent to the respect for the long history
of the parish as a local unit with its representative vestry, and
to some extent to the desire to bring into the rural areas something of the movement of democratic reform which was one
of the political achievements of the latter part of the nineteenth
century.

The country dweller has perhaps a greater awareness of his
county and of his parish than of his rural district. He looks to
the county town, which is often the largest town in the county,
as the place where all sorts of important matters are dealt
with; important legal business is transacted there, there is
probably a market and a cathedral as well as a county hall
and a county council. The rural district may take its name
from some small town miles away which the villager does not
identify with his own immediate locality. In his daily life and
work he looks to his local village with its inn, church, village
hall and shop as the social grouping to which he immediately
belongs.

Recognition of this was doubtless in the minds of the legis-
lators who provided for the modern parish organization. The
villager, however, was, for many years, not greatly interested
in the parish meeting or the parish council. The conduct of
parish business inevitably fell into the hands of the more edu-
cated and more articulate persons, who were at the same time
generally speaking the more socially influential.

The impact of two world wars, the general awakening of
the countryside to modern urban influences, the spread of education and the diminution of social barriers, has resulted in
a greater interest in parish affairs. Many parish councils are
now representative of varied social types—the vicar, the post-

man, the ploughman and the squire. The powers and influence of parish councils and meetings are not very substantial,
but they provide the elemental nucleus of local democracy
whereby the individual citizen can be brought into participa-
tion in his own self-government.

## THE ADMINISTRATIVE COUNTY OF LONDON

There are three special types of local government authority
in the administrative county of London—the London County
Council, which exercises powers over the whole county, the
twenty-eight metropolitan borough councils, and the Court of
Common Council of the City of London Corporation.

*The London County Council* consists, like other county councils
of a chairman, aldermen and councillors. The chairman is
elected annually by the council from members of the council
or persons qualified to be members. The aldermen are elected
by the councillors for six years, and half of them retire every
three years. The councillors are elected by the local government electors for the administrative county. The councillors
serve for three years and all retire together. The number of
councillors is treble the number of London members of
Parliament. The total number of councillors is 126. The
aldermen are in number one-sixth of the councillors. There
are thus 21 aldermen. The total size of the council is accordingly 147, or, if the chairman is elected from outside the
council, 148.

There is power to appoint a vice-chairman and a deputy
chairman.

Aldermen may be elected from among the councillors or
from persons qualified to be councillors. There are no ceremonial robes or insignia other than a chairman's badge of
office.

The services provided by the London County Council are
not so great in range as those provided by the council of a
county borough; for the local government services in London
are shared between the county council and the minor local
authorities. Water supply in and around London is provided
by the Metropolitan Water Board. The county council is not
concerned in police administration.

The services which the county council does provide, however, are in scale greater than those of any other local authority in the country, by reason of the dense population of the county (about 3¼ millions in 1957) and the high rateable value of the area. The council's powers differ from those of other county councils particularly in regard to housing. The council may provide housing in any part of the county of London as well as outside. It has provided a large number of parks and open spaces, with facilities for sports and entertainments, and contributes substantially, with other authorities, to the establishment of the Green Belt around London.

For the administrative county of London (i.e., including the City of London) the council is the authority for education and the care of children, the fire brigade and for the licensing of places of public entertainment. It provides the main drainage and sewage disposal for the whole area and certain surrounding areas. It is the local health authority under the National Health Service, and is town planning authority, but has delegated some of its town planning functions to the Common Council of the City of London and the metropolitan borough councils. It provides institutional accommodation for the aged and indigent, and the local welfare service for the blind and disabled.

For the county of London (exclusive of the City), the county council is responsible for Thames bridges and other county bridges, major street improvements, the licensing of petrol stations, and the inspection of shops and weights and measures.

*Metropolitan Borough Councils* differ from other borough councils in that the metropolitan borough council itself is a body corporate consisting of the mayor, aldermen and councillors. Metropolitan boroughs were not created by charter but by statute. The inhabitants of the metropolitan borough are not incorporated.[15]

The members of the council may wear robes, although in many cases this is dispensed with.

The titular distinction of the Westminster City Council and the Council of the Royal Borough of Kensington makes no

---

[15] There are no freemen or burgesses, although metropolitan borough councils may confer the titular or honorary freedom of the borough on distinguished persons.

difference to their powers and functions as metropolitan borough councils.

The mayor is elected annually by the council from among the members of the council or persons qualified to be members. A deputy mayor may be appointed by the council.

The aldermen are equal in number to one-sixth of the councillors. Aldermen are elected from the councillors or persons qualified to be councillors. They sit for six years and half retire every three years.

Metropolitan borough councillors all retire together in every third year. There is no annual retirement of one-third of the councillors as in boroughs outside London.

The powers of the metropolitan borough councils are rather less than those of a non-county borough council. For one reason, the metropolitan boroughs have no charters; nor do they have power to provide water supply or to license petrol stations, inspect weights and measures or control the hours of opening of shops.

The metropolitan borough councils have considerable work to do, none the less; for each borough is fully built up, although they vary in size and in the type of development.

Street maintenance and sanitation form a principal function. Baths, libraries, cemeteries, and public gardens are provided. Food and drugs are inspected. Each borough council has power to provide housing in its own borough.

*The City of London Corporation*, although dealt with last here, is by no means the least of the London local authorities. In history, prestige, in powers and in constitution it is different from every other local government authority.

Its fame is world wide. Its wealth, pageantry, and civic hospitality place it in a position apart. The Lord Mayor of London is a figure of national interest.

As a local government organization the City Corporation is, in the ambit and scale of its functions, not in the first rank. The area and resident population of the City are small, and the City is not, like a county borough, administratively self-contained. Main drainage, education, and the licensing of entertainments are, in the City, carried out by the London County Council. The Corporation has, however, a number of powers, both under public and private Acts, which are not possessed by the metropolitan borough councils. It is not a local town planning authority but has certain important planning functions. It has its own police force; it maintains important Thames bridges within the City and is the port health authority. The Corporation has considerable private funds and estates out of which it provides and supports a number of educational and charitable foundations. From these private funds are also met the cost of the banquets and other civic hospitality for which the City is famous, and the salary (£15,000 in 1957-58) of the Lord Mayor.

The origin of the Corporation is lost in the mists of antiquity. It claims to be a corporation by prescription, although in the course of the centuries numerous charters have been conferred. It retains many of the features of the medieval municipal corporations, and was not 'reformed' by the Municipal Corporations Act of 1835.

The Corporation consists of the 'mayor, aldermen, commonalty and citizens of the City of London'. The functions of the Corporation are discharged through three assemblies—the Court of Aldermen, the Court of Common Council and the Court of Common Hall.

The Court of Aldermen consists of twenty-six aldermen (one for each ward of the City) of whom one is the Lord Mayor. Each alderman is elected by the inhabitants or occupiers of property in the ward he represents. Aldermen are elected for life and consequently do not, as in the case of borough aldermen, retire every six years. Each alderman is a magistrate, and the Court is a judicial body. It is concerned with the administration of the City Police Force and control of street traffic.

The Court of Common Council is composed of the Lord Mayor, alderman and 159 common councilmen who are elected, as are other local government authorities, by the inhabitants and occupiers of property in the City. The Court of Common Council is elected annually on St. Thomas's Day (21st December), has control of the Corporation's estates and of the Corporation's seal. It is the local government authority for the City.

The law relating to public elections to membership of the Court of Aldermen and Court of Common Council has been brought into line with that of other local government elections. Apart from this the structure of the Corporation has not been interfered with by Parliament, and the Corporation claims to have the power to remodel its own constitution.

The Common Hall is an assembly of all the liverymen of the City. These are those freemen of the City who are entitled to wear the livery of one of the various city companies (formerly the craft guilds). Freedom of the City is usually obtained through one of these companies. It is, as with the freedom of a borough, a special status and is not necessarily identical with that of an inhabitant or ratepayer. The Court of Common Hall elects the two City Sheriffs, and certain other officers.

The Lord Mayor is elected each year on September 29th. The Court of Common Hall nominates two aldermen from among those who have been sheriffs of the City. Of these two aldermen the Court of Aldermen selects one to be Lord Mayor. He is then presented to the Sovereign for approval and is later sworn in as a magistrate by the Judges of the High Court. His journey from the City to the Law Courts is accompanied by a pageant illustrative of some aspect of London life, and is popularly known as the Lord Mayor's Show.

The Lord Mayor presides over each of the three Courts of the Corporation. He is head of the City Lieutenancy, a body of persons which exercise the functions in the City of a lord lieutenant, he is the City's chief magistrate, and has a number of privileges and duties in relation to the Sovereign, the port of London, and the administration of justice.

There is no deputy Lord Mayor. If the Lord Mayor cannot attend any meeting of the Courts of the Corporation, he must appoint as deputy for the purpose an alderman who has been Lord Mayor. If the Lord Mayoralty falls vacant through death or otherwise, the business of the Corporation is generally suspended until a successor is appointed. Meanwhile the senior alderman acts in necessary and urgent matters in the place of the Lord Mayor.

# 3

## Special Local Organizations

F o r a number of services, in which local government authorities are concerned, and which are administered on the basis of local areas, special authorities have been set up. The extent of the concern of the local government authorities varies according to the particular service or the local position.

### ELECTRICITY SUPPLY

Under the Electricity Act, 1947, the supply of electricity became, as from 1st April, 1948, a nationalized service under the general responsibility of the central government. Previous to the coming into operation of the Act, electricity supply was provided in some areas by local government authorities, in other areas by commercial companies. Each of these various bodies, over 500 in all, had a virtual monopoly of supply in its own area. Their powers and responsibilities were provided for in Acts of Parliament which authorized the laying of mains and the execution of works. The service provided was not uniform throughout the country, although the central government did, to a considerable extent, exercise supervision. Rates of charge were controlled and limitations were placed upon the scale of profits and their disposal.

The establishment of a national body of Electricity Commissioners to promote and supervise electricity supply throughout the country illustrated the growing recognition of the essential nature of this service. Technical developments made it possible to transmit a supply economically over long distances, and in 1926 a Central Electricity Board was created to supply electricity in bulk, through a national 'grid' system of main cables and power stations, to the authorities and companies who were suppliers to the general public.

Under the Electricity Acts, 1947 and 1957, the supply of

electricity is the responsibility of a Central Electricity Generating Board, appointed by the Minister of Fuel and Power, to provide for bulk supplies, and (in England and Wales) twelve area boards, also appointed by the Minister, to provide for supply in their own areas. General supervision of the whole arrangement is in the hands of an Electricity Council composed of the chairmen of the Generating Board and of the area boards, and certain other members appointed by the Minister and by the Generating Board. Over all these authorities the Minister has general direction.

None of these authorities is elected by the public. There is no direct link between them and the public they serve as was the case when electricity was supplied by elected local government authorities. To provide such a link and for representation of the consumer interest, there is, in the area of each area board, a consultative council who may receive representations and complaints from consumers and make suggestions and reports to the area board and also make representations to the Generating Board, the Electricity Council and to the Minister.

Each consultative council is composed of a chairman and between twenty and thirty other members, all of whom are appointed by the Minister. At least two-fifths and not more than three-fifths of the members are to be chosen from a panel of persons nominated by associations representing local government authorities in the area.

The chairman of each consultative council is a member of the area board. The remainder of the members of the councils are required to be representative of agriculture, commerce, industry and the general interests of local consumers. The councils may appoint committees and officers. The cost is borne out of national funds.

### GAS SUPPLY

The Gas Act, 1948, makes provision for the nationalization of the gas supply industry, and sets up central and local bodies of somewhat the same kind as those established for electricity supply. Gas supply was formerly provided by local authorities and commercial companies having, under parliamentary powers, a monopoly of supply in their separate districts. These areas were considered to be too numerous, and, in many cases, of inadequate size and unproductive of sufficient resources for the efficient development of the industry. Accordingly the Act of 1948 provided for the division of England and Wales into eleven gas supply areas, the size and shape of which differ considerably from the areas for electricity supply. For each area an area gas board to undertake gas supply is appointed by the Minister of Fuel and Power. A central body, the Gas Council, also appointed by the Minister, is set up to advise him and to assist the area boards.

The elective principle does not apply to these bodies, and, as in the case of electricity supply, a consultative council is set up for each area for the purpose of making suggestions, and receiving complaints. A consultative council may make representations to the area board, to the Gas Council and to the Minister.

The consultative councils are composed of between twenty and thirty members and a chairman, all of whom are appointed by the Minister. Not less than half the members of each council are to be appointed from a panel of persons nominated from amongst members of local authorities in the area by representative associations of local authorities. The chairman of each council is a member of the local area board. The remaining members are required to be representative of commerce, industry, labour and the general interest of gas consumers in the area. Each council may appoint committees and officers. Expenses are paid out of national funds.

### WATER SUPPLY

Piped water is, in some areas, supplied by commercial companies and in other areas by local government authorities. Statutory powers have been conferred on these suppliers either generally or individually, to lay mains, break open streets, execute works and do other things necessary for their undertakings. The suppliers are under a duty to provide (subject to certain conditions) an adequate and pure supply for domestic purposes to every dwelling the owner of which has demanded a supply. Suppliers are also obliged (if their resources are sufficient) to supply water for non-domestic purposes. By-laws may be made by the supplying authorities and companies as to the type and use of water fittings and for the general protection of the water supply. If any watercourse, pond or well is used for human water supply, the local government authorities have, as part of their sanitary functions, power to order the discontinuance of the supply if the water is contaminated.

*London.* The Metropolis Water Act, 1902, set up the Metropolitan Water Board which took over the undertakings of private companies supplying water in and around London. The Board is indirectly elected, and consists of eighty-eight representatives of local authorities in the area of supply. It has statutory powers akin to those of other water undertakers.

*Water rates.* Water supplied for other than domestic purposes may be charged for according to the quantity supplied, but the charges for water for domestic purposes is not based upon the quantity supplied or consumed. Water supply is considered to be an essential factor in public health, and the occupier of domestic premises ought not (it is considered) to be in a position to refuse to use the water in order to save money. Accordingly the charge for domestic water is normally based upon the net annual value of the premises and is levied in the form of a rate in the £, much in the same way as the rates levied for general purposes by local authorities.[1] The net annual value is that appearing in the valuation lists for general rating purposes. If domestic water supply is used for such purposes as car washing, gardening and in the use of water softening and refrigerating apparatus, the supplier may make extra rates for domestic supply, and may agree with the consumer to furnish the supply on such terms, whether by meter or otherwise, as may be agreed. Disputes relating to rates and charges are determined by the local county court. There are certain differences of detail between water rates and a local authority's general rates. These differences relate to the mode of collection, the giving of discounts, and the making of allowances for periods of inoccupancy. The water rate is levied separately from the general rates.

*The Water Act, 1945.* Water supply is derived from natural sources which are dependent in each locality on the geographical and hydro-geological conditions. The resources of

[1] See chapter 6.

every area are not the same. Nor is the demand in each area the same; for the demand depends to a large extent on the incidence of population. Apart from the increased use of water in recent years due to improved standards of hygiene and sanitation, the divergence between local resources and local demands is, in populous areas, affected by the fact that rain (one of the natural sources of supply) which falls upon the roofs of buildings is carried off by surface water sewers instead of being allowed to percolate into the ground and refurnish the wells.

The Water Act, 1945, contains provisions designed to co-ordinate water supply throughout the country. The Minister of Housing and Local Government is given the express duties of promoting the conservation and proper use of water resources and the provision of water supplies, and of securing the effective execution by water undertakers, under his control and direction, of a national policy relating to water.

The Act requires the Minister to appoint a Central Advisory Water Committee to assist him, and in local areas, where necessary, joint advisory water committees representative of the local water undertakers and local authorities. The primary function of these advisory bodies is the formulation of proposals for the planning and co-ordination of supplies.

The Minister also has power under the Act to arrange either by agreement or by compulsion for the amalgamation of undertakings, for the furnishing of joint supplies by undertakers, for the setting up of joint authorities, for the variation of areas of supply, or for the supply by one undertaker to another of water in bulk. The Minister has power to make orders to control the abstraction of water and to control waste.

## PUBLIC TRANSPORT

With the invention and development of mechanical transport in the nineteenth century, a large number of local authorities and commercial companies obtained from Parliament, by public and private Acts, powers to provide local systems of public passenger transport. Statutory authority was required by both local authorities and companies for the installation in public highways of tramways and apparatus for trolley buses. To run omnibuses, local authorities required special statutory powers, while commercial companies required no special authorization from Parliament.

In some localities there was considerable competition between the various operators. The Ministry of Transport Act, 1919, gave the Minister of Transport (thereby newly created) general responsibility for the oversight of all forms of transport. Under the Road Traffic Act, 1930, the country was divided into traffic areas each of which was administered by Traffic Commissioners with power to regulate (but not to undertake) the running of public service vehicles, the number of services to be permitted, and the routes to be followed. In 1934 the passenger transport services in and around London were taken over from the local authorities and companies by the London Passenger Transport Board, an appointed body under the supervision of the Minister of Transport.

By the Transport Act, 1947, the railways were nationalized and taken over by the British Transport Commission, who were also empowered to provide road transport services. In 1948 the London Passenger Transport Board was supplanted by the London Transport Executive, appointed by the Minister. Local government authorities have the right to make representations to the Transport Tribunal in relation to schemes made by that Tribunal for fares and charges for passenger transport. The Traffic Commissioners for each area are renamed the Licensing Authority for Public Service Vehicles, and retain their powers, under the supervision of the Minister, to determine the routes, stopping places, and types of vehicle to be permitted on any route.

The Act provides for the establishment of a Central Transport Consultative Committee for Great Britain, and Transport Users' Consultative Committees for local areas, to consider representations made by transport users as well as any matters referred to the committees by the Transport Commission or the Minister. The members are appointed by the Minister to represent various interests and types of activity of which local government may be one. The size of the committees is not specified in the Act. Any staff required by the committees is provided by the Transport Commission.

## THE RELIEF OF POVERTY

Local public services for the assistance of the necessitous poor originated in consequence of the dissolution of the monasteries by Henry VIII, and the cessation of the opportunity for charitable help which those institutions provided. By the Poor Relief Act of 1601, the local justices were required to nominate certain inhabitants of ecclesiastical parishes who should undertake the duty of appointing overseers of the poor. These officers had to find work for the poor and furnish materials for them to work on. The cost was met by a poor rate levied on the parish. This parish organization, with its representative vestries, lasted until the nineteenth century, when it was replaced by elected Boards of Guardians for parishes or unions of parishes.

Relief was, broadly, of two types (i) institutional or indoor relief by way of admission to a work-house, asylum or infirmary, and (ii) out-relief, or the issue of goods and money to poor persons not resident in an institution.

A social stigma attached to the recipients of poor relief or 'paupers'. They were unable to vote at public elections. Social and economic adjustments since the first world war led to an alteration of this attitude. In 1920, county and county borough councils were authorized to make schemes for the training and welfare of blind persons, including the grant of financial help to the unemployable blind. This assistance was given outside the ordinary system of poor relief.

The present system of providing for the relief of poverty has been developed as a result of two main causes (i) the change of social attitude towards poverty, and (ii) the need for an equitable distribution of the cost.

The adoption of the Elizabethan notion that each locality should bear the cost of its own poor imposed a severe burden on the unprosperous areas, where rateable values were low and the number of poor persons high.

The amalgamation of parishes into unions in the nineteenth century had the effect of spreading the load of poor relief over wider areas. The transfer of poor law functions from the Guardians to the councils of counties and county boroughs in 1930 spread the load still wider. The acceptance by the central government of a very substantial share in providing for the unemployed and the needy spread the load wider still. The various national insurance schemes, for instance, made provision at the expense of the nation for needs which otherwise would have been dealt with through the medium of the poor law.

The councils of counties and county boroughs, when the functions of poor relief were transferred to them, were empowered to provide free services for poor persons other than by means of the poor law. The term 'public assistance' came into official use as a description of poor relief. Later the term 'social welfare' became common.

*National Assistance.* In 1934 the National Assistance Board was set up to provide, other than by way of poor relief, for the needs of the able-bodied unemployed. The National Assistance Act, 1948, abolished the poor law altogether, and gave the Board the general duty to provide assistance for all persons whose resources are insufficient for their needs.

The Board's duty under the Act is to provide monetary assistance or, in special circumstances, assistance in kind, by (for example) the issue of orders for goods on local tradesmen.

It is also the duty of the Board to provide reception centres for the provision of temporary accommodation for persons without a settled way of life (e.g. vagrants), and to make provision whereby those persons may be induced to lead a more settled life. The Board may transfer to the councils of counties and county boroughs the duty of providing and maintaining these centres at the cost of the Board.

In addition, the Board may provide re-establishment centres at which persons who, through lack of regular occupation or lack of training, are in need of instruction may receive it so as to fit them for regular employment.

*Local Authorities' Services.* The Act requires the councils of counties and county boroughs to provide residential accommodation for persons in need of care and attention which is not otherwise available for them. Charges must be made for this accommodation according to the recipient's ability to pay. The charge must not be less than a prescribed minimum; if the applicant is unable to pay this the Board will assist him. The Assistance Board may demand accommodation in urgent cases. The same local authorities are also required to provide a welfare service for persons who are blind, crippled or otherwise physically handicapped. Workshops and training and recreational facilities may be provided. Charges may be made according to ability to pay. Husbands and wives are responsible for each other's maintenance and for that of their children.

When a local authority provides assistance for persons not ordinarily resident in its area, the cost can be charged to the authority of the area where the assisted person normally resides.

The practical application of the provisions of the Act involves considerable liaison between the National Assistance Board and the local authorities. The Minister of Health exercises general supervision.

The Board is, for the purpose of securing the advice and assistance of persons having local knowledge and experience in matters affecting the functions of the Board, required to set up Advisory Committees throughout the country for such areas as the Board thinks fit. The constitution of these committees is not prescribed in the Act; appointments are at the discretion of the Board.

## HOSPITALS AND MEDICAL SERVICES

Until the middle of the nineteenth century there was no official provision for hospital or medical treatment other than through the poor law. The Public Health Act, 1875, gave local government authorities power to establish hospitals, but little use was made of the power. This essential public service was left largely to the poor-relief authorities and voluntary bodies. By subsequent legislation local government authorities were empowered to make provision for maternity and child welfare, mental disorders, tuberculosis and venereal disease.

The taking over in 1930 by the councils and county boroughs of the functions of the Boards of Guardians, and the poor-law infirmaries and asylums, provided the opportunity for the reorganization of the various local public medical services into a municipal hospital and medical service side by side with the voluntary hospitals and charitable agencies.

The municipal medical service was not, however, uniform throughout the country. Local resources did not always match local needs. Moreover, developments in medical science necessitated the use of special equipment or special hospitals for the proper treatment of certain types of case, and few authorities had sufficient demand within their areas for these special types of provision to make it economical to provide the range of hospitals, clinics and apparatus desired. Mutual agreements were made between authorities and with the voluntary hospitals to meet these needs, and joint committees and boards of various kinds were set up.

Official provision for medical practitioner services was made through the national health insurance scheme organized by the central government.

The National Health Service Act, 1946, aimed at the establishment of a national health service for medical treatment of all kinds.

Municipal and voluntary hospitals, except in a few special cases, were, by the Act, transferred to and financed by the state. The country is divided into regions in which the hospitals of the various types can be grouped so as to provide the necessary range of facilities in each region. The provision of hospital and specialist services in each region is administered by a Regional Board appointed by the Minister of Health. Each hospital is managed by a Hospital Management Committee similarly appointed. To advise the Minister there is a Central Health Services Council with standing advisory committees.

The councils of counties and county boroughs are 'local health authorities' under the Act. Where necessary the Minister may, for the area of two or more of these authorities, set up a joint board representative of them to act as local health authority for the joint area. These local health authorities are responsible for providing for maternity and child welfare, midwifery, home nursing, vaccination and immunization, ambulances, preventive services, after-care, home-nursing and domestic help for the sick. They must also provide health centres where practitioners can provide treatment, with any special apparatus required, and where films, lectures and other public instruction on health matters can be given.

Medical practitioner, dental, pharmaceutical and ophthalmic services in the area of each local health authority are organized by local Executive Councils, each composed of twenty-five members, eight of whom are appointed by the local health authority and the remainder by the Minister and by the local practitioners.

Local authorities are not represented on the Central Council, Regional Boards or Hospital Management Committees. Five of the forty-six members of the Central Council must be laymen with experience in local government. In appointing the Boards and Management Committees the Minister must consult the local health authority.

## POLICE

The provision of police services has for many centuries been associated with the administration of justice. The parish constables and high constables of medieval times were, as the feudal system decayed, brought increasingly under the control of the justices of the peace and were subject to their appointment.

In boroughs, watchmen were appointed to supplement the parish constables and to provide the 'watch and ward' required in all walled towns by the Statute of Winchester of 1285. The preamble to the Metropolitan Police Act, 1829, explains that these arrangements were found inadequate in and near the metropolis 'by reason of the frequent unfitness of the individuals employed, the insufficiency of their number, the limited sphere of their authority and their want of connection and co-operation with each other'. Special provision for the metropolitan area was accordingly made.

In 1835, when the boroughs were 'reformed' by the Municipal Corporations Act of that year, each borough was required to set up a borough police force. The Municipal Corporations Act, 1882, provided that each borough police force should be administered by a watch committee appointed by the borough council. Of this committee the mayor (who is head of the borough justices) must be a member.

In 1839 the justices of the peace in quarter sessions (then the local government authority for each county) were empowered to establish local police forces in the counties. When, by the Local Government Act, 1888, county councils were established, the management of the police force in each county was transferred from the quarter sessions to a standing joint committee composed of equal numbers of justices and of members of the county council.

By the Police Act, 1946, the police forces in non-county boroughs are to be amalgamated with the county police force except where the population of the borough in 1939 was more than half the total population of the county. The Act enables two or more police authorities, whether of counties or of boroughs, to make voluntary schemes, with the approval of the Home Secretary, for the amalgamation of their forces, and for the constitution of a combined police authority representative of the combined authorities to administer the combined force. The Home Secretary may himself make compulsory schemes for the same purposes.

These arrangements for borough and county forces have one feature in common, namely, that no local police force is directly controlled by a publicly elected authority. The watch committee of a borough has virtual independence of the borough council in the management of the borough force.[2] The standing joint committee in a county, and a combined police authority where forces have been combined contain, it is true, representatives of local government authorities, but the councils themselves play no part in the control of the forces and have no obligation in the matter other than to provide, out of the rates, the funds necessary for pay and equipment.

It is thought inadvisable to allow a service essential to the maintenance of law and public order to be directly and entirely under local popular control. At the same time it is felt to be appropriate that the local government authorities, who have to provide funds for police services, should have some representation upon the bodies controlling the local forces.

*London.* The City of London has its own police force controlled by a Commissioner appointed by the City Corporation, subject to the approval of the Home Secretary. His powers of control over the force are wide and are subject only to a general supervision by the Court of Aldermen and the Home Secretary.

Outside the City a number of boroughs, urban districts, rural districts and parishes within, roughly, fifteen miles of

[2] See chapter 11.

45

Charing Cross form the Metropolitan Police District. Police services in this District are provided by the Metropolitan Police Force under a Commissioner of Police for the Metropolis who is appointed by the Crown and acts under the immediate direction of the Home Secretary. Funds are obtained by precepts levied according to rateable value upon the local government authorities in the district; these precepts are met out of rates levied by those authorities.

*Private Police.* A number of public authorities, such as the British Transport Commission and harbour and dock authorities, maintain private police forces at their own expense for the protection of their property and undertakings.

### HARBOURS AND PORTS

When the British Transport Commission on 1st January, 1948, took over, under the Transport Act, 1947, the ownership of the railways, the Commission at the same time took over the docks and harbour undertakings formerly owned by the railway companies, as well as the undertakings of a number of companies and bodies having the management of canals and inland waterways.

There remained a number of harbour undertakings owned by public authorities and private companies. The Act of 1947 provides that 'trade harbours' may be taken over by the Commission under schemes made for that purpose. Those harbours where facilities are provided only for pleasure steamers, yachts and fishing vessels are not subject to this provision. Pending the making of any scheme for trade harbours the existing authorities remain in function.

Harbour facilities in some of the smaller ports are provided by the local borough or district council or commercial companies. Facilities at the larger ports, such as London and Liverpool, are provided by specially established public bodies representative of local authorities, the central government and users of the ports. Statutory powers have been granted to carry out works, make by-laws, levy tolls and charges, and regulate the use of the harbour accommodation. Finance is provided by the charges made for the facilities.

*Port Health Authorities.* Under the Public Health Act, 1936, the Minister of Health may by order constitute port health districts consisting of the area of any neighbouring local authority or authorities. For each district he may set up a port health authority. This authority may be either the local authority or one of the local authorities in the district, or a joint board representative of the local authorities in the district. The port health authority has jurisdiction over land and water within the district, for such matters as quarantine, medical inspection of ships and immigrants, and the examination of imported food and drugs. Within the port health district no other local authority normally having functions of the kind exercised by the port health authority may exercise those functions. A port health authority may, however, delegate any of its functions to a riparian local authority whose area is within or abuts on the port health district.

The expenses of a port health authority which is also a local government authority are borne as part of the authority's normal expenditure. Where a joint board has been constituted expenses are borne by contributions obtained by precepts on the constituent authorities.

The Minister of Health has power to act in default of a port health authority.

The City of London Corporation is the port health authority for the Port of London.

### LAND DRAINAGE AND THE CONSERVATION OF RIVERS

At the time of the passing of the River Boards Act, 1948, the control of freshwater fisheries and navigable rivers, the drainage of land and the prevention of pollution of water-courses were in the hands of a variety of authorities.

That these matters were of importance and of public interest had long been recognized. Owners of property on the banks of rivers and streams have a legal right to the use and flow of the water, but the public has also a general concern.

Powers of management and control over particular rivers have been conferred on a number of bodies of a public or semi-public type, known by various names—conservators, trustees, commissioners of sewers and the like.

The pollution of a river or stream by the discharge into it of noxious matters such as rubbish, sewage, or refuse from manufacture had been made illegal. The Rivers Pollution Prevention Acts conferred power on local authorities to take proceedings against offenders, but provided that where the pollution was due to manufacturing or mining processes the consent of the Minister of Health should be required, and the Minister should have regard to the industrial interests involved and the circumstances and requirements of the locality.

For the purpose of land drainage (as distinct from the drainage of buildings) a number of catchment areas had been defined. Each catchment area was intended to include the area drained by a main river and its tributaries, and was administered by a catchment board appointed by the Minister of Agriculture and Fisheries and by the councils of counties and county boroughs in the area. The catchment board was responsible for the general supervision of the area and for the execution of works in connection with the main river.

In addition, a number of smaller land drainage districts had been defined. These were such areas as would derive benefit or avoid danger as a result of drainage operations. Each district had a drainage board elected by owners and occupiers of land in the area. Where a drainage district was within a catchment area it was called an 'internal drainage district' and the board was an 'internal drainage board' and was under the supervision of the catchment board. A drainage district could, however, exist outside a catchment area. All drainage boards had duties of providing drainage works within their districts and could levy drainage rates.

For the protection of freshwater fisheries, the Minister of Agriculture and Fisheries had appointed fishery boards each of which had power, within a defined fishery district, to issue licences to anglers, prescribe the conditions under which fishing might take place, and impose fines. Local anglers were represented upon these boards.

*River Boards.* The River Boards Act, 1948, authorized the Minister to set up a number of river boards each having jurisdiction over a 'river board area', to exercise the functions of catchment boards and fishery boards and duties of prevention of pollution. Catchment boards, fishery boards and bodies

48

of commissioners, conservators and others having concern with the management of rivers cease to exist within the area of a river board. Internal drainage boards, however, remain in function.

Each river board may comprise not more than forty members, one of whom is appointed by the Minister. Of the remaining members a majority are appointed by the councils of counties and county boroughs in the area. The remaining members are appointed by the Minister to represent local drainage boards and fishery interests. A river board has powers of supervision of the local drainage boards, and may issue, upon the councils of counties and county boroughs in the area, precepts proportioned according to their rateable value for contributions towards the expenses of the board.

*The Thames, the Lee and London.* The Thames Conservancy, a body appointed by government departments and local authorities, and the Lee Conservancy Catchment Board, somewhat similarly appointed, have special powers to deal with the catchment areas of the rivers Thames and Lee. The London County Council has special powers to deal with flood prevention in the county. The existence of these various powers made it unnecessary to provide in the Act of 1948 for a river board for these areas in the first instance, but the Minister has, under the Act, power to bring in these areas into the same position as the rest of the country if need be.

*Land Drainage Boards* are elected by owners or occupiers of land on which a drainage rate has been levied in the year immediately preceding the election. The boards are elected every three years under rules made by the Minister of Agriculture and Fisheries. Each elector has votes according to the rateable value of his property, i.e., one vote for each £50 up to £250, six votes if his property is between £250 and £500, eight votes for property between £500 and £1,000, and ten votes for over £1,000. The chairman may be paid, and members may be repaid their travelling expenses. Officers may be appointed.

The boards have, subject to the supervision of the river board or catchment board for the area, power to execute works, remove obstructions to watercourses, and compel owners and occupiers of land to carry out their obligations with regard to watercourses and drainage. The expenses of the boards are met by drainage rates levied by the boards upon occupiers and owners of land in the drainage district. The rate is assessed according to the annual value for income tax under Schedule A. Agricultural land is assessed at the full gross value, but other land is assessed at one-third of the gross annual value. Appeal against a drainage rate lies to quarter sessions. Recovery of the rate is enforced by distress upon the defaulter's property, and, if the distress is insufficient, by committal to prison. No person may be committed, however, if his failure to pay is due to circumstances beyond his control.

*Sea Fisheries.* For the purpose of protecting inshore fisheries the coast of England and Wales has been divided by the Minister of Agriculture and Fisheries into a number of sea-fisheries districts, each of which is controlled by a local sea fisheries committee. These committees are committees of the local county council or borough council, as the case may be. If two or more councils are concerned in a district, a joint committee may be provided. Each of these committees must include members appointed by the Minister to represent local sea fishing interests. These appointed members must not exceed in number the members representing the local government authorities.

A sea fisheries committee may make by-laws to regulate the methods of sea fishing, and to protect the breeding of shellfish, may destroy pests, contribute to the cost of harbours for fishing vessels, and take proceedings for offences. Expenses of a sea fishery committee are borne out of the rates as part of the expenditure of the council or councils appointing the committee.

## THE DEVELOPMENT OF SPECIAL AREAS

The growth of the concept of national planning and the increasing acceptance of the idea that economic problems such as unemployment, shifts of population, and distribution of industry, were not matters to be left to the interplay of so-called laws expounded by classical economists, but were matters for direct state intervention and influence, led to the setting up of special bodies with power to stimulate industrial development in appropriate areas.

Local government authorities have, of course, various powers to undertake the development of their areas by the construction of roads, sewers, housing estates and the rest. These powers are, however, exercised to meet a demand already existing. Local authorities hesitate to venture heavy capital expenditure on development when there is little prospect of immediate recoupment.

The direct stimulation of industrial development has been undertaken by the central government in respect of two types of area, (i) certain areas already developed but which are by reason of trade depression or industrial changes in need of assistance, and (ii) areas of little or no development in which the establishment of new towns is appropriate.

*Development Areas* were the subject of provisions in the Special Areas (Development and Improvement) Act, 1934, and subsequent Acts now replaced by the Distribution of Industry Acts, 1945 and 1950. The particular areas to be dealt with, four in number, and situated in North-East England, Cumberland, South Wales and Scotland, are specified. Under the earlier Acts bodies of commissioners were set up with powers to undertake and assist development. By the Act of 1945 these arrangements are terminated and the functions of the commissioners have been taken over by the Board of Trade and are to a great extent exercised through regional controllers of the board assisted by the local regional officers of other government departments concerned. Estate companies have been set up with financial assistance from the government. If any development area is deficient in a basic service such as lighting, heating, power, housing, health or other services, financial aid may be granted by the government to meet the deficiency. Grants may also be made by the government to local authorities or to non-profit-making companies to enable them to re-develop derelict land in a development area.

*New Towns.* Under the New Towns Act, 1946, the Minister of Housing and Local Government may take direct action to establish new towns by means of development corporations financed by the government. Before designating any area as appropriate for a new town the Minister must consult the local authorities. The corporations may themselves be authorized to carry out operations normally performed by local authorities, such as the construction of roads, houses, sewerage and other public services, and may make contributions towards the expenses of local authorities in providing services in a new town. The income of the development corporations, apart from government subventions, derives from rents and profits on estate development. The Act of 1946 enables a corporation to transfer any part of its undertaking to a local authority or statutory undertaker on agreed terms. The New Towns Act, 1959 set up a Commission for the New Towns and requires the Minister, on the winding up of a new towns corporation, to transfer (after consultation with the councils of the county and county district) the undertaking of the corporation to that Commission.

## JOINT AUTHORITIES

For a number of services, in localities where the area of any one local government authority, or its resources, are not such as to make for an efficient and economical management of the service, recourse has been had to the device of setting up joint authorities.

Provisions for setting up these joint authorities are contained in numerous Acts of Parliament relating to particular services. For example, the Town and Country Planning Act, 1947 (for planning purposes), the Education Act, 1944 (for education purposes), the National Health Service Act, 1946 (for local health services), the Water Act, 1945 (for water supply) and the Public Health Act, 1936 (for general public health services) all give power to the appropriate Minister to set up a joint board for carrying out services in combined local areas.

The Police Act, 1946, empowers the Home Secretary to make Orders, with or without the agreement of the councils concerned, for the amalgamation of local police forces and for the setting up of a combined police authority for the combined area of the constituent authorities. The Fire Services Act, 1947, contains similar provision for the amalgamation of fire brigades.

The effect of these various arrangements for joint boards or combined authorities is to create a joint body as an independent entity, whose existence and activities are not controlled by the constituent authorities. The creation of the joint body is by an Order of the appropriate Minister, not by an act of the constituent authorities, and, once in existence, the joint body can operate, within the limits of the powers given to it by the Order, without interference by the constituent authorities.

These joint bodies have no power to levy rates. Their finances are derived from contributions made by the constituent councils, upon whom the joint body has power to make due demands or issue precepts. The contributions are not within the discretion of or variable by the contributing authorities but are assessed according to the terms of the Order.

It is in these features that a joint board or combined authority differs from a joint committee. A joint committee is the creation of the constituent councils and is subject to whatever limitations and controls those councils may impose.

# 4

## Administration of Justice

THROUGHOUT England and Wales the local organization for the administration of justice is in a number of ways associated with the system of local government.

In medieval times, local government services of the modern type were practically non-existent. A general obligation was placed upon every man to share in the maintenance of highways, bridges, and military service, as well as in the ordinary duties of complying with the law of the land and of keeping the peace. Compliance with these obligations was enforced by means of the local feudal courts and by the locally elected constables. There were county courts or assemblies of the freemen in each county, and these courts had certain judicial functions and provided the opportunity for the consideration of matters of common interest. In each county the sheriff appointed by the King carried out periodical visits of inspection (the sheriff's tourn) to see that the judicial organization was functioning properly and to punish offenders.

With the decay of the feudal system and the growth of the royal influence, conservators of the peace, later known as justices of the peace, were appointed by the Crown by means of a commission of the peace issued for each county. By the fourteenth century these justices were carrying out extensive duties of a judicial kind. Their more important duties were performed at quarterly meetings—the courts of quarter sessions. Under the Tudor Kings another county office was instituted, that of lord lieutenant, appointed by the Crown to take over the sheriff's duties in regard to the supervision of military service. The lord lieutenant was head of the county justices and keeper of their records (*custos rotulorum*).

Side by side with these developments a number of towns obtained, by royal charter, exemption from the local feudal arrangements, and were authorized to set up their own local courts; some were granted separate commissions of the peace, and were allowed to appoint their own sheriffs and coroners. Some towns in fact became counties of themselves.

The pattern of the local organization for the administration of justice thus became one of counties and boroughs.

Over this local system there were the judges of the King's own courts, His Majesty's Judges, who toured the country and held assizes for the trial of the more important offences and disputes.

This framework still remains. The ancient offices of lord lieutenant, sheriff, coroner, and constable still exist, although the powers attaching to these offices have altered considerably. The lord lieutenant still takes ceremonial precedence over other office holders in a county at large.[1] He holds office during the pleasure of the Crown. Appointments of justices of the peace are made on his recommendation. He is, in most counties, *custos rotulorum*, and his official concern with military matters is largely confined to the auxiliary and cadet forces. The sheriff, appointed annually for each county by the Crown, and, in boroughs which have their own sheriffs, by the borough council, has the duties of summoning juries and of carrying out the execution of writs and processes of the courts. The coroner for a county or a borough is appointed, and paid, by the council of the county or borough; his duties include the holding of inquests and the disposal of treasure trove. The office of high constable of a county or borough is now replaced by that of chief (or head) constable, who is the paid officer appointed as head of the local police force. Elected parish constables have ceased to exist.

The tours of the judges of the High Court are arranged in circuits based on groupings of counties and boroughs.

Justices of the peace have, to-day, power to hold magistrates' courts to try a wide range of minor cases. For some purposes a justice is competent to sit alone as a court of summary jurisdiction, and for other purposes in petty sessions composed of two or more justices. The council of any borough having a separate commission of the peace, and a county council, may

---

[1] A Lord Lieutenant is not normally appointed for the county of a city or county of a town.

petition the Crown to appoint a stipendiary magistrate, paid by the council, who, when sitting alone, has the power of a petty sessional court.

Quarter sessions deal with more important cases and act as a court of appeal from the magistrates'courts and stipendiaries.

Boroughs with the status of a 'county of a city', or 'county of a town' still exist. They have their own quarter sessions, commissions of the peace, sheriffs and coroners. Borough courts of quarter sessions are presided over by a recorder, appointed by the Crown and paid by the borough corporation. Some of these boroughs have their own separate courts of assize attended by the judges of the High Court when on circuit, and can thus be, for judicial purposes, independent of the county at large.

Of the remaining boroughs, some have separate commissions of the peace; others have not. In either case the borough justices are competent only to hold magistrates' courts of summary jurisdiction and petty sessions.

Every mayor of a borough and every chairman of a county council or county district is a justice of the peace by virtue of his office.

The chief official of a court of quarter sessions is the clerk of the peace. In counties he is appointed by the quarter sessions; he is usually the clerk of the county council. In a borough he is appointed by the borough council and is often (though not always) the town clerk.

*Administrative business of the Justices.* From the sixteenth to the nineteenth centuries the justices in quarter sessions had considerable administrative work. When, under Elizabeth I, the parishes were made the local units for poor relief and the maintenance of highways, the county quarter sessions were given duties of supervision over the parish authorities and had power to impose penalties for neglect of parochial obligations. The justices thus became concerned not only in dispensing justice but also in the administration of local services. In the course of time the non-judicial functions of the quarter sessions were increased, and, by the nineteenth century, quarter sessions had become the local government authority for the county, with duties in relation to bridges, lunatic asylums, weights and measures and other matters.

The Local Government Act, 1888, which created county

councils and county borough councils, transferred to those authorities the administrative (non-judicial) business of quarter sessions. Quarter sessions, then, ceased to be concerned with the administration of local government services.

The justices of the peace have, however, certain functions, partly judicial and partly administrative, in relation to the issue of various licences. Premises where intoxicating liquors are sold require, in addition to a licence from the excise authorities, a licence from the licensing committee of the local justices of the peace sitting in annual licensing meetings and special sessions. New licences require confirmation by a committee of quarter sessions, which is also the authority for determining the amount of compensation to be paid when an 'old' (pre-1904) liquor licence is extinguished. The licensing of moneylenders is also a function of the justices. In some parts of the country the licensing sessions deal also with the issue of licences for theatres, cinemas and public music and dancing—a function which in other parts of the country is performed by the council of the county or county borough.

Justices of the peace are also concerned with the visitation of prisons and of institutions for the mentally defective.

*Expenses.* The cost of providing and maintaining court houses and their equipment,[2] and the salaries of the recorders, stipendiary magistrates, coroners, clerks of the peace and other staff are borne by the local government authorities. The cost of borough courts is borne by the borough council, and that council may also have to make a contribution towards the county fund to the extent to which the borough makes use of the county system of justice.

In counties there is a standing joint committee composed of equal numbers of justices representing quarter sessions, and of members of the county council. This committee provides the accommodation and staff for the justices' courts and quarter sessions. The county council meets the expense. The standing joint committee is also concerned in the management of the county police and may, by delegation from the county council, deal with the licensing of sporting tracks on which betting takes place.

[2] Other than of the county courts set up to deal with civil cases. These courts, and the Supreme Court of Judicature, are maintained out of national funds.

In counties and county boroughs there are magistrates' courts committees composed of justices with the duty of maintaining an adequate and efficient organization of magistrates' courts, the provision of accommodation, and the appointment of justices' clerks. Costs are borne by the county or borough council.

# 5

## The Nature and Ambit of Local
## Government Functions

THERE is no general code of legislation from which a complete statement can be obtained of the powers and duties of any type of local government authority; they have been conferred piecemeal and in respect of particular services as the need arose, and have been adjusted from time to time in accordance with the development of public services and the changing trends of national policy.

The functions exercisable by the local authorities cover a very wide range. Some are concerned with human material—the welfare of mother and child, the education of people of all ages, the care of the helpless and afflicted. Other functions are concerned with inanimate things—the management and construction of roads, the control of the erection of buildings, the planning of town and country development, the protection of buildings from fire. There are functions which relate to the carrying on of trades and businesses, namely the licensing of cinemas, the registration of nursing homes, the control of offensive trades, the inspection and testing of weights, measures, food and drugs. Other functions relate to the landscape and the natural world, such as the protection of wild birds, the prevention of cruelty to animals, and the provision and management of commons and open spaces.

All the functions of each local authority are exercisable only in relation to the area of that authority. There are a few cases in which a local authority may exercise functions outside its own area by providing, for example, a housing estate, an open space, a residential school, or a sewage disposal works, outside the area; but, for the most part, a local authority may exercise its functions only within the area. These functions must, however, in some way be related to the needs of the area. Local authorites have no capacity to alter, define or affect the rights, capacity or responsibilities of citizens in any way which is unconnected with the authority's area, as is the case with the laws relating to marriage and divorce, the status of infants and married women, and the rights of inheritance, which are matters for the concern of national governments.

The powers of an individual local authority are largely, but not entirely, dependent upon the class to which that authority belongs. The councils of county boroughs have a wider range of functions than any other type of local authority, for the reason that no other local government authority has jurisdiction within the area of the borough. In an administrative county, where functions are distributed among the authorities of various classes—the county councils, district councils and parish authorities—the class to which each individual authority belongs is a general guide to the scope of its functions. Thus the county council provides services such as the management of county roads, the provision of fire brigades and ambulances, which can be more appropriately organized over wide areas and which, if these services were more greatly localized, might in some instances prove unduly burdensome in cost to the authorities of a smaller area.

The district councils exercise functions of a local character relating to such matters as street maintenance and cleansing, local sanitary services and housing. Differences in function exist between the urban and the rural district councils due to the differences between urban and rural conditions, and to the fact that in the rural districts the parish authorities have functions in their own parishes. Non-county borough councils, by virtue of the existence of their borough charters, stand in a somewhat different position from the councils of the other county districts. As for the parish authorities, their powers vary according to whether the authority is a parish council or a parish meeting.

*Private and adoptive Acts.* The status of any local authority is not, however, a complete guide to its functions. Among authorities of the same class the functions of individual authorities vary.

Most of the functions of local authorities have been given to them by public general statutes, which indicate in each case the functions to be exercised by each class of authority. In addition to these general statutes, many individual authorities have obtained private or local Acts conferring particular and additional powers. Every local authority, other than a parish authority, may promote a Bill to obtain special powers for itself, to carry out public works, to conduct a particular enterprise, such as a municipal bank, or to control certain businesses or activities such as domestic employment agencies or street trading, or in other ways to deal with the particular requirements of the locality.

In addition to these public and private Acts, Parliament has passed a number of Acts usually known as 'adoptive Acts' and chiefly relating to public health, the provisions of which may be applied to a particular locality by the decision of the local authority itself or by an Order of the appropriate Minister. The application of different provisions to different authorities adds further to the disuniformity of functions as between one authority and another.

*Delegation, surrender and transfer of powers.* A number of Acts of Parliament which confer functions upon particular classes of local authority make provision for alternative means whereby these functions may be exercised. Thus the Education Act, 1944, which makes each county council a local education authority, empowers a county council to agree to arrangements under which the councils of boroughs and urban districts in the county may take a share in the work of public education. County councils may also, under the guidance of a Minister, delegate functions relating to planning and to the provision of certain local health and welfare services.

Other statutes empower a county council to delegate outright particular duties to district authorities. The Local Government Act, 1933, gives a county council outside London power to delegate to the council of any county district in the county any function of the county council except a function for which the county council is required to appoint a committee, and except the power to borrow money or to issue a precept. In some statutes power has been given whereby a minor authority may surrender its powers to a county council.

The Minister of Housing and Local Government has under the Local Government Act, 1933, general powers to confer functions of parish councils on councils of boroughs and urban districts, to confer functions of urban district councils on rural district councils, and to confer the functions of a parish council on a parish meeting. He may also, under the London Government Act, 1939, with the consent of the authorities concerned, transfer powers as between the London local government authorities.

The Minister may also, by provisional order subject to confirmation by Parliament, transfer to a county or county borough council the functions of local public bodies such as conservators operating in the county or borough concerned.

County and county borough councils may delegate their functions in relation to the licensing of theatres and cinemas to justices of the peace, and a county council may delegate its functions in relation to the licensing of sporting tracks on which betting takes place to the standing joint committee of justices and of the council.

In addition to all this, a number of statutes provide opportunity for the making of schemes under which functions normally carried out by one type of authority may be exercised by other authorities, or by combined authorities specially created. Powers have been given to different Ministers under various Acts to set up joint boards to perform, in the area of two or more authorities, particular functions normally carried out by the local authorities for those areas.

Moreover, any local authority may concur with any one or more local authorities in appointing a joint committee for any purpose in which they are jointly interested and may delegate functions to the joint committee other than the power to levy a rate or borrow money.

For all these reasons there is considerable variation in the functions exercisable by each local government authority.

*Exercise of functions.* Besides the variation in function, there are wide differences in the extent to which each local authority exercises the functions assigned to it. Local provision must be suited to local needs, which vary from place to place. Some authorities make much use of powers for which other authorities have little need. The functions of local authorities fall into two main classes—powers and duties. Some statutory provisions make it obligatory upon a local authority to carry out a certain function or to provide a certain type of service. In other cases the provisions of the statute are permissive. The result is that while there are certain services which are provided everywhere (those which are obligatory), there are other services which are provided in some localities only.

And further, apart from the variations in the powers and duties of local authorities, there are local variations in the degree of efficiency, and of the standard of service provided, according to the local demand, the ability of the authority, and its financial capacity and willingness.

For all these reasons it is not possible to indicate other than broadly the distribution of functions between the various types of local authority, nor is it possible to say without considerable research or inquiry of the local authorities themselves, the extent to which particular functions are exercised in any locality or which authority exercises which function.

It is possible, however, to describe broadly the field of local government operations, and to provide a general picture of the ambit and nature of local government functions.

## PUBLIC HEALTH

The term 'public health' may be used in respect of a large group of services concerned with the physical well-being of the public. The earlier public health legislation contained provisions on a number of matters indirectly related to physical welfare such as open spaces, streets and buildings, and in respect of which the statutory provisions have been so extended as almost to form separate codes. In its widest sense public health merges into other spheres of local government, such as housing and physical education. It is not easy to draw a clear line of division. As generally used to-day the term 'public health' embraces the 'sanitary' and 'environmental health' services, such as sewerage and refuse disposal and the prevention of disease, and the 'personal health' services which relate particularly to medical treatment.

In the early years of the nineteenth century there was little or no provision for public health. The ancient municipal corporations were often negligent and the justices of the peace, as the county authorities, had little power in health matters beyond the suppression of nuisances. Commissioners of Sewers had been set up for land drainage in some areas. In the country-side there was virtually no sanitary government, and in most of the towns sewage was untreated and discharged into open streams, water was impure, garbage was thrown into streets, and epidemics were severe. These conditions were accentuated by the growth of the towns with the industrial revolution.

In the course of the century from 1830 onwards, great developments in the field of public health took place. Popular alarm and the social conscience were aroused. In 1831 an epidemic of cholera led to the creation of a Central Board of Health, with temporary local boards. In 1834 the poor law was reformed. In 1835 the municipal corporations were re-organized. In 1871 the Local Government Board was set up as a central government department. Under the Public Health Act, 1872, the country was divided into urban and rural sanitary districts. The Public Health Act, 1875, consolidated public health law. Since then the number of provisions relating to public health have continually increased, side by side with the reform of the local government structure. The Ministries of Health and of Housing and Local Government have replaced the Local Government Board. In the administrative counties the sanitary services are largely in the hands of the authorities of the county districts, the parish authorities also having a small share. Local medical services are (broadly speaking) with the county councils as local authorities under the National Health Service Act, 1946. The councils of county boroughs operate sanitary services and are local health authorities under the Act of 1946. Hospital and specialist medical services are administered by the special authorities set up under that Act.[1]

*Sanitary services (i)—Sewerage and drainage.* It is the duty of each borough, urban and rural authority to make sufficient provision for the proper sewerage of its district, and to provide sewage disposal works and public sewers. A sewer is a conduit which takes effluent from more than one house or property. A drain is a conduit leading from one house or property into a sewer. The term is also applied to channels for conducting surface water. When a building is a hundred feet or less from a public sewer, the authority may require the owner to

[1] See chapter 3.

discharge the sewage from the premises into the public sewer. In built-up areas, therefore, all sewage is discharged into public sewers, but in rural areas private cesspools are more usual. The local authority may (and if required by the Minister of Housing and Local Government must) undertake throughout the whole or any part of their district the cleansing of cesspools and earth closets either free or on payment, but there is a general obligation upon the occupier to maintain the premises in a sanitary condition. Private sewers and drains may be constructed by an owner for his own use, but must be suitably maintained to the requirements of the local authority. Private sewers and drains may be taken over by the local authority.

Trade effluents may be discharged into public sewers only by arrangement with the local authority. In London the London County Council provides main sewerage

Local authorities have considerable powers of control over the construction of buildings and the provision of sanitary arrangements. By-laws may be made and enforced. The authorities have power to provide public lavatories.

*Sanitary services (ii)—Refuse collection. Street cleansing.* The borough and district councils may, and if required by the Minister of Housing and Local Government must, undertake to remove house refuse in either the whole or any part of their areas. Where this service has been so undertaken the authority is under an obligation to remove the refuse free of charge within seven days of a written request from the occupier of the premises. A charge may, however, be made for collection at more frequent intervals and in cases where the authority are under no obligations to remove the refuse. The authorities may require, or provide on payment, regulation dustbins for house refuse. An authority may undertake the removal, at a charge, of trade refuse.

The same authorities may, and if required by the Minister must, undertake the cleansing of streets, and may undertake the watering of streets.

*Nuisances and offensive trades.* Each borough and district council must appoint one or more public health inspectors, and must carry out periodical inspections of the district to see whether there are any nuisances likely to be prejudicial to health, such as filthy ditches or deposits, insanitary premises and animals, efflu-via from factories, unventilated or overcrowded workshops, smoke pollution, contaminated water supply, or unfenced quarries. The authority may take steps to abate the nuisance and may institute legal proceedings against offenders.

The establishment of certain offensive trades without the consent of the borough or district council is an offence. The authority may make by-laws to regulate the manner in which these trades are carried on. Examples of offensive trades are. blood or bone boiler, fat melter, glue or size maker, soap boiler, tallow melter, tripe boiler, rag and bone dealer.

The Clean Air Act, 1956, empowers local authorities to establish 'smoke control areas' and to undertake research into aerial pollution.

*Food and drugs.* The law relating to food and drugs lays down standards as to purity and quality of certain foods such as bread and flour, margarine and butter, and milk.

Milk purveyors must be registered with the local authority. Slaughterhouses must be licensed. The district medical officer must be notified of any cases of food poisoning. Markets and premises where food is sold or prepared are subject to inspec-tion. Adequate precautions must be taken in the manufacture, packing, storage and sale of food against its contamination. By-laws may be made by local authorities relating to these matters. Samples of food and drugs may be taken for analysis by the public analyst, and unsound food may be seized and condemned.

For all these purposes local authorities appoint inspectors and may institute legal proceedings against offenders.

Local authorities may provide public markets, slaughter-houses, cold-air stores and refrigerators.

These various powers are largely exercised by the councils of boroughs and county districts. County councils have, how-ever, with other local authorities, the duty to appoint public analysts, may provide facilities for bacteriological and other examinations and may take proceedings for the enforcement of the law relating to food and drugs. A county council, and a borough or district council, may provide facilities for the cleansing of shell-fish.

*Infectious disease, notification, disinfection.* The Minister of Health has wide powers to make regulations for the prevention of infectious diseases, and may specify the local authorities which are to carry out and enforce the regulations.

Cases of 'notifiable disease' must be notified to the borough or district medical officer of health. The list of these diseases is varied from time to time according to need.

Borough and district councils may provide disinfecting stations at which any articles may be disinfected free of charge. These authorities may also cleanse and disinfect premises, and may provide temporary accommodation for persons voluntarily or compulsorily removed from infected premises.

In addition, county councils, in common with other local authorities, may cleanse verminous persons or premises.

*Baths and wash-houses.* Borough, district and parish councils may provide public baths (for personal cleansing) and wash-houses where housewives may do their own domestic laundry, with or without drying grounds, and may make reasonable charges. These authorities may also provide public swimming baths and bathing places. The swimming baths may be closed during the winter months and may be let for dances, meetings and concerts.

*Local personal health services.* The National Health Service Act, 1946, which nationalized hospitals and medical services (see chapter 3), requires the councils of counties and county boroughs, as local health authorities, to make arrangements, with the approval of the Minister of Health, for carrying out certain local services as part of the national health service. The detailed arrangements therefore vary in each locality and may or may not include the delegation of some part of an authority's functions to minor authorities or voluntary bodies. The functions conferred on local health authorities are as follows:

(i) *Health Centres* are to be provided and equipped at which facilities are to be available for the use of medical and dental practitioners and pharmacists for the examination and treatment of patients, and where practitioners can collaborate in 'group practice' and make use of equipment not easily obtainable by the individual practitioner.

At these centres the authority may provide lectures, films and other instruction on health and disease and publish information.

(ii) *Care of mothers and babies.* Local health authorities must arrange for the care (including dental care) of expectant and nursing mothers and of children under five who are not attending primary schools. (Children attending school come within the purview of the school medical service.[2]) These duties include the supply of special food and maternity outfits and provision of ante-natal and post-natal clinics, day nurseries and residential nurseries. Maternity homes are provided by the hospital authorities. Charges for these services may be made according to the means of the recipients of the service. The authority must be notified of all births in its area. Local health authorities are also concerned in the care and protection of children apart from medical care.[2]

(iii) *Midwives.* Local health authorities have duties of supervision over practising midwives. The authorities must ensure that an adequate number of midwives is available, either by the employment of midwives by the authority itself or by the making of arrangements with hospital authorities or voluntary bodies.

(iv) *Health visiting.* Local health authorities must provide for the visiting of sick persons in their homes by health visitors employed either by the authorities or by voluntary organizations.

(v) *Home nursing* facilities must be arranged for by local health authorities either by the employment of nurses or by arrangement with voluntary organizations.

(vi) *Vaccination, etc.* Local health authorities must make arrangements with medical practitioners for the vaccination and immunization of persons against smallpox and diphtheria and may, with the Minister's consent, make similar arrangements in respect of any other disease.

(vii) *Ambulance services.* It is the duty of every local health authority to secure that sufficient ambulances and other transport are available for the conveyance of sick persons, mental defectives and expectant and nursing mothers.

(viii) *Prevention and after-care.* To the extent approved by the Minister of Health a local health authority may make, at charges suited to the means of the recipients, provision for the prevention of illness, and for the care of persons suffering or

[2] See later, p. 72.

who have suffered from illness or mental defect. This provision may not include the payment of money to these persons except by way of remuneration for work done by them, as, for example, in the case of their employment in a rehabilitation centre.[3]

(ix) *Domestic help*. A local health authority may make such arrangements as the Minister may approve for providing domestic help for households where it is required through there being in the household a person who is ill, or is lying-in, or who is an expectant mother, or mentally defective, or aged, or is a child under school age. The authority may make charges for these services according to the means of the recipient.

*Private nursing homes*. A nursing home must not be carried on unless it is registered with the council of the county or county borough in which it is situate. The authority may refuse or cancel registration if the premises or their staffing and equipment are not suitable.

## EDUCATION

Previous to 1870 public education was provided (apart from the universities) by charitable bodies, voluntary societies, grammar schools supported by endowments, by private schools run at a profit and by the well-known 'public schools'. The Elementary Education Act, 1870, provided for the creation of school boards with power to establish elementary schools and compel attendance. The Education Act, 1902, abolished these boards and made the councils of counties and county boroughs the local education authorities, with power to provide elementary and higher education. The larger non-county boroughs and urban districts were at the same time given power to provide elementary education in their areas.[4] Since then the public education service has been widely developed. It is no longer limited to the providing of academic instruction, but has become a social service capable of exercising an important influence over persons of all ages from two years old upwards. Meals, milk and medical attention are provided for school

[3] As to facilities provided by local authorities for handicapped and physically defective persons through the welfare service, see chapter 3, p. 41.

[4] These powers arose under Part III of the Act, and these borough and urban authorities were popularly referred to as 'Part III authorities'.

children, trade schools and technical colleges, facilities for physical training and recreative activities for persons of all ages, and adult education by means of evening classes and otherwise are provided.

The Education Act, 1944, took away from the councils of non-county boroughs and urban districts any elementary education functions formerly exercised by them, and gave the councils of counties and county boroughs, as 'local education authorities' the duty 'to contribute towards the spiritual, moral, mental and physical development of the community' by securing that efficient education throughout the three stages of primary, secondary and further education should be available to meet the needs of the population of their areas.

The absorption by the county councils of the functions of elementary education formerly possessed by the councils of certain county districts enables greater co-ordination to be secured between the various stages of education throughout the county as a whole with its greater financial resources, wider area and greater range of child population. The higher and more specialized forms of education, requiring special classes and establishments, can only be adequately provided in areas where there are sufficient pupils to justify the special provision. The Act of 1944 not only raised the compulsory school age to fifteen years (with opportunity for the Minister of Education to raise it to sixteen), but provided that no fees should be charged for any schools (including secondary schools and county colleges) maintained by local education authorities. The term 'elementary education' (for children up to the age of fourteen) has been discontinued. The modern term is 'primary education' for children up to the age of ten and a half. Above the age of twelve all children are to have, up to the higher age limit, 'secondary education' of a type suited to their aptitudes.[5]

But while the Act of 1944 places county councils in the same position as councils of county boroughs in that they are, as local education authorities, responsible for all forms of public education throughout the whole of their areas, the Act permits any local education authority to make schemes of divisional

[5] i.e. not necessarily of the 'grammar school' type. The type of education between ten and a half and twelve is what is expedient in the circumstances.

administration under which functions relating to primary, secondary and further education may be delegated to bodies of persons constituted as 'divisional executives' for parts of the authority's area. Where any non-county borough or urban district has either a population of 60,000 or an elementary school roll of 7,000, the borough or district council may ask that their area may be an 'excepted district' exempted from the county council's divisional arrangements. If this is agreed to by the Minister, the borough or district council may make their own scheme of divisional administration after consultation with the county council.

Under the Local Government Act, 1958, the status of an 'excepted district' may be obtained without a school roll of 7,000 if the Minister considers there are exceptional circumstances.

*Nursery schools.* Compulsory school age starts at five years, but local education authorities may provide primary schools known as nursery schools for children between the ages of two and five.

*Special schools* for children suffering from disability of mind or body may be provided.

*Voluntary schools.* In addition to establishing its own schools a local education authority may maintain schools established by other persons and bodies. These latter schools are referred to in the Act of 1944 as 'voluntary schools'. The degree of control by the local education authority over these schools varies according to the financial assistance given. In any event the authorities of a voluntary school have a certain freedom as to the religious instruction to be given in the school.

*Public and private schools.* Outside the system of public education are the well-known 'public' schools and many colleges and private schools. Local education authorities are empowered to enter into arrangements with the authorities of these various establishments, as need be, for meeting the educational needs of the area. A number of these bodies receive grants direct from the central government on condition that they shall admit a certain proportion of their pupils from public primary schools.

*Further education* can take two forms, (i) the establishment of county colleges at which young persons over school age can be required to attend courses of instruction or receive part-time education up to the age of eighteen, and (ii) provision by way of classes, evening schools, polytechnics or other means, including co-operation with universities and the award of scholarships.

*Ancillary services.* Local education authorities are under a duty to provide periodical medical inspection and free treatment for pupils in their schools. The authorities must also arrange for the supply of milk and meals to school children on terms prescribed in regulations made by the Minister. Board and lodging and clothing may be provided free or at charges to suit the parents' means. Children may be examined for cleanliness, and appropriate remedies applied in necessary cases. Arrangements for free transport of children to and from schools may be prescribed by the Minister. Education must not be limited to scholastic instruction; provision must be made for recreation, and social and physical training, by the establishment of holiday camps, playing fields, gymnasiums, organized expeditions and other facilities.

*Employment of children.* Local education authorities have power to prohibit or restrict the employment of children in any manner which is prejudicial to health or likely to hinder education. A notice of prohibition or restriction may be served upon the employer of any child. For disregard of a notice the employer may be fined.[6]

*Public libraries.* The Public Libraries Acts are adoptive, and may be applied by a county borough council in respect of the borough and by a county council in respect of the whole or any part of the county. Non-county borough and urban district councils and parish meetings may also adopt the Acts if the county council's adoption does not include their areas. After adoption of the Acts the powers conferred by them are carried out by the adopting authority, and include power to provide public libraries, museums and art galleries.

## THE WELFARE OF CHILDREN AND YOUNG PERSONS

In addition to their duties as education authorities, the councils of counties and county boroughs have a statutory duty to concern themselves in the welfare of the young.

---

[6] As to by-laws relating to the employment of juveniles, see p. 73.

If a child under the age of seventeen has no parent or guardian capable of looking after him (or her), or is abandoned or lost, and intervention appears to be necessary in the interests of the child, the council of the county or county borough is, under the Children Act, 1948, under an obligation to take the child into its care until the age of eighteen. The council may assume full parental rights over children in its care.

Children and young persons may also come into the care of these local authorities through the courts of law. A court has power to commit persons under seventeen to the care of a 'fit person'. The court may designate the council as a 'fit person'.

The council must provide, for children which come into its care through any of these causes, accommodation in a home or hostel provided by the council or a voluntary body, or by boarding out the child with foster parents.

A council may contribute towards the maintenance of persons between the ages of eighteen and twenty-one who have, since ceasing to be of compulsory school age, been in the care of a council. Persons who, on arriving at the age of eighteen, are in the care of a council may be given financial help towards their education or training.

Contributions in respect of children in the care of a local authority up to the age of sixteen may be required from the child himself if earning, or from his parents, stepfather, stepmother or putative father.

The councils of counties and county boroughs have powers of inspection of voluntary homes and nurseries in which children are accommodated. Any person undertaking for reward the maintenance or care of a child of compulsory school age without its parents must notify the council, and be subject to visitation on behalf of the council. The council may regulate the number of children to be kept in any premises, and may take steps for the removal of a child from unsuitable conditions. Periodical inquiry must be made by a council to find out what foster parents acting for reward are in the area of the council.

*Employment of juveniles.* Councils of counties and county boroughs may make by-laws regulating the employment of persons under the age of eighteen,[7] and may also issue licences permitting children to take part in entertainments.

The hours and conditions of work of persons under eighteen employed in shops, hotels, and places of amusement, and in running errands and delivering goods, are the subject of statutory provisions. Councils of counties, boroughs, the City of London and certain urban districts have duties of enforcement of these provisions and may appoint inspectors.

Local education authorities may be empowered to provide a youth employment service and to administer in that service unemployment benefits and national assistance for persons under eighteen.

*Adoption of children.* Societies which arrange the adoption of children may not operate unless they are registered with the council of the county or county borough. A council may refuse registration. Adopted children must be visited and inspected on behalf of the council. The council may be appointed guardian *ad litem* of a child in proceedings relating to the adoption of the child.

*Approved schools and remand homes.* Councils of counties and county boroughs are under a duty to provide remand homes for the reception of children and young persons committed to custody by the courts, and may provide 'approved schools' to which children may be committed by order of the court.

### ROADS AND BRIDGES

*Highway authorities.* In medieval times the duty to take part in the repair of highways rested upon every man as part of his feudal obligations. Roads were 'repairable by the inhabitants at large'. By the Highways Act, 1555, the duty was organized by the parish authorities.[8] In the eighteenth century a number of turnpike trusts were created to build roads at private expense as commercial ventures; traffic was allowed on these roads on payment. In towns various bodies of commissioners were created to pave and repair streets.

During the nineteenth century, elective local highway boards

---

[7] In the City of London these powers are exercised by the City Corporation. As to powers of restricting employment which hinders education see *ante*, p. 72.

[8] See chapter 6, p. 97.

were set up in some areas, and in other areas the urban sanitary authorities were given highway powers. The competition of the railways made many turnpike trusts insolvent, and by 1895 all turnpike roads had been taken over by public authorities.

When the modern local authorities were created they were all given, in relation to highways, powers varying with the status of the authority. The Ministry of Transport was created in 1919 with powers of supervision over (*inter alia*) the country's road system.

The division of responsibility among public authorities in respect of highways depends to a large extent upon the type and classification of the highways. At one end of the scale the Minister of Transport is responsible for the construction and maintenance of main and trunk roads, but he may delegate his functions, upon terms, to local highway authorities. At the other end of the scale parish councils have powers of street lighting, and may acquire and repair rights of way other than along roads; their consent is required to the diversion and stopping up of highways.

*County Councils* are responsible for 'county' roads and bridges. These powers may be delegated or transferred to other authorities.

*Rural District Councils* have in some districts power to provide street lighting, but they have no other highway powers except by arrangement with the county council.

*Non-county Borough and Urban District Councils* are responsible in their areas for roads other than 'county' roads. If the population of the borough or district is over 20,000 the council may claim to exercise the functions of maintenance and repair of any county road in the area.

*County Borough Councils* are responsible for all roads in their boroughs, other than trunk roads and roads maintained by the Ministry.

The powers of highway authorities include repair, paving, lighting, drainage, widening, improvement, the creation of new roads, and the furnishing of highways with road crossings, trees, sign-posts, street refuges, and protective fences, and the protection of the highway from obstruction. By-laws may be made. 'Special roads' may be provided for special classes of traffic.

*In London* the county council executes major road improvements, and the metropolitan borough councils execute minor improvements. Road maintenance is performed by the borough councils.

*Building line.* In respect of roads under their care, highway authorities may prescribe how near to the road any form of building is to be allowed. No building may be erected so as to project nearer to the road than the prescribed building line without the consent of the authority.

*New streets.* Borough, urban and rural authorities, and the London County Council, have power to determine the widths, levels and directions of new streets laid out by private developers for public use.

*Private streets; adoption by local authority.* Private roads, such as a carriage drive, or a forecourt to a shop or petrol filling station, are not repairable by the highway authority, although the public may in practice have access to these places. A private road may, however, become a public highway by dedication by the owner, by his formally handing it over to the local authority. Dedication may also be presumed by long usage by the public.

If a private road is in need of repair, the highway authority may undertake repairs at the cost of the owner or owners. The authority may also formally adopt a private road, once the road is made up to the satisfaction of the authority. If the road is not satisfactorily made up, the authority may make up the road, and charge the expense proportionately upon the owners of property fronting on the road. The authority may itself agree to bear a part of the cost. A road once adopted by the highway authority becomes a public road in perpetuity. These powers of adoption of private roads are exercised by borough, urban and rural district councils and, in London, by metropolitan borough councils.

*Street naming and numbering.* Outside London, borough and district councils, and, in London, the London County Council, have power to name streets, alter street names, and number, and re-number the buildings along streets.

*Road bridges.* Highway authorities have, in relation to road bridges, powers somewhat similar to those in respect of highways. Restrictions may be imposed as to the weight of traffic allowed on a bridge. There are 'county bridges' built and maintained by county councils. These include bridges carrying county roads. The borough, urban and rural authorities in the county may, by delegation, exercise powers over these bridges.

County borough councils are responsible for all public bridges in their areas.

The councils of non-county boroughs and urban districts have the powers of maintenance and improvements of minor bridges in their areas.

There are a number of bridges privately constructed to which the public have access, such as bridges built over railways and canals, which are repairable by the owners of the bridges.

## POOR RELIEF

The duties of county councils and county borough councils to provide residential accommodation and welfare services for persons in need are dealt with in chapter 3.

## FIRE BRIGADE

Previous to 1941, the organization and equipping of fire brigades were performed by borough and district councils outside London and by the London County Council. Some brigades were organized on a voluntary basis. The Fire Brigades Act, 1938, empowered local authorities to combine and co-operate in their fire brigade arrangements. In 1941 all local fire brigades were absorbed into the National Fire Service, so as to facilitate the concentration and mobilization of fire-fighting forces of adequate size to deal with serious fires caused by air raids. Under the Fire Services Act, 1947, the National Fire Service was discontinued, and the obligation to provide local fire brigades was placed upon the councils of counties and county boroughs. In addition to maintaining efficient forces of personnel and equipment, these councils are required to ensure that a sufficient supply of water is available for fire-fighting, and are under a duty to obtain information for fire-fighting purposes about the buildings and property in their areas, and to give advice about fire protection in buildings.

### FUNCTIONS OF GENERAL CONTROL

*Licensing of entertainments—Theatres.* In certain parts of London and in some other cities, premises kept for the performance of stage plays must be licensed by the Lord Chamberlain. In other parts of the country, licences are issued by the county council or county borough council.

*Cinemas.* A cinematograph exhibition in public must be licensed by the council of the county or county borough in which the exhibition is held. This function may be delegated to local justices, or to district councils.

*Music and dancing.* Dance halls, concert halls and other premises where public music, singing or dancing is performed must in London and the Home Counties be licensed by the council of the county or county borough. In some parts of the country special local Acts apply, in other parts (i.e. those areas in which the local authority has adopted Part IV of the Public Health Acts Amendment Act, 1890) the local licensing justices issue licences. In the rest of the country no licences are required.

*Racecourses.* Horse racing within ten miles of Charing Cross must not take place unless the racecourse is licensed by the county council.

*Betting.* No betting or bookmaking may take place on any sporting track where races (other than horse-races), athletic sports or other sporting events are held, unless the track is licensed for betting facilities. Licences are issued by the councils of counties and county boroughs, but this function may be delegated to the standing joint committee of justices and of the council. These various licences are issued subject to conditions as to the safety and proper conduct of the premises.

*Employment agencies.* Theatrical employers and agencies offering theatrical employment must be registered with, and agencies offering to supply nurses (other than associations for the supply of non-resident district nurses) must be licensed by, the council of a county or county borough, or of the City of London.

*Petroleum storage.* Petrol filling stations and other premises where petroleum is stored must be licensed in the City of London by the Common Council, elsewhere in London by the London County Council, and outside London by the borough or district council.

*Explosives.* County, borough and urban district councils, and certain harbour authorities, have power to license firework factories and premises where gunpowder is stored, and may provide magazines for the storage of explosives.

*Fertilizers and feeding stuffs* must comply with prescribed standards of quality. County and county borough councils have the duties of enforcing the requirements by inspection, analysis and the taking of legal proceedings.

*Shops.* The Shops Act, 1950, contains provisions relating to the hours of work and holidays of shop assistants, the hours of closing of shops, sanitary conditions in shops, and similar matters. Provisions are also contained in the Acts, and in the Young Persons (Employment) Act, 1938, as to the hours and conditions of work of persons under eighteen in shops, hotels, clubs and places of entertainment and in running errands and in delivering goods. The duties of inspecting shops and other premises, and of taking legal proceedings for non-compliance with these Acts, rests upon the London County Council and the City of London Corporation, borough councils, councils of urban districts with a population of over 20,000 or more, and elsewhere the county council.

*Weights and measures.* County councils, the City of London Corporation, county borough councils, and some non-county borough councils are required to appoint inspectors of weights and measures, and to take proceedings to enforce compliance with the law relating to weights and measures and to the sale of coal by weight.

*Licensing of motor cars and drivers.* The issue of licences for mechanically propelled vehicles, and for drivers of these vehicles, is performed on behalf of the central government by the councils of counties and county boroughs. The councils are reimbursed by the government the cost of collection.

*Protection of animals.* Local authorities have powers of inspection of riding establishments with a view to safeguarding the welfare of horses on the premises. Trainers and exhibitors of performing animals must be registered with and are subject to supervision by a local authority. Local authorities must take steps to prevent contagious diseases among animals, and are responsible for the enforcement of the Acts and Orders relating to the protection of wild birds. The local authorities having these various powers and duties are the councils of counties, county boroughs and of the larger non-county boroughs and urban districts.

## BURIAL AND CREMATION

Cemeteries and crematoria may be provided by the councils of boroughs, county districts and parishes, either within or without their respective areas. Mortuaries and post-mortem rooms may also be provided by these authorities.

## PUBLIC RECORDS

*Keeping of records.* The lord lieutenant of a county is, as *custos rotulorum*, generally responsible for the oversight of records of counties outside London. Subject to such directions as he may give, the clerk of a county council has the duty of keeping all documents relating to the business of the council. Town clerks of boroughs and clerks of district councils have the charge and custody of charters, deeds and other records and documents belonging to their councils. Parish documents are, in urban parishes, to be deposited in such custody as the borough or urban district council may direct. County councils outside London are required to make periodical inquiry as to the manner in which records under the control of parish authorities are kept.

In London the clerk of the county council is responsible for county records other than those relating to quarter sessions and the justices. These latter records are kept by the clerk of the peace.

Borough, district and parish councils may provide depositories for public books, papers and documents for which no other provision is made.

*Births, deaths and marriages.* Registration officers are appointed, and local offices provided, in London by the City Corporation and the metropolitan borough councils, and outside London by the councils of counties and county boroughs. The arrangements are under the general supervision of the

Registrar-General and the duties and functions of the registration officers are prescribed by him.

*Electors' registration.* The clerks of county councils and the town clerks of boroughs and urban districts are responsible for the preparation of registers of electors.

*Local land charges.* In view of the fact that all councils (other than parish councils) have considerable powers over private property by way of imposing building restrictions, planning requirements, road charges, and the like, these councils are required to keep a public register of the various charges and restrictions imposed by them on individual properties. The registers are open to inspection, and certificates showing the entries against particular properties may be obtained for a small fee from the council concerned. These registers are intended to assist intending purchasers of property in ascertaining what restrictions and limitations have been imposed on the property.

## PUBLIC MONUMENTS

Local authorities have no general powers to provide public statues, monuments and war memorials, but powers have been obtained by some authorities in Private Acts. All local authorities may, however, maintain statues and monuments.

Drinking fountains and cattle troughs may be provided by borough, urban and rural district councils.

The Minister of Works prepares from time to time a list of ancient monuments and may take appropriate steps to safeguard any monuments listed; county and borough councils may acquire or become the guardians of an ancient monument and maintain it at their expense.

Councils of counties and county boroughs, as local planning authorities, may make orders requiring the owner of a building of special architectural or historical interest to preserve it and may contribute towards the expense of restoration or preservation. The Minister of Housing and Local Government is required to publish, for the guidance of the local planning authorities, lists of buildings of historical or architectural interest. No building in these lists may be altered without prior notice to the local planning authority, so that they may be able to take any necessary steps under their town planning powers.

## ENTERTAINMENT

The councils of boroughs and county districts, the London County Council and the City of London Corporation may themselves provide, or contribute towards the provision of, entertainments of any type, including theatres, dance halls, concert halls, the maintenance of a band or orchestra, and the provision of refreshments and programmes in connection with the entertainments.

These authorities may set aside limited portions of their parks or pleasure grounds for the provision of entertainments.

These powers are in addition to the powers of local authorities to provide facilities for games, recreations and sports in public open spaces.

Some local authorities, under powers conferred by the Civic Restaurants Act, 1947, carry on a public restaurant service.

Local authorities, other than parish authorities, may spend money on official visits and hospitality to distinguished visitors.

## PUBLICITY

Local authorities of all types, other than parish councils, may set up information centres or make other provision whereby members of the public can, on application, obtain information about the local government or national services in the area.

These authorities may also issue publications, provide lectures, discussions, films, exhibitions and similar publicity for affairs of local government.

Some authorities, particularly those for health resorts and watering places, have special powers to advertise the amenities of their areas.

## SMALL-HOLDINGS AND ALLOTMENTS

County councils outside London are under a duty to provide, according to local demand and conditions, small-holdings for letting to persons with agricultural experience who desire to become farmers. Land may be acquired for this purpose, equipment may be provided and improvements carried out by the local authority. Small-holdings so provided must be let at the full fair rent.[9] These powers may, on the application of the council of a county borough, be applied to the borough by the Minister of Agriculture and Fisheries. The Minister may himself provide small-holdings in any area.

*Allotments.* The councils of boroughs, urban districts and parishes are required to provide, if there is sufficient local demand, allotments for letting to local residents. County councils are required to co-operate with other local authorities in the county in meeting any local demand. A county council may assume the powers of a district or parish council and itself provide allotments.

## BY-LAWS

County councils and borough councils have power to make by-laws for the good rule and government of their areas, and for the prevention and suppression of nuisances. These by-laws relate chiefly to public order and behaviour, such as loitering, street music, defacing of signposts, noisy animals, spitting, hawking, and street litter.

All local authorities have powers to make by-laws relating to particular functions exercisable by those authorities.

Notice of the intention to make by-laws must be advertised in the local press and be open to public inspection. The by-laws must be confirmed by the appropriate 'confirming authority' usually the Home Secretary, Minister of Housing and Local Government or other member of the central government, and do not come into force until so confirmed. Copies of by-laws must be placed on sale.

## ACQUISITION OF LAND BY LOCAL AUTHORITIES

All local authorities have power to acquire land by agreement, whether by purchase, lease, or exchange, provided that the land is required for the purposes of their functions as local

[9] The Minister may make loans to small-holders to provide them with working capital.

authorities. They may also lease any land in their possession and may sell any land which is surplus to their requirements. The consent of the Minister of Housing and Local Government is required to sales, to leases by parish councils, and to leases for over seven years by other local authorities.

Local authorities, other than parish councils, may, with the consent of the Minister, purchase by agreement land in advance of immediate requirements.

*Compulsory purchase.* Local authorities also have power to acquire land by compulsory purchase for a large variety of purposes. It is a frequent practice to provide, in statutes which confer functions upon local authorities, that the authorities shall have power to acquire land compulsorily for the purpose of carrying out the functions conferred. Thus for educational purposes, for highways, for public health, fire brigade, town planning and other purposes, the appropriate local authorities have this power to purchase by compulsion. Land for the use of parish authorities may be purchased compulsorily on their behalf by the county councils.

The procedure by which the power is operated varies according to the purpose. The Acquisition of Land (Authorization Procedure) Act, 1946, has largely regularized this procedure.

No compulsory purchase can take place unless the local authority has powers of compulsory purchase conferred by Parliament in relation to the purpose for which the land is required. Where power has not already been conferred, then parliamentary powers must be sought. These powers can be obtained in two ways, (i) by the promotion of a special private Act in Parliament or (ii) by provisional order made by a Minister, subject to approval by Parliament. When powers are obtained in this way, they relate to particular lands within a defined limit, and the procedure by which the purchase is carried out is indicated in the Act or Order.

Certain statutes, however, allow an authority to exercise powers of compulsory purchase by means of an order made by the appropriate Minister. The Local Government Act, 1933, and the Act of 1946 above-mentioned have provisions of this kind.

The procedure for the exercise of compulsory powers by these various methods has certain features in common. The proposal must be advertised in the local press; a map showing the land to be acquired must be made available for public inspection;[10] generally (but not always) notice must be served on owners and occupiers of the land; opportunity must be given for objections to be heard; usually a public local inquiry is held at which objectors can, in person or by legal representatives, state their objections; after disposal of objections the order must be confirmed by a 'confirming authority' (frequently the Minister of Housing and Local Government).

In special cases where the land is urgently required, this procedure can be shortened by reducing the press advertisements, by shortening the time for the hearing of objections, and by dispensing with the public local inquiry.

*Lands Tribunal.* Under the Lands Tribunal Act, 1949, a lands tribunal has been set up as an appellate body for settling disputes of various kinds in relation to land, including the amount of compensation on compulsory acquisition, the modification of restrictive covenants, and other similar matters.

## PROMOTION OF LEGISLATION

Local authorities other than parish councils are expressly empowered to promote private Bills in Parliament, and to enter opposition to private Bills promoted by other persons or bodies. Bills are promoted by local authorities to obtain an extension of their powers according to the needs of the locality. A local authority will offer opposition to private Bills when the powers sought in those Bills adversely affect the property or functions of the authority or the public interests in the area of the authority.

Before an authority may promote or oppose a Bill, a resolution to that effect must be passed by a majority of the whole number of members of the authority. A resolution to promote a Bill must, when passed, be advertised in the local press, and the approval of the Minister of Housing and Local Government must be obtained to the promotion. Any local government

[10] In the case of land required for town planning purposes the planning authority is required to show, in its published development plan, what land it considers should be subject to compulsory purchase. This requirement is in addition to the other notices, advertisements, etc., required in the course of the actual making of a compulsory purchase order.

elector in the area of the authority may make objection to the Minister. After the Bill has been deposited in Parliament a confirming resolution must be passed by the authority.

In respect of Bills promoted by the London County Council for the provision of public works or the provision of open spaces this special procedure is not required.

In the case of Bills promoted by borough and urban district councils the authority must, in addition to following the special procedure mentioned above, seek the approval of the electors of the area by summoning a public meeting. In certain circumstances a poll of the electors (in the manner of a public election) may be required.

## PARKS AND OPEN SPACES

All local authorities have power to purchase by agreement or accept gifts of land, whether within or outside their areas, for public gardens, walks, recreation grounds, parks and other open spaces. Statutory powers have been obtained by many authorities to obtain particular sites for open spaces by compulsory acquisition.

Land may also be acquired compulsorily or by agreement by a local authority by the exercise of its powers as a housing authority in order to provide open space as an adjunct to housing development. The powers of compulsory acquisition of town planning authorities may also be made use of to provide open spaces.

Disused burial grounds may, in certain circumstances, be used for public open space.

The power to provide open spaces includes the provision for recreational activities, such as sports and games, swimming and paddling pools, boats, seats and bandstands.

The Green Belt (London and Home Counties) Act, 1938, contains provisions enabling local authorities to secure as open space, or prevent building upon, land surrounding London to be made accessible to the public.

For the purpose of enabling streets to be used as playgrounds, local authorities may make orders, subject to confirmation by the Minister of Transport, restricting, wholly or partially, the traffic in any street.

The National Parks and Access to the Countryside Act, 1949, which set up a National Parks Commission for promoting national parks, gives local authorities certain powers to co-operate, and requires them to carry out or assist in the survey of public rights of way and the publication of definitive maps.

## HOUSING AND SLUM CLEARANCE

The housing service is one in which local authorities of all types have a share. The duties of providing houses and of dealing with the clearance of slum areas rests upon the councils of boroughs, county districts, the City of London Corporation and the London County Council. Other county councils may, to assist a rural district council, by agreement take over the functions of that council in relation to housing, and may also be authorised to act in default of a borough, urban or rural district council. A parish authority has a statutory right to make representations to other authorities calling upon them to exercise their housing powers.

Housing functions fall into two main groups, (i) the provision of new houses, and (ii) the amelioration of bad housing conditions. It was in the middle of the nineteenth century, in the course of the industrial revolution, that the first housing legislation was passed as part of the general movement for the improvement of public health in the growing urban areas. In 1851 local authorities were given powers of control over lodging houses and were authorized to erect lodging houses for the labouring classes. In 1868 urban authorities were given power to deal with unfit houses, and in 1875 powers were given to acquire and demolish houses in insanitary areas, without power to provide new accommodation.

Since then, the housing powers of local authorities have been much extended and have received great impetus from the lack of housing accommodation due to destruction through war damage and to shortages of labour and materials in the course of the first and second world wars. Two important factors which have contributed to the necessity for the development of housing powers and their use on a large scale by local authorities have been the tendency of private builders (whose natural desire is to make the fullest use and turnover of their capital) to build houses only for sale, and the difficulty, in times of shortage, of building houses to let at economic rents which working-class tenants can reasonably afford.

The code of Housing Acts, of which the Housing Act, 1957, is the main statute, accordingly not only confers on local authorities power to erect houses, but provides for the subsidization, both by the central government and by the local authorities themselves, of housing operations. In short, houses may be erected at the public expense, and let at rents which do not entirely recoup the public authorities for the expense of erection and maintenance.

Any sales of dwellings erected under housing powers can take place only with the consent of the Minister of Housing and Local Government, who may impose conditions.

Local authorities as a class are among the largest landlords of dwelling houses in the country. Every town has its municipal housing estate, almost every village has its row of council houses. These houses need not necessarily be within the area of the authority which has provided them.

*Provision of housing accommodation.* A local authority may acquire for housing purposes land (whether inside or outside the area of the authority) by agreement or by compulsion, and may, with the consent of the Minister of Housing and Local Government, appropriate land already in its possession. The authority may erect new houses or acquire and convert old ones, and fit them out with requisite fittings and conveniences. It may also make grants to private owners to enable them to improve old houses or provide new ones. Water rights may be acquired and streets, open spaces, shops and other buildings be provided. Where the housing is not within the authority's own area, the local authority for the area concerned must be consulted with regard to any streets and other incidental works constructed.

With the consent of the Minister, land obtained for housing may be sold or leased by the housing authority to other persons for the provision of places of worship, factories, places of recreation and other purposes connected with the development of the land as a building estate. The authority may, instead of erecting houses itself, sell or let the land for building development by private developers. The authority may delegate the management of its houses to a Housing Management Commission appointed by it.

Local authorities may promote and assist voluntary Housing Associations in providing houses by acquiring land for them, by agreement or by compulsion, and by granting financial assistance and financial guarantees.

*Review of housing accommodation.* Local housing authorities are required to make from time to time a review of the housing conditions in their areas, and to submit, as necessary, proposals to the Minister of Housing and Local Government for the provision of new houses.

*Overcrowding.* Housing authorities must also have their areas inspected to see whether any houses are overcrowded, and, if so, to take legal proceedings against occupiers and landlords for the abatement of overcrowding, and to submit proposals to the Minister for the provision of houses to meet the situation.

*Slum clearance.* The medical officer of health of a local authority is under a duty to make to the authority an official representation concerning any houses which are unfit for human habitation, and any areas in which the housing conditions are injurious to health. The authority may, on consideration of such a representation or any other information in their possession, define such an area so as to exclude houses which are not unfit, and declare that area to be a 'clearance area'. The authority may then make an order for the demolition of buildings in the area. This order must be publicly advertised and be brought to the notice of persons interested in the property, in order that they may raise objections. The order must then be submitted to the Minister of Housing and Local Government, who, after hearing objectors, may confirm it, whereupon it becomes effective. If the owner does not clear away the bad buildings, the local authority may do so. The authority may, alternatively, buy the land in the area and clear it themselves. Compensation for bad buildings is paid at the site value only, although *ex gratia* payments may be made in appropriate cases.

*Redevelopment areas.* If an area contains fifty or more working-class houses, and at least one-third of the working-class houses are overcrowded or unfit, the local housing authority may, if the area is one suitable for working-class housing, declare it to be a 'redevelopment area' and, after due advertisement and notice to owners, may submit plans to the Minister for the redevelopment of the area as a whole by the local authority.

When the Minister has (after dealing with objections) confirmed the order, the local authority may redevelop the area according to the plan (acquiring any land necessary for the purpose) or make arrangement for the redevelopment of property in the area by the owners.

Owners of property may themselves submit proposals for redevelopment, and if the local authority approves the proposals, the redevelopment is left to be dealt with by the owners.

*Individual unfit houses.* The general requirement of the law is that no house shall be let for human habitation unless it is fit for that purpose. Local authorities must carry out inspections and may require owners to execute repairs or demolish houses which are unfit. By-laws as to the condition of houses may be made and enforced by a local authority.

*Small dwellings acquisition.* Local authorities have power to advance money on loan on favourable terms to enable persons to buy, repair, construct or alter houses.

*Local housing authorities in London.* The London County Council, the metropolitan borough councils and the City of London Corporation all have powers, as housing authorities, to build houses and deal with clearance and redevelopment areas.

The City Corporation is the authority for clearance and redevelopment areas in the City. In the rest of the county the clearance of areas with ten houses or less is the function of the borough council, but the county council may itself choose to deal with the area; the county council is the authority for redevelopment areas, but may allow the borough council to deal with any area. In practice smaller areas are left to the borough councils; larger areas are done by the county council.

The city and borough councils deal with individually unfit houses. The overcrowding survey is performed by the city and borough councils, and the provision of houses to relieve the overcrowding is the duty of the City Corporation and the county council, but the borough councils may provide such houses by arrangement.

All these authorities may provide new houses in their own

areas. The county council and the City Corporation may also provide houses outside their respective areas.

The City Corporation and the county council make by-laws relating to houses, but the enforcement of the county council's by-laws is performed by the borough councils.

### CONTROL OF BUILDING WORK

Local authorities may make by-laws relating to the stability of all types of buildings, the materials to be used, the height, windows, sanitary arrangements and similar matters. A local authority may require the submission of plans of any intended constructions. Dangerous and neglected structures may be ordered to be repaired or demolished. In London, the London Building Acts provide a special code relating to the stability and structure of buildings.

### COMMON LODGING HOUSES, ETC.

The provision of lodging houses for the working class is one of the functions of housing authorities. Apart from this, the London County Council and borough and district councils have power to make by-laws as to houses let in lodgings. Common lodging houses and seamen's lodging houses are subject to registration with borough and district councils, who may exercise supervision and impose conditions as to the accommodation and conduct of the premises.

Canal boats used for human habitation are subject to similar control.

Tents, sheds and vans, and camping sites, are also controlled by local authorities by by-laws or by licences issued subject to conditions.

### TOWN AND COUNTRY PLANNING

The general planning of town and country as a function of local government is a concept of the twentieth century. Public authorities have, since towns were first created, made endeavours, as desire and opportunity arose, to bring about in a limited way ordered developments in urban areas, by means of street improvements, the provision of public buildings, or by the planned lay-out of particular local features such as public squares, monuments and gardens. Owners of private property have also made endeavours of a similar kind as part of the process of estate development. This type of civic planning, related mainly to architecture, is, however, only one narrow aspect of town and country planning in the modern sense.

The numerous plans for reconstruction prepared and issued by civic authorities after the second world war exemplified the growing acceptance of the idea that planning should not be merely an incident to architecture, or associated only with road improvements or building operations, but should embrace the general control of land use from every aspect, including the co-ordination of social services, transport and communications, the disposition and inter-relation of agricultural, industrial and residential areas, the density and trends of population, the lay-out and provision of streets and open spaces, and the siting of schools, churches, community centres and buildings of all kinds.

The first legislative provisions dealing with town planning were in the Housing, Town Planning, etc., Act, 1909. That Act enabled local authorities to make schemes as respects any land 'in course of development' or 'likely to be used for building purposes'. Schemes were therefore limited to the planning of the layout of new housing estates or suburbs. Local authorities had power to remove or alter buildings which did not comply with an approved scheme.

Later legislation empowered local authorities to grant permissions for the erection of buildings by private owners pending the formal approval of a scheme. This originated the system known as 'interim development control'.

The Town Planning Act, 1925, consolidated previous legislation and made a new departure in separating planning from housing as a subject of legislation. The Act related, as did previous Acts, to the planning of undeveloped land only.

It was not until the Town and Country Planning Act, 1932, that planning could be applied by local authorities to land which was already built up.

The local planning authorities under that Act were the City of London Corporation for the City, the London County

Council for the rest of the administrative county, and, outside London, the borough and district councils. County councils could become planning authorities by the surrender of planning powers by the minor authorities. Planning authorities were empowered to give to owners permission to develop their land subject to conditions designed to secure conformity with planning requirements. Compensation was payable to owners whose property was interfered with or 'injuriously affected' by planning operations. It is generally the case that, in an area where development has been unplanned or badly planned and where, for that reason, a planning scheme is the more desirable, the greater will be the prospect that restrictions will have to be imposed, or the use of property altered, in order to bring the area into a properly planned condition. In built-up areas, therefore, where property values were high, and the development of property was intensive, the carrying out of a planning scheme was likely to involve the local authority in a huge liability for compensation.

The Act of 1932, in extending planning powers to built-up areas, did not, however, impose on local authorities any obligation to make a scheme. The powers were permissive, and the prospective claims for compensation deterred many local authorities from using their planning powers. Moreover, the influence which town planning authorities were able to exercise was largely negative. Undesirable new development could be prevented, but existing bad development could only with difficulty and at great cost be altered. Further, local authorities had themselves little power actively to promote good development. Schemes merely indicated what development could be carried out when an *entrepreneur* was found ready and willing to undertake the approved development.

In 1943 the whole country was put under 'interim development control' irrespective of whether any local authority had resolved to make a planning scheme or not. An Act of 1944 gave local authorities power to undertake the redevelopment as a whole of areas of war damage.

The Town and Country Planning Act, 1947, inaugurated a new series of planning powers and duties. Councils of county districts ceased to be planning authorities, and planning functions in counties were given to county councils. The Minister of Housing and Local Government may, however, authorize or direct the delegation of planning functions to the minor authorities. The councils of county boroughs remain planning authorities as under previous legislation.

Under the Act of 1947, each planning authority is required to prepare, and review at five-yearly intervals, a development plan showing the intended position of proposed roads, public works, and open spaces, and allocating areas for agricultural, industrial, residential and other purposes. The plan may also designate areas of land as subject to compulsory purchase for the purposes of carrying out the plan.

The Act further provides that no new developments of land or material changes in the use of any buildings may take place without the prior consent of the planning authority, who, in granting permission, may impose conditions.

The Act also enables local planning authorities, subject to the approval of the Minister, to carry out development themselves in a general way; to require, on payment of compensation, the alteration or removal of existing buildings which are out of accord with planning requirements; to control advertisements; and to make orders for the preservation of trees, woodlands and buildings of historical and architectural interest.

The Act further gives planning authorities powers of compulsory acquisition of land for planning purposes including the carrying out of developments by the authorities themselves, and authorizes the payment of grants by the central government to local planning authorities in respect of the expense of acquisitions of land, of compensation to owners, of the clearance of land for redevelopment and other matters.

The provisions of the Act leave largely unaffected the powers of local government authorities in relation to their general functions such as the provision of highways, open spaces and housing, and the making of by-laws to control the stability and structure of buildings. The general intention, however, is that the development plans shall govern all operations in respect of the use of land whether by public authorities or by private owners. Once areas have been designated in the plan for housing, open space or other public purposes, the actual carrying out of those purposes may be performed by major or minor authorities according to their statutory powers within the limits of such conditions as the plan or the planning authority may determine.

The Act provides for consultation between a county council and the councils of county districts at various stages, and further provides that each planning authority may appoint a planning committee to exercise functions on behalf of the authority, and that these committees may appoint sub-committees on which (in case of a county council) the district councils may be represented.

The Act also empowers any two or more local planning authorities to appoint joint advisory committees to advise the authorities on the planning of their areas. This is in addition to the normal power of local authorities to appoint joint committees. The Minister may himself appoint a joint advisory committee for any area and may also set up joint boards as planning authorities for the areas or parts of the areas of any two or more local planning authorities. He may also appoint a joint body consisting of the representatives of two or more local planning authorities to hold any land acquired for planning purposes.

Subsequent planning legislation has dealt with the procedure on appeals against planning restrictions, and with the payment of compensation. Compensation for planning restrictions is payable only in a very limited set of circumstances; compensation for compulsory acquisition is, however, based on the 'market value' having regard to the possible development of the property in accordance with planning requirements.

The Town Development Act, 1952, enables the Government and local authorities to give financial assistance towards the cost of 'town development' in country districts in order to relieve congestion in existing town areas.

# 6

## Local Government Finance

THE income of a local government authority comes from three main sources, (i) from receipts, rents, fees and charges made for services, (ii) from rates levied upon inhabitants of the area of the authority, and (iii) from grants made by the central government and from contributions from other local authorities. The income which each local authority receives from these sources varies both in amount and in proportion.

### INCOME FROM FEES, ETC.

Income from rents of houses, fees for licences, charges for recreational facilities and other similar receipts, which make up what might be called the 'earned income' of a local authority is normally set off against the cost of the service to which the income relates. If there is a surplus or 'profit' this can be used in relief of the non-remunerative services, or, in other words, be used to keep down the rate-borne expenditure.

### RATES AND RATING[1]

Rates are contributions required to be made by occupiers of property in a local government area towards the expenses of local services provided in that area. Each item of occupied property is given a value for rating purposes—the rateable value. The amount of contribution payable by the occupier is proportioned according to the value. The proportion (or rate) is settled periodically by the appropriate local government authority for the area.

This system of rating originated in the medieval parishes.

[1] What is said in this chapter relates particularly to the rates levied by local authorities, and not to the rates levied by Land Drainage Boards and water suppliers, as to which see chapter 3.

The parishioners, assembled in the vestry, agreed to pay, each according to his means, contributions towards the upkeep of the local church. This method was adopted under the poor law of Elizabeth I, and local inhabitants were required to make contributions towards the relief of the poor of the parish. The Highways Act of 1555 had already obliged the inhabitants of parishes to contribute their personal service towards the upkeep of local roads. The justices of the peace in quarter sessions were given the duty of seeing that this parochial obligation was duly performed. If it were not, a fine could be levied on any inhabitant for the general default of the parish. The fines were used to defray the cost of road repairs. By an Act of 1691, parishioners who were thus fined were authorized to exact contributions from their defaulting fellow parishioners, and the justices were empowered to settle the rate of contribution. This in due course developed into a system of rates levied in respect of highway maintenance.

There has for centuries been a conception that, when public works are provided which result in a benefit to an owner's land, he and other owners so benefiting should contribute towards the cost of the works according to the value of the benefit. Thus, as early as the reign of Henry VI, Commissioners of Sewers were authorized to levy contributions upon owners, according to the value of their properties, for sea defence and similar works undertaken by the Commissioners. This conception found expression down to modern times in the various local sewers rates.

By the nineteenth century there were a number of separate rates, the poor rate, the highways and sewers rates, and various other special rates for lighting, police, libraries and other purposes. The position has now been much simplified.[2] Local authorities and companies supplying water levy their separate rates upon occupiers of premises to which a supply is given.[3] Land drainage authorities may levy and collect a drainage rate upon owners whose properties are within the drainage area.[3] For all other local government purposes there is, in boroughs and urban districts, one consolidated 'general rate' which is raised for all purposes.

In rural districts there is a certain complication; for, although

[2] i.e. since the Rating and Valuation Act, 1925.     [3] See chapter 3.

one general rate is levied for all services which the district as a whole receives, there frequently are certain parts of the district which are better provided for in respect of certain services such as street lighting, for which it is justifiable to charge the cost only upon the area receiving the benefit. For these special expenses items are added on to the general rate levied in the parishes or other local areas (known as contributory places) in which the special expenses have been incurred.

Similarly, in administrative counties, the councils of certain boroughs and county districts may have power to provide various local services which would otherwise be provided by the county council. The expenses of a county council are therefore divided into 'general county expenses' for which the whole county is chargeable, and 'special county expenses' which are chargeable only on parts of the county. The county council accordingly makes a rate for general county purposes, and a rate for special county purposes.

For these reasons the level of rates in an administrative county is not uniform throughout the whole of the county.

Differences in rates may also occur when the area of a local government authority has been extended. The standard of service and the level of rates may be lower in the newly added portion, and, until the services in that portion come up to the standard throughout the whole area, it is fair to give the ratepayers of the added portion some concession. It is usual, therefore, to arrange that, for a number of years, the rates levied in that portion shall be different from those in the rest of the area. To this practice is given the term 'differential rating'.

*Property liable to be rated.* The types of property in respect of which rates are payable do not fall into any easily definable class. Broadly speaking, the property liable to be rated consists of land, and certain constructions upon land or uses of land. Thus buildings, tramway lines, hoardings, harbours, mines and quarries, gas mains and similar works, sporting rights over land, and various tolls and tithes are rateable. Income and profits are not, as such, rateable, although they may in certain cases be taken into account in assessing the value of property to be rated. Moveable property such as stock-in-trade and furniture are not rateable, but certain types of machinery and plant of a more or less fixed character are rated. The various items of property so liable are known as 'hereditaments'.

*Occupation.* Since rates are chargeable upon the occupier of a 'hereditament' it follows that the property must be in occupation. To constitute occupation for rating purposes the person liable must have exclusive right of possession, and make some beneficial use of the property. A guest (being not in exclusive possession) is not liable to rates. The owner of a building which is entirely disused is not rateable. But if the occupier of a house goes away, leaving his furniture there and with the intention of returning, he is liable to be rated during the period of absence. Empty houses to let or for sale are not rateable.

*Exemptions from rating.* Agricultural land, air-raid shelters used exclusively as such, churches, chapels, lighthouses, and the premises of certain scientific societies are exempt from rates levied by local government authorities. Relief is also given to charitable and other organizations not conducted for profit. No rates are payable upon property in the occupation of the Crown, but *ex gratia* payments are made in lieu of rates.[4]

*Basis of assessment.* Each hereditament is given an annual value. This value is the net benefit which the occupier can be assumed to get by his occupation of the property. The law requires that this benefit is to be estimated by reference to the rent which a hypothetical tenant would pay for the property on a tenancy from year to year, the tenant paying the usual tenant's rates and taxes.

In the case of land and buildings this hypothetical rent is estimated on the assumption that the landlord will pay for repairs and insurance. The rent so estimated is the 'gross annual value'. Since the landlord is assumed to pay for repairs and insurance, it is also assumed that he would make the rent large enough to include these items. Accordingly deductions are made, on a prescribed scale, from the gross value. The result, after the deductions have been made, is the 'net annual value', and is, for this type of hereditament, the 'rateable value'.

The intention of the legislature behind these provisions

[4] As to railways and electrical undertakings, see later in this chapter.

apparently was that there should be some correspondence between the rateable value and the actual rent being paid or likely to be paid for the property. This correspondence did not, however, always exist, especially where fluctuations in the market values of property took place. The valuations for rating tended to take on a static quality and were by no means always in accord with the actual current rents.

*Rating of dwelling-houses.* The great shortage of houses due to the two world wars, the imposition of rent control in respect of certain types of dwellings and the provision of houses by local authorities at subsidized rents had the effect of creating a great disparity between the rents actually paid for comparable properties, and made it difficult in many cases to assess what would be the rent payable by the 'hypothetical tenant' of a dwelling-house.

Houses are now valued by reference to the rents which were actually paid for comparable premises in August, 1939.

From the gross values, deductions according to a prescribed scale may be made to arrive at the net annual (or rateable) value.

*Other properties.* In the case of shops, offices and other premises capable of being let at a rent, the old rule applies, and the annual value will be estimated by reference to the hypothetical rent. To avoid too great a disparity, however, between the valuation of houses (based on 1939 rents) and the valuation of those other properties (based on a post-war hypothetical rent), it has been provided that, until 1963, the rateable value of these latter properties shall be reduced by one-fifth, the expectation being that, by then, the effect of the abolition of rent control would enable appropriate valuations of all these properties, including houses, to be made on the old basis of hypothetical rent.

Other forms of rateable property such as water mains, mines and harbours are also required to be assessed on the basis of a hypothetical rent; but there may in fact be no rent actually paid, nor any comparable properties let at a rent. In such cases an estimate of the annual value may have to be arrived at by taking into account the profits earned by the undertaking, or the capital cost of the works, or the output produced, as the case may be.

With these types of property a gross value is not first ascertained and subjected to prescribed deductions. The annual value is the hypothetical rent which a tenant would pay if he (and not the landlord) paid for repairs and insurance. Thus the net annual value is arrived at straight away. From this net annual value, certain deductions in respect of certain types of property are made in order to arrive at the rateable value.

The principal example is that of industrial and freight-transport hereditaments. In these cases a deduction of 50 per cent. of the net annual value is made in order to arrive at the rateable value. In this way occupiers of these hereditaments are relieved of half of the rates they would otherwise pay.

Where an undertaking extends over several local government areas, the undertaking is usually valued as a whole, and the total valuation is apportioned among the rating authorities of the areas concerned.

*Railways*. The Local Government Act, 1948, makes special provision for the nationalized railways. Dwelling-houses, hotels and other properties which are used in connection with these services and which are capable of being separately assessed will be treated in the ordinary way and rated according to annual value. The remainder of the nationalized railway undertakings are exempted from rating, but annual contributions in lieu of rates are payable.

Payments are variable according to changes in circumstances, including the rise or fall in the average rates levied throughout the country. These annual payments are for the benefit of all local authorities in England and Wales and are distributable among those authorities according to the rateable value of their respective areas.

*Gas and electricity*. Each area gas board is given a basic total of rateable value, related to the aggregate of the rateable values of gas properties (other than houses, show-rooms and certain water undertakings occupied by a Board) as they were on the vesting day for nationalization. This basic total is to be adjusted from year to year by reference to increases or decreases in the quantities of gas supplied; and the adjusted total is to be apportioned among the rating areas covered by the Board according to the quantities of gas made and sold in the respective rating areas.

Electricity generating and area boards are also given a basic rateable value related to their generating and distribution activities; this rateable value is apportioned among the local authorities concerned.

On the rateable value thus apportioned, the respective rating authorities levy rates on the gas and electricity authorities.

*Making a rate—Poundage.* The sum total of the values of the properties in a local government area form the rateable value of the area. From this total, the local authority can ascertain what rate will have to be levied in order to produce a given sum, after due allowance has been made for costs of collection, defaults in payment by individual ratepayers, empty properties and other factors. The produce of (for instance) a penny rate, or, in other words, the produce of a rate of a penny in the pound, will be the amount obtained by requiring each occupier to pay one penny for each pound of the annual value of the property he occupies in the area. Thus, if his property is valued at £50 a year, the levying of a penny rate will oblige him to pay 50*d*. On a rate of a shilling in the pound he will pay 50*s*. Rates are always expressed and levied as so much in the pound of the annual rateable value. The poundage of the rates will therefore vary from area to area according to the rateable value of the area and the sum to be raised in that area out of rates.

An area of low rateable value will require a higher rate poundage to produce a given sum than an area of high rateable value. The rate poundage, or level of the rates, in any area is not, therefore, of itself, an indication of the extravagance or economical management on the part of the local authority, although these factors will, of course, affect the rate poundage; for, whatever the rateable value of the area, any rise or fall in the total expenditure to be borne out of rates will cause a corresponding rise or fall in the rate poundage.

*Making a rate.* Rates for local government purposes (i.e. other than land drainage and water rates) are made and levied by the councils of county boroughs, metropolitan boroughs and county districts. These authorities are 'rating authorities'. County councils and parish councils do not make or collect rates, although a considerable part of the expenditure of these authorities comes from rates. A county council, having ascertained how much of its expenditure is to be rate-borne, works out the amount of the rate poundages required to produce the necessary sums for 'general' county purposes according to the rateable value of the whole county, and for 'special' county purposes according to the rateable value of those parts of the county liable to bear those special expenses. The county council then issues, to the various borough and district councils in the county, demands, known as precepts, asking those authorities to obtain and remit to the county council the produce of the rate poundages so ascertained.

Parish councils issue precepts upon the council of the rural district in which the parish is situated.

Precepts upon the rating authorities are also issued by certain special bodies which have independent financial powers but have no authority to levy a rate upon the public. Thus precepts are issued by the authorities of the Metropolitan Police, by river boards, and by various joint boards formed to exercise functions normally carried out by local government authorities.[5]

The rating authorities, after receiving these various demands, levy in their respective areas a consolidated rate sufficient to meet these demands and the requirements of the rating authority itself. Thus the ratepayer receives one demand for all local authority purposes.[6] Rates are normally made half-yearly.

*Collection of the rate.* Demand for the payment of rates is made normally upon the occupier. Where a building is occupied in parts, and one part is used as a dwelling, and the remainder for other purposes, the whole building may be treated as one hereditament, and the rates will be then payable by the person receiving the rents of the parts.

In the case of properties of small rateable value (£18, or in certain circumstances £25) the owner may (if the rating authority so decides) be made liable to rates instead of the

---

[5] See chapter 3. Standing Joint Committees (the police authorities in counties) do not issue precepts upon the rating authorities, but make requisitions upon the county councils. In the Metropolitan Police District the police authority issues precepts upon the rating authorities in the district. Other joint committees, set up by agreement between local authorities, are dependent for their funds upon the subscriptions of the constituent authorities, but have no power to make any demand or precept.

[6] i.e. other than for water supply, or land drainage.

occupiers. Owners who are thus compulsorily rated must be given a discount of 10 per cent., or, if the rating authority so decide, up to 15 per cent. on the rates payable. In this way the owners of small properties become the collecting agents for the rating authorities. Owners may also agree to pay the rates on their properties. The owner may either agree, for a discount, to act as collector for the rating authority, or he may, for a larger discount, make a 'compounding agreement' by which he will pay the rates whether the properties are occupied or not.

If rates are not paid, the defaulting ratepayer (i.e. the occupier) may be summoned before two justices of the peace, who may issue a warrant for distress and seizure of his goods, and may commit him to prison. The justices may remit the rates in whole or in part if they think fit to do so. The rating authority has also itself power to reduce or remit rates on account of the poverty of the person liable.

*Process of valuation and assessment.* Since the liability to pay rates is assessed in relation to the value of property, it follows that the process of valuation is a critical part of the rating system. Part III of the Local Government Act, 1948, contains important provisions relating to the carrying out of this process.

*The old system.* Under the pre-existing law, the duty of making the valuations of rateable property had been placed upon the 'rating authorities', i.e. the councils of boroughs and county districts. Assessment committees composed of representatives of the rating authorities and (in the administrative counties) of the county councils were set up to hear objections and approve the valuations. Appeals from their decisions lay to the courts of quarter sessions. County Valuation Committees for each administrative county, and a Central Valuation Committee for the whole country, were set up to secure uniformity of methods of valuation.

Under this system the local authorities who assessed and collected the rates were themselves responsible for the valuations. The rateable value of a local authority's area is obviously of great concern to that authority; for the rate poundage and the rate revenue are closely related to the rateable value. Moreover, the rateable value of an area is frequently used as a measure of a local authority's liability to contribute towards expenses for which it may be, with other local authorities, jointly liable. Further, the rateable value of an authority's area is one of the factors which determine the share which the local authority receives of certain important subventions from the central government. In order that each authority's liability or entitlement (as the case may be) may be fairly measured, it is essential that the rateable value of every area shall be arrived at in the same way and by uniform methods. In spite of the existence of County Valuation committees and the Central Valuation Committee, absolute uniformity was not secured. Accordingly, the Local Government Act, 1948, laid down a new procedure by which officers of the Board of Inland Revenue, and not the rating authorities, carry out the valuations of property for rating purposes. From the date of the coming into operation of the relevant provisions of the Act, the assessment committees, and county and central valuation committees ceased to operate.

*The new system of valuation.* The valuation officers are required to make every five years for each rating area a valuation list showing the hereditaments in the area and the values placed on each. This list is sent to the local rating authority and is published and open to public inspection. Objections may be made to it, and appeals from the valuation officer's decisions on the objection may be made to local valuation courts composed of members chosen from a panel. Appeal from decisions of the valuation courts may be made to the county court.

Alternatively, instead of appealing to a local valuation court or a county court against any proposed valuation, an objector may agree to have the matter settled by arbitration.

It is the duty of every council of a county or county borough to make and submit for the approval of the Minister of Housing and Local Government a scheme for the constitution of the local valuation panels.

*Criticisms and advantages of the rating system.* The notion, which was at one time current, that the rates paid by an individual recipient of local services should bear a direct relation to the actual benefit received by him through those services, does not completely accord with modern conceptions and practices. The old drainage rates, for instance, were based upon the actual acreage of the land drained. Now, however, that rate is levied on all the properties in the land drainage district according to annual value. In the early days of rating it may have been fair to assume that the occupier of a large estate received more benefit from such works as roads, bridges and sewers than the occupier of a smaller property. This notion can hardly have been valid in respect of the poor rate, which could only have been paid by those who were in need of no poor relief. Nevertheless, the fact that local authorities spend their rate income largely on providing public services may tempt the ratepayer to make a comparison between what he pays and what he gets. 'The citizen,' it is said, 'pays his taxes in sorrow, but his rates in anger.' If this be true, it is probably because the prosperous ratepayer, paying substantial sums in rates, has less need of a number of services such as public education, local welfare, and council housing than his poorer neighbours whose individual (although not collective) contributions to the local rate income may be small.

Rates cannot, however, now be regarded any longer as a contribution to be measured according to value received. A justifiable cause of irritation may still remain in the minds of the ratepayer in that the amount he has to pay is not assessed according to his income or financial capacity, but is based upon the value of the house, shop or office he occupies. The father of a large family, needing a sizeable house, with a correspondingly sizeable value, may pay more in rates than the childless occupant of a cottage or small flat with an equivalent income. The rates paid by a business man in respect of his shop or office may be relatively high compared with those payable by a person whose vocation does not necessitate the occupation of business premises. Moreover, the business man treats the rates on his premises as part of the overhead expenses of his business. They are accordingly reflected in the prices charged to customers of the business, with the result that the incidence of the rates in those cases ultimately falls on the consumer. Another criticism of the rating system is that in numberless cases the poor man pays, in rates, a larger proportion of his earnings than the rich man.

The several types of national taxes, collected as they are in different ways, may avoid or incur these criticisms in varying degree. One substantial advantage which the rating system has is that the method of assessment and collection is relatively easy. Rates are charged upon property which is immovable and is readily capable of valuation. The amount to be paid does not depend on any statement, return, or accounts of the person liable, and cannot therefore be evaded or affected by falsification or omissions.

## GRANTS

Up to the beginning of the nineteenth century, local government services, such as they were, depended for their finances upon local sources with little or no aid from the central government. The great expansion of local services in the nineteenth century, when, with the industrial revolution and the awakening of the social conscience, public health, public education, poor relief, police, highways and other services were greatly developed, made it clear that to finance local services entirely out of local rates was not only unfair, but was likely to lead to serious discrepancies in the standards of service provided in the different local areas.

The rate income of local authorities varies considerably. The poorer areas, where the bulk of the population are at a low income level and property values are low, are the areas which, generally speaking, are most in need of local public services, such as housing, public health, public education and local welfare. A great deal of the work done by local authorities has been given to them in pursuance of national policy and for national rather than local purposes. An efficient police force, for instance, is an essential national need, and its efficiency in any area ought not to suffer through any inadequacy of local financial resources. In this, and in other local public services, the central government is concerned to see that the standard of service is of a certain level of efficiency throughout the country. Consequently it has been thought fair to subsidize local authorities from national funds.

The practice of granting financial aid to local authorities gained increasing acceptance as local government developed in the latter half of the nineteenth century and onwards, not only because of the interest of the central government in the efficiency of local services and because the government imposed increasing duties upon local authorities, but also because the government has, in pursuance of national policy, taken action which has seriously affected the income and resources of local authorities. The Local Government Act, 1929, for instance, exempted agricultural land entirely from liability to general rates, and reduced the liability in respect of industrial and freight-transport hereditaments. The Education Act, 1944, abolished the power of local education authorities to charge fees for secondary education. This type of action in itself justifies the grant of financial aid to local authorities.

*Former grants.* In the early and middle years of the nineteenth century, government grants were few and took the form of payments of a proportion (or percentage) of the cost of local services such as police and the administration of justice. In 1888, when county councils and county borough councils were created, the old percentage grants were largely replaced by a system of 'assigned revenues' under which the government diverted to the use of local authorities the income arising from certain state taxes, such as licence duties on male servants, armorial bearings, dogs and guns, part of the probate and estate duties, and the surtaxes on beer and spirits. The assumption was that, as an area developed and became more prosperous, the local income from these particular taxes would increase and help to pay for the expanding local services.

The system was found inadequate, and, by the early years of the twentieth century, the old practice of making grants on a percentage basis had come into considerable use. The Local Government Act, 1929, however, brought in a new system of government grants. Many former percentage grants, and most of the assigned revenues, were discontinued, and a system of 'block grants' was instituted, with the intention of meeting the needs of local authorities in respect of the functions they had to perform, and to provide some compensation to the authorities for the loss of income through the de-rating of agricultural and other hereditaments.

The Act provided that the government should make an annual General Exchequer Contribution, the amount of which was to be fixed by the government and periodically revised. This Contribution took into account the losses suffered through de-rating, the discontinuance of former grants, and the nation-alization of certain services.

The total Contribution was divided among the councils of counties and county boroughs.

In each county the county share was divided among the county councils and the councils of the county districts.

This system of providing financial assistance to local authorities by Exchequer grants based on a General Exchequer Contribution related to the actual expenditure of local authorities was abolished by the Local Government Act, 1948, and a new system of financial assistance was instituted by which the government paid 'equalization grants' to those counties and county boroughs whose financial resources fell below a certain minimum. Each county council (whether or not entitled to an equalization grant) had to pay to each county district in the county a 'capitation sum' related to the population of the district.

The system of grants was further revised by the Local Government Act, 1958, by the instituting of 'general grants' and 'rate-deficiency grants', as to which see below.

*Present methods of providing financial assistance.* The general object of the system of government grants is to supplement the resources of local authorities so as to enable those authorities to provide services adequate to the requirements of the locality.

An ideal system of government grants would take into account the local needs of an area, the financial means of the local authority, and the cost of providing necessary services in the area. These factors vary in each case and are difficult to assess.

On particular matters it may be possible to lay down general standards by reference to which the lack or sufficiency of a local service can be measured. Thus the width and construction of roads are capable of being prescribed, and estimates of cost per mile, according to local conditions, can be ascertained. But how is it to be determined whether a new road in a particular situation is actually needed or not?

And suppose that it were possible, by elaborate regulations as to the size of classes, the construction of schools, the salary scales of teachers and the rest, to ascertain what it ought to cost in any area to educate a child, how is it possible to measure whether the local education authority can afford, with its other services, to furnish education of the standard required?

It is in fact extremely difficult to assess the proper needs and resources of an area. Conditions and costs vary from place to place. Rateable value is not a true guide to the financial strength of an area; the only true guide would be an assessment based on the financial capacity of the individual ratepayers. Moreover, expenditure on local government services, and the government contribution towards them, must be related to the resources of the nation as a whole.

Our present grant system attempts in different ways to take into account these various considerations.

*Percentage grants.* For road works, including the cost of new roads, road improvements, road maintenance, bridges, subways, traffic signs and the like, the government pays grants to local authorities on a percentage basis. The percentage varies with the nature of the work. The plans and proposals of the local authority and the estimates of cost are subject to the prior approval of the government. Thus the central government can assure itself not only that the construction will be of the approved standard, but that the cost will be appropriate. The government's share of the cost can be apportioned according to the extent to which the road works will serve a national or local need.

The government pays 50 per cent. of the cost of local police services, and pays grants up to 100 per cent. in respect of school milk and meals.

*Present assigned revenues.* The councils of counties and county boroughs still receive the licence fees on guns, game licences and dogs. This is the last remnant of the old assigned revenues.

*Housing grants.* The grants in respect of housing have been of various kinds, and have been changed from time to time according to the attitude of the central government towards housing needs.

The usual type of housing grant (subsidy) now used is on the 'unit cost' basis. Housing is a service which is normally expected to yield an income by way of rents. These rents are seldom economic, and are, indeed, not always intended to be.

Housing operations are, in general, financed out of borrowed money repaid in instalments, with interest, over a long period of years (usually sixty). Since the rents do not cover the entire cost of loan charges, annual capital repayments and maintenance, the government subsidies take the form of annual payments to the local authority over a long period in respect of each dwelling. The government subsidy varies according to circumstances, costs and national policy. The amount paid has varied from £10 to over £50, payable over a period of sixty years.

Special provision has been made for increased subsidies where needs are unusually high or sites are unusually expensive, and also in respect of agricultural dwellings erected in sparsely populated rural districts.

A county council may lend money to a district council in the county for housing purposes, and any local authority providing housing in the area of another authority may, with the consent of the Minister of Housing and Local Government, advance money to that other authority for providing incidental and necessary works such as sewers and roads.

*The general grants.* Under the Local Government Act, 1958, a new grant called 'the general grant' is to be payable to the councils of counties and county boroughs. These general grants replace former percentage grants payable in respect of education, the fire service, local health and welfare services, the care of 'deprived children', town planning and some other matters.

The aggregate amount of the general grants for any year is to be fixed by the Minister of Housing and Local Government after taking into account a number of factors, including the latest information about expenditure on local services, the current level of prices and costs, and foreseeable variations, changes and developments in local services, and general economic conditions.

The general grant payable to each county and county borough is divided into a 'basic grant' ascertained according to the population and the number of children under fifteen years of age in the area of the recipient authority, and a 'supplementary grant' calculated according to the number of people over 65 years of age, the density of population and any recent decline in it, the school population, the number of children under five, the road mileage, and, in the case of authorities in Greater London, the higher level of prices and costs in and around London.

The details of the method of distribution and the amounts to be paid are set out in General Grant Orders made by the Minister and confirmed by Parliament. Each Order will cover two or more years.

A local authority receiving a general grant may spend it on any service it wishes, and not necessarily on those services for which percentage grant was formerly paid. These grants can, therefore, be said to give the local authority greater freedom in the management of its finances. None the less, if a local authority fails to achieve or maintain a reasonable standard in the provision of the services in respect of which the general grant has replaced the former percentage grants, the appropriate Minister may report to Parliament recommending that the grant be reduced.

Moreover, the central government, in order to exercise general supervision over local authorities and keep in touch with their activities and ensure that their spending is not out of accord with the national economic interest, requires local authorities to submit for approval programmes of capital expenditure, proposals for borrowing money for local projects, and various reports and financial returns. In this way the central government can keep watch over the activities of the local authorities and exercise a broad general control.

A county council is not obliged to share any of its general grant with the councils of county districts.

*Rate-deficiency grants.* The Local Government Act, 1958, also revised the system of Exchequer equalization grants. These are now termed rate-deficiency grants, and are payable direct to county district councils and metropolitan borough councils who qualify by reason of their rate resources being below the national average, as well as to eligible county and county borough councils.

The condition for the payment of a rate-deficiency grant to an authority is that the product of a penny rate for its area must be less than the 'standard penny rate product'. Rate resources are, therefore, measured by reference to rate product, and not by reference to rateable value. The 'standard penny rate product' for an area bears the same proportion to the product of a penny rate over the whole of England and Wales as does the population of the local area bear to the total population of England and Wales.

The amount of the rate-deficiency grant is related to the normal expenditure of the authority in the same ratio as the actual penny rate product bears to the 'standard penny rate product', the idea being to bring the local rate product up to the national standard.

In the Administrative County of London there are special arrangements for adjusting the precepts of the London County Council upon the metropolitan borough councils (who are the rating authorities) so as to equalize to some extent the financial burdens falling upon the poorer boroughs.

All these changes are intended to bring the amount of the general government grants into closer relationship with the financial capacity of each local authority. They do not, however, entirely overcome the underlying flaw in the rating system, namely that rates are paid on the basis of the value of property occupied, not on the personal income of the occupier. To assess the individual capacity of the ratepayer would involve the making of inquiries and returns similar to those for income tax. This would destroy one of the prime advantages of the rating system, namely, the simplicity and inescapability of assessment of liability. Moreover, the whole of a person's income does not always arise in one local government area. A system of 'local income tax' might involve difficult questions as to the respective portions of a person's income to be taken into account in each of the local areas concerned.

*General conditions attaching to grants.* The various percentage and unit cost grants are made on condition that the government department concerned is satisfied as to the reasonableness of the expenditure and of the efficiency of the service provided. As a result, the payment of these grants gives the department concerned the opportunity to review the local services in respect of which the grant is made. This, and the threat of withdrawal of the grant if the service is not satisfactory, provides one of the important methods by which the central government exercises influence over the operations of local authorities.

Moreover, general grants and rate-deficiency grants to any

local authority may be reduced by the appropriate Minister, with the approval of Parliament, if that authority fails to achieve or maintain a reasonable standard of efficiency and progress.

*Contributions by local authorities to each other.* County councils may make contributions to the expenditure of district councils. Moreover, a number of statutes give local authorities express powers to contribute towards the expenses of a project, e.g. the provision of an open space, which is provided by another authority and which will be of advantage to the contributing authority.


## BORROWING BY LOCAL AUTHORITIES

All local authorities have power to borrow money for carrying out their duties. Borrowing is usually resorted to where capital expenditure is involved, as in the case of the acquisition of land, or the building of roads, bridges and other permanent works. Repayment over a period of years is required; sixty years is a usual period.

In this way the cost of permanent works, instead of being borne entirely at the time of construction, is spread over the succeeding generations who will share the benefit of the works.

A county council may borrow money in order to lend it to a parish council.

*Consents to the exercise of borrowing powers.* No money may be borrowed without the prior sanction of a higher authority. The London County Council is in a special position. Its financial operations are under the general supervision of the Treasury. To obtain authority to borrow, the Council obtains each year from Parliament a London County Council (Money) Act, which gives Parliament itself the opportunity of looking into the Council's expenditure.

All other local authorities must obtain the sanction of the Minister of Housing and Local Government before borrowing.

*Modes of borrowing.* Local authorities other than parish authorities may borrow from the public by mortgages, the issue of stock, or by debentures on the security of the general property and revenues of the authority, and by temporary loan or overdraft from a bank.

Parish councils may borrow by mortgage only.

During and since the second world war the central government has assumed a greater control than formerly over capital investment generally throughout the country, and, in consequence, the Treasury exercises supervision over the borrowing operations of local authorities. This does not dispense with the need for the prior sanction of the Minister as mentioned above.

A local authority may borrow from itself by utilizing (subject to repayment) any unused capital funds it may have available and intended for other uses.

## FINANCIAL PROCEDURE OF LOCAL AUTHORITIES

*The General Fund.* All local authorities, with the exception of parish councils, must set up a general fund called, in the case of county councils, the 'county fund' and, in the case of other authorities 'the general rate fund', to and from which all receipts and expenses must be paid.

*Spending procedure.* (*i*) *County councils.* These authorities are subject to special statutory provisions in regard to their spending processes. A county council must have before it each financial year an estimate of its income and expenditure for that year. The annual estimates are normally prepared and submitted by the county council's finance committee.

(ii) *Borough councils and district councils.* There is no obligation to frame an annual budget. Annual estimates are, however, framed as a matter of practice and are, indeed, essential in order that the council may know what rates to levy.

All payments to and from the general rate fund of a borough must be made to and by the borough treasurer.

(iii) *Parish councils* are not required to set up a general fund. Their funds are obtained by precept upon the county council. A parish council may, in general, incur expenditure up to the amount of a rate of 4*d.* in the £ of the rateable value of the parish, but the parish meeting may authorize expenditure up to 8*d.* in the £. The Minister of Housing and Local Government may increase these limits. Every cheque or order for payment must be signed by two members of the parish council. If there is no parish council the chairman of the parish meeting is responsible for expenditure and must keep proper accounts.

*Accounts.* All local authorities are under a general legal obligation to keep proper accounts; if their public moneys are misapplied, proceedings may be taken by the Attorney-General against the authority, its members and officers.

The accounts of county councils and rural district councils are complicated by the fact that certain expenses are not chargeable over the whole area of the authority. Thus a county council must keep separate accounts of 'general county expenses' (which are chargeable over the whole county) and of 'special county expenses' which are chargeable only upon certain parts of the county. Similarly rural district councils must keep a 'general district account' of expenditure chargeable over the whole district, and a 'special district account' of expenses falling to the charge of individual parishes.

*Audit.* With the exception of certain accounts of boroughs outside London, the accounts of all local authorities are subject to the audit of an official of the central government—the district auditor. Accounts are made up normally to 31st March. The date of each local authority's audit is advertised in the locality, and the accounts are made available for public inspection. Any ratepayer may appear before the auditor and make objection to any item.

*Surcharge.* The auditor is concerned not only with the accuracy of the accounts; he must be satisfied that the authority has acted within its legal powers. If he is not satisfied as to the legality of any item he must strike it out, and may surcharge the amount of the item upon those members of the authority who voted the expenditure, and upon officers by whose carelessness or neglect of duty money has been mis-spent or improperly applied. Persons surcharged in this way become personally liable to repay the amount to the council, and are liable to arrest and to the seizure of their property if the amount is not duly repaid.

It is provided, however, that no surcharge shall be made if, before the expenditure was made, the Minister of Housing and Local Government had given consent to the expenditure. Local authorities in doubt about the legality of any intended expenditure therefore make a practice of obtaining the Minister's prior consent. This consent, although it stops the district auditor from making any surcharge in respect of the item, does not prevent any interested ratepayer from taking legal proceedings to challenge its legality.

Surcharge for a sum of over £500 disqualifies a person from being a member of a local authority for five years.

A person surcharged may appeal to the High Court if the amount exceeds £500 or, if the amount is less than that, to the Minister of Housing and Local Government, on the grounds that the district auditor was wrong, or that, even if the surcharge was correct, the person surcharged ought to be excused on the grounds that he acted reasonably in incurring the expenditure.

*Borough audit.* In respect of certain services, the accounts of borough councils outside London are audited by the district auditor, with the usual right of surcharge. Other accounts are audited in various ways according to the wish of the borough council.

The council may decide to submit all its accounts to the district auditor, in the same way, and subject to the same conditions, as other authorities.

Or the council may appoint, and pay, a professional auditor. He would have no right of surcharge.

Thirdly, if the council does not adopt either of the above-mentioned courses, it must apply the old-fashioned method of elective audit. Under this system the council appoints annually two auditors, and the mayor appoints a third from among the members of the council. These three together conduct the audit. They need not have any professional qualifications and have no powers of surcharge.

In all cases where the audit is not conducted by the district auditor, the borough treasurer must print and publish, on completion of the audit, an abstract of the accounts of the borough.

*Local financial returns.* All local authorities are required to send to the Minister of Housing and Local Government annual returns of income and expenditure.

# 7

# The Relationships Between Local Authoritics

The presence throughout England and Wales of a large number of authorities, both national and local, engaged in providing public services, necessarily brings these various authorities into official relationships with each other. In every part of the country the citizen finds more than one public authority administering to his needs. In the administrative counties there are at least two local government authorities, the county council and the council of the county district. In the rural areas there are parish councils as well. These, however, are not the only public bodies with services to perform for the citizen's benefit. Hospital services, electricity supply, transport and poor relief are the concern of national authorities operating in all localities. Even in the county boroughs, where there is only one local government authority, the county borough council, these national bodies will have functions to perform. And in any area there may be set up some special combination of authorities, a joint board or joint committee for example, to which the citizen can look for some public service which otherwise would be provided by the local government authorities themselves.

It is hardly possible, where such a complex pattern of authorities exists, for any one authority, whether national or local, to operate in complete isolation or ignorance of the others. The functions of public authorities impinge upon each other in many ways. Housing schemes of local government authorities involve the provision of electricity, water and gas. Local road maintenance and improvement, and traffic control by the local police, cannot fail to interest the national authorities organizing road transport.

The hospital service provided by the Regional Hospital

Boards, the clinical and environmental health services and the institutional care for the poor and aged provided by local government authorities, and the work of the National Assistance Board, can hardly be dissociated; for the citizen (for whose benefit these services exist) may be old, sick and poor all at the same time, and his needs may come within the ambit of the functions of more than one authority.

The public good demands co-operation and coherence as between authorities of various kinds even when the authorities are legally independent of each other and their functions are defined and distinct.

*The Administrative County.* In the administrative counties the organization of local government authorities in a two-tier or three-tier structure brings those authorities into special relationships. In an average sized administrative county there may be a dozen or so rural districts, a score or more of urban districts, several non-county boroughs, and, it may be, a hundred or more parishes. In London there are the City of London and twenty-eight metropolitan boroughs. While each of these divisions of a county is administered by a separate authority, the whole group of areas making up the county is under the administration of a county council. The group of authorities in the county may be likened to a family of individuals each varying in size and importance, each with his own rights and duties, in all of whom the county council as the presiding member has a certain interest and over whom it can exercise certain powers of influence.

As in the case of human families the influence of the county council is greater towards those members of the group which are of lesser rank than over those of superior stature. The hand of control exercised by the county council is particularly intimate over the parish authorities, but may be hardly felt at all by the councils of non-county boroughs.

*County Councils and the Parishes.* The creation of parish councils lies in the hands of the county council, and the county council may group parishes or dissolve any group and may, subject to confirmation by the Minister of Housing and Local Government, alter parish boundaries and divide parishes. A county council may confer on a parish meeting any functions of a parish council. A county council may divide a parish into wards for election purposes. The change of name of any parish is within the competence of the county council. It is by the instrumentality of the county council that a parish council acquires land by compulsory purchase. The county council has the right to inquire into the methods by which parish records are kept. A county council may remove, in the case of a parish councillor, a disability arising from pecuniary interest.

*Rural district and parish authorities.* Liaison between the rural district council and the parish authorities is provided by the setting up of 'parochial committees'[1] and by the inclusion of the rural district councillors for the parish on the 'representative body' for the parish where there is no parish council.[2]

Rural district councils may delegate to a parish council any functions which may be delegated to a parochial committee, i.e. any functions which the rural district council may exercise in the parish except the power of levying a rate or the borrowing of money.

A parish council may institute official complaints to the rural district council, through the medical officer of health for the district, about the insanitary or unfit condition of any houses in the parish, and may complain, as may a parish meeting also, to the county council that a rural district council has not carried out its duties under the Housing Acts.

*County Council and District Councils.* The relations between the county council and the councils of county districts are chiefly in respect of the distribution of functions, election arrangements, financial affairs, and the taking of action in cases where a district authority has failed to carry out its duties.

A county council may delegate some of its functions to a council of a county district; and the council of a county district may surrender certain of its powers to a county council. The county council may contribute towards any expenses of the councils of county districts, and the county council has the duty of formulating proposals for securing (by combination of districts or otherwise) that a medical officer of health of a county district shall not engage in private practice.

[1] See chapter 11.    [2] See chapter 2, p. 27.

A district medical officer must furnish the county medical officer with all official information which the county medical officer may reasonably require.

For election purposes a county council may, with or without a request from a district council, divide an urban district into wards, divide rural parishes into wards or combine rural parishes; and may fix the number of councillors for each ward or parish. An urban district council may, in respect of its own district, make proposals on these matters to the county council, and if the county council does not agree with the proposals the urban district council may appeal to the Home Secretary.[3]

On the request of an urban or rural district council, the county council may order that the councillors shall all retire together every three years, instead of one-third annually. The county council may also rescind any such order.

The financial arrangements between local government authorities in administrative counties have been dealt with in a previous chapter. Where any joint committee has been set up representative of district or parish councils, and disputes arise as to the apportionment of expenses among the constituent authorities represented on the joint committee, the county council has power to determine the dispute.

A county council's concern in the alteration of areas of district councils is dealt with in chapter 15.

*Action in default.* When the council of any county district makes default[4] in the carrying out of its duties in relation to public health, the county council may draw the attention of the Minister of Housing and Local Government to the matter, and the Minister may, after a local inquiry, confer upon the county council the powers of the defaulting authority, or may himself assume the powers.

If a rural district council makes default in its housing duties the county council, after due inquiry, may itself take over the powers of the rural district council.

These opportunities of taking action in default give the

---

[3] A county council has no powers in these various matters over a non-county borough; for the constitution and electoral arrangements of boroughs is a matter for the charter of incorporation.

[4] As to the Minister's powers to take action in default, see chapter 8.

county council a general function of oversight into the activities of the district councils. Action in default is rarely taken by a county council, but the existence of the opportunities places the county council in a position of pre-eminence over the minor authorities.

Two other matters may be mentioned as illustrative of the relationships between county and district councils. An urban or rural district can change the name of the district, but the consent of the county council is required. A county council may make by-laws for the 'good rule and government' of any part of the county outside a non-county borough.[5] The county council's by-laws are, however, enforced by the urban and rural district councils.

There is therefore, among the local authorities in an administrative county, an inter-action and reaction in respect of each other's operations which makes county administration something more than assemblage of local authorities in juxtaposition.

*London.* The position in the Administrative County of London, while showing some resemblance to that of other administrative counties, is rather different. There are no parishes or county districts in London. The Corporation of the City of London has fewer local government functions than a county borough council, but has some functions which the usual non-county borough council does not exercise. The status of the metropolitan boroughs may be said to be somewhere between that of a non-county borough and of an urban district. The Metropolitan Boroughs' Standing Joint Committee, representative of all the boroughs and of the City, is advisory only, but does serve to promote a great measure of harmony and co-operation in the functioning of the respective councils.

The London County Council has power in certain cases to act in default of a metropolitan borough council. Provisions exist for the transfer of powers as between the county council and the city and borough councils.

*General relations between all local authorities.* Apart from the special relationships which exist between local authorities in administrative counties, relations may and do arise between local authorities of all classes, including the councils of county

[5] A borough council makes its own by-laws for these purposes.

boroughs. These relationships arise from the operation of the various local services.

In addition to the general power of local authorities to set up joint committees for purposes of mutual concern there are special provisions in various statutes, particularly the Police Act, 1946, and the Fire Services Act, 1947, enabling local authorities having functions under those Acts to combine for the purpose of carrying out those functions. Somewhat similar powers have been conferred on the Ministers of the Crown to arrange for the setting up of joint boards of local authorities for carrying out particular duties.[6] When set up, these joint boards, or combinations of authorities, become virtually independent local authorities for the particular purposes for which they were created.

Where the operations of one authority are likely to affect another authority there is provision in a number of statutes for the making of official representations by the local authority affected. On certain matters local authorities are empowered to enter into agreements with each other for the carrying out of public services or to make contributions towards each other's services, or to obtain recoupment from each other.

It is by virtue of arrangements such as these that local education authorities (upon suitable financial adjustments) accept into their schools pupils normally resident outside the area in which the school is situated. Mutual arrangements for the obtaining of books by one library authority from the public library of another authority are frequently arrived at. Schemes for the rendering of mutual assistance by fire authorities may be made. The Green Belt around London is an instance of the co-operative effort and expenditure of a number of local authorities. The National Assistance Act, 1948, enables local authorities to agree to reimburse each other any expense incurred by one authority in providing accommodation for assisted persons ordinarily resident in the area of another authority.

Local authorities may in certain cases make contributions towards the expenses of other local authorities.[7]

*Associations of local authorities.* For the purpose of representing and protecting their common interests the various groups of local authorities have formed Associations. Statutory recog-

[6] See chapter 3. Joint authorities.     [7] See chapter 6, p. 114.

nition has been given to the existence of these bodies,[8] which
are active in matters of mutual concern to the authorities they
represent. Representatives of these Associations are frequently
brought into consultation with Ministers and government departments, and, on matters affecting local government as a
whole, joint consultations and joint action by the Associations
in combination are arranged.

The County Councils Association represents the county councils (other than London), the Association of Municipal Corporations represents the boroughs outside London, a Metropolitan
Boroughs' Standing Joint Committee represents the metropolitan city and borough authorities, there is an Urban District
Councils Association, a Rural District Councils Association,
and a National Association of Parish Councils. There are also
a number of associations representing authorities according to
particular functions. The Association of Education Committees,
the Association of Health and Pleasure Resorts, are of this class.
There are also local associations of authorities in particular
areas.

*Local authorities and nationalized services.* Local authorities, as
bodies representative of local public opinion, and as authorities
concerned with the operation of public services in their respective areas, are given special recognition in the statutes which
deal with the nationalization of certain public services. In the
setting up of Regional Hospital Boards and Hospital Management Committees under the National Health Service Act, 1946,
the Minister of Health is required to consult local health authorities. Local authorities have an influence in the appointment
of consultative councils for the purposes of gas and electricity
supply (see chapter 3). The National Assistance Act, 1948, requires the National Assistance Board to set up local advisory
committees for utilizing the advice and assistance of persons
having local knowledge and experience in matters affecting
the functions of the Board. There is no requirement that these
persons shall be members of local authorities, but it is in

---

[8] See, for instance, the Electricity Act, 1957, Sched. I, which provides that
a certain proportion of members of Consultative Councils under that Act shall
contain persons nominated by associations which appear to the Minister to
represent those authorities.

The Local Government Act, 1948, s. 129, authorizes local authorities to sub-
scribe to representative associations of authorities and of local government officers.

practice almost inevitable that members of local authorities will be among those chosen.

*General relationships between public authorities.* So long as public bodies continue to bear well in mind that their purpose is to carry out their functions for the service of the citizen, so long will use be made of the various opportunities for co-operation between local and other public authorities and for harmonizing their various operations. Even where the authorities are not specially authorized or required to enter into official relationships or agreements, common sense and practical convenience often dictate that authorities which operate services which affect other services in the same locality shall consult with each other. There is accordingly a great deal of inter-communication and conference between the various public bodies.

This does not mean, however, that the highest co-operation is always secured. Public authorities, like private individuals, have independent points of view which cannot always be reconciled. It is indeed the purpose of local government to allow for individuality of views according to local needs, local tradition and local capacity. It is quite possible that an authority may not, for various reasons, financial, political or otherwise, find itself in complete accord with the proposals of other authorities.

This is a risk implicit in any system which allows for the administration of services by different authorities. When in any matter a number of authorities are concerned or consulted, the inevitable result is a certain delay and a risk of disagreement.

This provides the supporters of the county borough system with one of their principal arguments.

When all the local government services in the borough are managed by one body only, the borough corporation, there is no occasion for the development of differing points of view, as might be in the case where services are administered by different local government authorities. In the county borough system disharmony is disposed of by co-ordination of the various departments and committees within the borough council's own organization.

The two-tier system, it is alleged, makes for division of responsibility with its attendant risks of delay and discord. To this it may be answered that the conception of the single multi-purpose local authority, running all local services, as typified by the county borough corporations between 1930, when poor law and hospital services were transferred to them, and 1948, when the same services with others were taken away from them, is no longer valid. The taking away of hospitals, public assistance out-relief, electricity and other public services from those authorities has had the effect of breaking up the simple pattern of local administration in those areas and has set up, in the county boroughs, the necessary regional and area boards side by side with the borough corporations. The single multi-purpose local authority no longer exists.

To this the supporter of the county borough system may well answer that the breakdown of the system in part by the setting up of local boards and committees for the nationalized services is no excuse for perpetuating the comparatively complex two-tier and three-tier systems of local authorities in the administrative counties.

County boroughs are, however, always compact areas of concentrated population, where administration of all local government services may be more practicable than in the average administrative county which (London being a startling exception) is a fairly wide area of diffuse population. Accordingly there are, in counties, a number of services which can be administered best on a county basis, and a number which are appropriate for more local treatment. Even in London where the urban concentration is intense and it would be technically feasible to convert the whole of the Administrative County into one county borough (abolishing the minor local authorities), there is much to be said for maintaining the two levels of local authorities. This, it has been said, provides both for the large perspective (the county view) and the more intimate perspective (the 'town hall' view).

In other words, the system gives the citizen, within his immediate locality, a minor authority providing a first point of contact with local government, and a focal point for civic interest and local patriotism. At the same time the system allows for the administration over wider areas of those services such as main roads and planning for which a large area is appropriate.

The two-tier system inevitably means a separation between

major county functions and minor local functions, and a certain amount of what may be called administrative untidiness is probably unavoidable. It is virtually impossible to devise a completely clear-cut division between the functions of a county authority and those of the minor authorities. In spite of anomalies here and there, the system is generally workable and, being largely embedded in tradition, is broadly acceptable to the local public.

Anyone who tries to devise a completely clear-cut division of functions between county and minor local authorities, or indeed between local and national authorities, will have a difficult task, for the reasons indicated at the beginning of this chapter. Public services are inter-related and cannot be administered with complete mutual indifference. This may be a valid argument for keeping the number of public bodies in any area as few as possible. Supporters of the two-tier system allege none the less that the existence of two levels of local authority serves to keep local government alive, by the stimulus of rivalry, and by the interaction of the responsibilities of the various authorities. In such a system local government can never go dead or become moribund.

This advantage remains and (it is said) is emphasized in those cases where the authorities at different levels are concerned in providing similar or concurrent services, as, for instance, in London where both the county council and the city and borough authorities have powers to provide housing, or as in the provinces where both county and minor authorities carry out duties in relation to road maintenance and the provision of open spaces.

Further, the two-tier and the three-tier systems allow greater opportunities than the single-tier system for citizens themselves to take part in public affairs and to obtain experience in the art of local self-government.

In a county borough, local government, traditional associations and the civic sense are in strong alliance. The citizen's interest from all directions can be focused upon the one public body, and is not diffused, as it must be, in a county where a number of authorities take part in local government.

To this, the protagonist of the two-tier system may reply that the concentration of a number of public services in one county borough authority has the result that the elected members must of necessity delegate much of their work to officers, or call in non-elected members by co-option to help in the borough council's work, whereas the distribution of functions among the various authorities in a county makes the respective role of each authority easier to perform, and the burden upon members is thereby lighter. The effect is that more work is done by the elected representative, and does not have to be given to non-elected co-opted members or officers. In that sense, therefore, the county system may be considered to be the more democratic.

To all these arguments there is one general reply—that each system has its advantages, that variety is a principal feature of English local government, and the existence of alternative methods of performing local government enables the needs of the local situation to be met more suitably than if there were no such alternatives.

# 8

# The Central Government and
# Local Authorities

No local government authority[1] is completely autonomous.
None of them can do just as it likes. In the first place, all of
them are dependent upon the central government for the conferment of powers. The government, through Parliament, settles
what functions each local authority shall have. In the same
way these powers may be added to or withdrawn.

In the second place, each authority is, within the ambit of
the powers conferred on it, subject to certain external controls
in the exercise of those powers. Each authority is, of course,
publicly and periodically elected, and is therefore in the performance of its lawful functions subject to the wishes of the
electors. Apart from this, the central government has a considerable interest in and influence over the manner in which
the functions of local authorities are carried out.

The central government is responsible for national administration. The powers conferred by Parliament on local bodies
may leave them a wide discretion in some respects, but no
central government could, without neglecting its own responsibilities, safely allow that discretion to be entirely unlimited.
There are some local services the efficient administration of
which is essential to the welfare of the country as a whole. Public
education, public health and police are in this class. It would
obviously be undesirable for services such as these to fall below
a certain standard of efficiency in any local area. A measure
of uniformity and co-ordination is necessary. A minimum overall standard having been achieved, it is then allowable for each

[1] What is said in this chapter refers only to the elected local government
authorities. The various local bodies, such as Regional Hospital Boards, Electricity Area Boards, and the rest, which operate nationalized public services in
local areas are part of the central government's organization, and are constituted
and conditioned by the government and are completely under its control.

local authority to develop and adjust the operation of its services according to local needs, within the national framework.

For these reasons the central government must retain a certain interest in the activities of local authorities. The control and influence of the government vary with particular services. Where the functions of the local authority are permissive this control and influence are relatively light. In the matter of the provision of a town or county hall, for instance, the discretion of the local authority is almost unfettered; it can be almost as extravagant or as parsimonious as it (bearing in mind its responsibility to the local electors) desires to be. Where the functions of the local authorities are obligatory the control and influence of the central government are greater, and are, in some matters, close and detailed.

*General supervision.* A number of Ministers of the Crown have been given a clear statutory duty to exercise supervision over particular public services in which local authorities have a share. Thus the Minister of Education is given the duty 'to promote the education of the people of England and Wales . . . and to secure the effective execution by local authorities, under his control and direction, of the national policy for providing a varied and comprehensive educational service in every area'. The National Assistance Act, 1948, provides that the functions of local authorities under the Act (of providing accommodation for the needy) and a welfare service shall be exercised under the general guidance and control of the Minister of Health. The Children Act, 1948, which makes local authorities responsible for the care of children deprived of a normal home life, provides that the local authorities shall exercise their functions in that regard under the general guidance and control of the Secretary of State (the Home Secretary). The Ministry of Health Act, 1919, by which the Ministry was first established, gave the Minister of Health the duty of 'promoting the health of the people throughout England and Wales'. An Act of the same year gave the Minister of Transport the duty of 'improving the means of and facilities for locomotion and transport'.

This type of general duty gives the Minister in question the right to interest himself in the work of local authorities. Even in cases where no general duty has been laid upon a Minister, it is the common practice for every Government Department to interest itself in those branches of local government which are in any way concerned with the Department's work. Circular letters of advice, explanatory instructions, information and statistics are sent out to local authorities. In return the Departments will ask for reports and information about the work of local authorities.

*Inspection.* Ministers who have the duty of supervising particular local services make a practice of appointing inspectors or other officers to keep the local services under review and provide a point of contact between the local authorities and the Minister. In some cases this practice is authorized by statute. Thus the Minister of Education is required to cause inspection to be made of every educational establishment; inspectors of fire brigades may be appointed to assist the Home Secretary to supervise the fire services of local authorities; he may also appoint inspectors for the purposes of the enactments relating to children and young persons; inspectors of the Minister of Health may be appointed to inspect disabled persons' and old persons' homes provided by local authorities. Inspectors of the Ministry of Housing and Local Government may attend meetings of a district council, as and when directed by the Minister, and may take part in the proceedings but may not vote.

Apart from any express statutory authority to appoint inspectors, the inspection and supervision by officers of the central departments having concern with local services is an obvious convenience. Thus the inspection of local police forces, of local roads, and of local town planning arrangements are performed by officers of the central departments. A considerable influence may be exercised over local authorities through the medium of these officers. Not only do they help the authorities by advice and suggestions, but their reports to their departments on any proposals by a local authority which may involve a financial grant by the government are usually a deciding factor in the payment of the grant.

*Administrative schemes and arrangements.* In respect of some services local authorities are required to obtain a Minister's approval to their administrative arrangements. Thus establishment schemes to deal with the personnel of local fire brigades must be submitted to the Secretary of State. Local health authorities must submit to the Minister of Health for approval proposals for carrying out the midwifery, ambulance and other services under the National Health Service Act, 1946. Schemes for the making of arrangements for the local welfare services under the National Assistance Act, 1948, must also be submitted to and approved by the same Minister.

This method of making local arrangements by means of approved schemes absolves Parliament from the attempt to legislate in great detail, and, by leaving the local authority to take the initiative in suggesting the form of the arrangements, makes possible a close accord with local conditions. At the same time the method gives opportunity for intervention by the central department, and to that extent tends to limit the discretion of the local authority, in the organization of its own affairs.

Schemes and orders for the setting up of joint authorities or joint boards for certain purposes may be made by a Minister. Thus the Secretary of State may make schemes for the provision of joint fire brigades or police forces for the areas of two or more local authorities; and the Minister of Housing and Local Government may make provisional orders for the union of areas for water supply or sanitary purposes, and for the constitution of joint boards for such services.

And although local authorities have a general power to form joint committees, this power may be exercised in relation to certain services, such as education and fire services, only with the approval of the appropriate Minister.

The concern of a Minister in a local authority's arrangements extends in some cases to the functioning of a local authority's committees. For example, the arrangements for setting up an education committee must be approved by the Minister of Education; the terms of reference of the statutory children's committee and of the committee set up under the National Assistance Act, 1948, by a local authority may be varied (with certain limited exceptions) only with the consent of the Secretary of State and the Minister of Health respectively. The constitution of a county fire brigade committee (other than in London) may be determined by a management scheme approved by the Secretary of State.

*Reports and returns.* The Minister of Housing and Local

Government and the Secretary of State have a general power to require all local authorities to submit reports and returns about their work. Other Ministers have similar powers in respect of particular services.

*Officers.* Certain statutory appointments of officers of local authorities[2] are subject to the supervision of a Minister.

*Bills and by-laws.* When a local authority promotes a Bill in Parliament for the conferment of powers upon the authority, the promotion must first be approved by the Minister of Housing and Local Government. When the Bill comes before Parliament, the government departments concerned report to Parliament upon the merits of the proposals in the Bill.

All by-laws made by a local authority require the sanction of the appropriate Minister.

*Particular acts of local authorities.* In a number of instances a local authority may exercise its powers on a particular matter only with the prior approval of a Minister. Thus the compulsory acquisition of land by a local authority requires Ministerial approval. The consent of the Minister of Housing and Local Government is required in order that a local authority may sell or exchange land, or may appropriate land for a purpose other than that for which it was acquired; a similar consent is required to the purchase of land not immediately required for a statutory purpose.

There is a variety of other matters in which the prior consent of a Minister is necessary before the local authority can lawfully act. Important examples of this class of case are the development plans which local planning authorities are required to make under the Town and Country Planning Act, 1947. These plans require the approval of the Minister of Housing and Local Government, and may be modified by him as he thinks fit.

*Appeals to a Minister.* When a local authority is given power to interfere with private property, or to act in any way that may adversely affect another public body, it is common to provide that there shall be an appeal against the actions of the local authority. In a number of cases these appeals will be heard by the courts; in other cases they will be heard by the appropriate Minister. Where, for instance, a local authority

[2] See chapter 13.

seeks to acquire land by compulsory purchase, opportunity is afforded to persons affected to make objections to the Minister of Housing and Local Government, who is required to take these objections into account. A similar right of objection to the Minister is given in respect of property affected by town planning schemes; the Minister also hears appeals against decisions of a local town planning authority as to the use to which premises may be put.

In some matters the law provides that any person aggrieved by an act or neglect of a local authority may complain to a Minister, who make take suitable action to deal with the complaint.

*Local inquiries.* Where any proposals of a local authority requiring the consent of a Minister appear likely to concern a number of persons, or have an effect on the locality as a whole, or when a number of objections have been put in against the proposals, it is frequently the practice for the Minister, before deciding the matter, to hold a local inquiry. These inquiries are of the nature of informal lawsuits, held under the chairmanship of an officer of the Ministry. The parties for and against the proposals appear in person or by legal representative.

*Regulations.* Many of the Acts of Parliament dealing with local government functions empower the appropriate Minister to make regulations in supplementation of the statutory provisions. In these regulations such matters as the standard of service to be provided, the fees to be charged, the forms to be used, the procedure to be followed and the notices to be given are prescribed.

*Conferment and transfer of powers.* The Minister of Housing and Local Government has power to confer on rural district councils the functions of an urban district council, and may confer on an urban or a rural district council the functions of a parish council. The Minister may also, with the consent of the authorities concerned, rearrange powers as between the London County Council, the City of London Corporation and the metropolitan borough councils. The Minister may also, by provisional order (to be confirmed by Parliament) transfer to county and county borough councils the functions of local conservators or other local public bodies.

*Action in default.* In Acts of Parliament which impose a duty upon local authorities it is usual to provide that, if the local authority fails to do its duty, the appropriate Minister may take action in the matter, by declaring (after due inquiry) that the local authority is in default. The steps which may then be taken by the Minister vary according to the provisions of the relevant statutes. In some cases the Minister may himself perform the local authority's function.

For instance, where an authority has failed to make building by-laws, the Minister may himself make by-laws for the local authority's area.

In other cases the Minister may issue a formal order directing the defaulting authority to do any necessary acts within a specified time. If the order is not complied with it may be enforced by obtaining an order of the court (mandamus) against the authority, and the ultimate consequence may be that the members or officers of the authority may be fined or arrested for contempt of court if the order is not complied with.

A third course which may be followed in some cases is for the Minister to transfer the powers of a defaulting authority to another authority. For example, where a county district is in default in its public health or housing duties the Minister may transfer the duties to the county council.

The London County Council has power, in relation to certain health matters, to take action in default of a metropolitan borough council, to carry out any necessary duties and charge the defaulting council with the cost.

The Education Act, 1944, contains an unusual provision empowering the Minister of Education to give to local authorities appropriate directions when it appears to him that the authority have acted, or propose to act, unreasonably in regard to their functions under the Act.

All these various methods of action in default of a local authority are very seldom used. It is obviously necessary that there should be opportunity for some effective action where a local authority is neglectful. It is said that the mere existence of default powers, and the threat implied in their existence, is sufficient to keep local authorities reasonably assiduous. It is probably fairer to contend that default powers are seldom exercised because, where the authorities are democratically elected, and the electors take an interest in the doings of the local council, the pressure of public opinion and the fact that the elected representative is anxious to do well, are sufficient safeguards against default.

*Financial control.* The fact that the district auditor is a government official, together with the powers given to the Minister of Housing and Local Government to remit surcharges, or to sanction expenditure with a view to avoiding a surcharge, may be regarded as giving the central administration some interest in the financial affairs of local authorities.

The central departments have, however, very little concern with the amount which a local authority may spend out of rate income. There are instances where the law imposes a limit on the rate which may be levied for particular purposes (the provision of entertainments by local authorities, for instance). These instances are few. For the most part local authorities, so long as they perform their proper functions, have a free hand as to the amount of rate-borne income they will spend on any project.

Where a project is to be financed by borrowing money, the control of the central department is considerable. Except in a few limited cases, no local authority may borrow money without the sanction of some higher authority, which is usually a government department.[3] The department satisfies itself that the purpose of the loan is desirable (a local inquiry may even be held) and that the amount is reasonable. The refusal of sanction still leaves the local authority free to finance the project out of rate income.

In practice, the most powerful form of financial influence exercised by the central departments over local authorities is by way of the various percentage and other grants paid by the government towards particular local services or projects. It is a condition of the payment of these grants that the service shall be efficient or the project shall be approved by the department concerned. The threat of withdrawing grant gives the department a weighty influence in the matter.

*General effect of central control.* By all these various means, the central government can make its influence felt in local affairs. Ministers of State may not only intervene in cases brought to

[3] See chapter 6, p. 114.

their notice; they (or their officers) may actively inquire into and inspect the work of local authorities and may exercise a check upon their activities either by refusing sanction or approval, by withholding a grant, or by overruling a local authority on appeal. Should any authority fail to do its duty, powers exist to remedy the default. By regulations, local authorities may to a considerable extent be directed as to what they shall do and how they shall do it.

In spite of all this, local authorities must not be assumed to be puppets without will, tied at every turn by the restrictions of the central departments. The concern of the central government is to see that local government works, not to hinder it from working. Over a large part of the activities of local authorities central control is light and indirect. Moreover, all the various modes of central control still leave to the local authority the function of evolving proposals, of taking the initial steps. It is the local authority which forms the first estimate of what the locality needs in the way of local services, the mode of making provision, and the timing and rate of speed. Town plans, housing schemes, drainage works, local road improvements are not in the first instance thought out by a government department. The local authority does that. The Minister only intervenes to see that the authority is doing its work properly. And when the schemes and plans come to be carried into execution, the necessary works are carried out under the direction of the local authority.

Even though proposals of an authority may be subject to Ministerial approval, it must not be supposed that a local authority, in submitting its proposals, is entirely passive. A great deal of discussion, often forceful, takes place between local authorities and the various Ministries.

Contact between central and local government is constant and continuous. Deputations from local authorities attend upon Ministers to present a local case, explain the local point of view and to make suggestions. Frequent conversations take place between officers of local authorities and government departments. In matters which affect local authorities collectively the representative organizations of local authorities[4] use their efforts to bring national and local policies into accord.

[4] See chapters 7, p. 123, and 12, p. 192.

*Legislative proposals.* It has become an increasing practice in recent years, when the central government propose to introduce legislation affecting local authorities, for the government to discuss its proposals in draft with the local authorities concerned or with their representative associations. In this way, the views and suggestions of the authorities who are to be concerned in the proposed legislation, and will share in its administration when it becomes law, are laid before the Minister concerned, and the Minister has the opportunity of explaining to the authorities what his aims and intentions are. These discussions frequently lead to the amendment of the draft legislation, and help both Ministers and local authorities to bring their respective points of view into closer adjustment. By this means also the time of Parliament is saved in that much that would otherwise be said and done upon the draft legislation in its course through Parliament is disposed of before the legislation is introduced.

While it is true that the central government has its due influence over the local authorities, it is also true that the local authorities, both alone and in combination, are not without influence over the central departments. Central control is necessary in every system of local governments. In the English system it is tempered with that spirit of compromise which is said to form an essential element in the British character.

# 9

## Local Government Elections

ONE of the principal features of the English system of local government which distinguishes it from a number of foreign systems is the fact that all the members of each local government authority are, without exception, publicly elected by people in the area administered by the authority.

Under some systems of local government there is, in each local area, some official appointed by and representative of the central government and having authority to exercise, by veto or otherwise, influence over the affairs of the local authorities.[1]

Moreover, it is a practice in some European countries for the mayor, burgomaster, or other leading representative elected in each local area to be approved by the central government before he enters upon his local government duties.

There are no such arrangements to the English system. Local government authorities are composed entirely of persons elected in the locality in which they serve. There are no appointed members, nor is the election of any member of a local council subject to the influence or approval of the central government.[2]

This does not mean to say that all the members of each local council are elected by the popular vote of the local residents. The bulk of the members of a council, namely, the councillors, are elected by the general public of the locality, but the chairman, or mayor, and the aldermen (where there are any) are elected, not by the public at large, but by the

[1] The inspectors appointed by government departments, as to which see chapter 8, have no powers of control or veto over local authorities. In respect of certain services under the direct control of the central government (see chapter 3) various local organizations exist, which are directly supervised by the government, but these are not part of the local government system properly so called.

[2] As to the approval of the central government to certain appointments of officers, see chapter 13.

councillors.[3] The procedure of election to membership of a council differs therefore according to the position which the member is to occupy.

*Parish meetings.* A parish meeting is an assembly of the local government electors of the parish. Every elector may attend. There is no election to be made other than to appoint a chairman for the year. Nominations are made orally, voting is by show of hands. If, however, a poll is demanded, the election takes place by secret ballot as for an ordinary local government election.

## THE ELECTION OF COUNCILLORS[4]

*Electoral areas.* For the purpose of the election of county councillors, every administrative area is divided into electoral divisions for each of which, in counties outside London, one county councillor is elected.[5]

In London, each electoral division for parliamentary elections is a division for county council elections, and in each division the number of county councillors to be elected is treble the number of members of Parliament.[6]

Boroughs and urban districts may be divided into wards for electoral purposes, in which case there is an election in each ward. The number of councillors to be elected for each ward in a borough is fixed by the borough charter or may be fixed or altered by Order in Council upon a petition presented by the borough council. In urban districts the number of wards and councillors for each is determined or altered by order of the county council after a local inquiry.[7]

If the borough or urban district is not divided into wards,

---

[3] Aldermen in the City of London are, however, elected by the local government electors.

[4] What is said in this chapter is not generally applicable to the City of London, which has its own peculiar local organization. See chapter 2, p. 31.

[5] The divisions outside London may be varied by order of the Home Secretary on representations made by the county council or the council of a county district.

[6] The electoral divisions for the London County Council being the same as for parliamentary elections may be varied only with the consent of Parliament under the House of Commons (Redistribution of Seats) Act, 1944, as amended by the Representation of the People Act, 1948.

[7] If the urban district council asks the county council to make an order, and the county council refuses, the urban district council may apply to the Home Secretary for an order.

one election is held for the whole borough or urban district.

Rural districts are divided for electoral purposes into areas which are either parishes, groups of parishes or wards of parishes. The areas and the number of councillors for each are determinable or alterable by the county council.

In fixing the number of councillors to each ward or division regard must be had to the fact that in boroughs and in some urban and rural districts one-third of the councillors retire each year. The number of councillors for each electoral area should in such cases accordingly be divisible by three.

For the purpose of parish council elections the county council may, if the area or population of a parish is so large, or different parts of the population are so distributed, as to make a single election of parish councillors inconvenient, or if it is otherwise desirable that certain parts of a parish should be separately represented on the parish council, make an order dividing the parish into wards for electoral purposes. Where the parish is divided into wards, separate elections take place for each ward.

The electoral areas form, as it were, the ground plan for the election campaign, and show the constituencies to be contested and the number of seats to be fought for in each.

*The conduct of the election.* Elaborate provisions and rules have been made for regulating in detail the process of local government elections. It is essential that these elections should be conducted with scrupulous fairness, and that every step in that process should be duly prescribed[8] and that those conducting the election should have no opportunity of favouring, or of being suspected of favouring, one side or the other.

A council always remains in office until its successor is appointed. At the time when an election for a new council is in progress there is accordingly always an old council in existence and in function. Although the members of this council may be deeply concerned in the results of the election, and, although the personnel and policy of the council may be vitally influenced by the outcome of the election, the council as a body has no part to play in the actual conduct of the election. The cost of the election (other than candidate's own expenses) is borne by the council; the cost of parish council elections is borne

[8] See, for instance, the Second Schedule to the Representation of the People Act, 1949, and Rules made by the Home Secretary for urban and rural district elections.

by the rural district council. The operation of the machinery of the election is, however, in every case entirely in the hands of the returning officer.

*The returning officer.* For county council elections each county council must appoint a county returning officer. He is usually the clerk of the county council. It is he who arranges for the printing of the ballot papers, for the provision of the ballot boxes and other apparatus, and the collection and counting of the votes. Where a county electoral division is wholly within a borough, the mayor of the borough is the returning officer for that division, but he must act under the instructions of the county returning officer. Deputies may be appointed.

At borough elections outside London, in boroughs divided into wards, an alderman is appointed to be returning officer for each ward; if there are no wards, the mayor (or, if he or the deputy mayor cannot act, an alderman) acts as returning officer for the whole borough. At elections for urban and rural district councillors the clerk of the district council acts. In a metropolitan borough the town clerk is returning officer. At parish council elections the returning officer is the clerk of the rural district council or someone appointed by him.

*Polling districts and places.* One of the first duties of the returning officer is to see that there are sufficient and convenient polling stations at which the electors may record their votes. These arrangements are, of course, usually made well beforehand. Schools and other places maintained out of rates may be used as polling stations free of charge.

*The register of electors.* Another duty which must be performed before an election is the preparation of the list of those persons who are to be entitled to vote at the election. The duty of preparing this list is performed by the registration officer of each parliamentary constituency. He is either the clerk of the county council or the town clerk of the borough or urban district. He makes inquiry throughout the area as to which persons are qualified to vote. He makes up his list in self-contained portions for each electoral unit. County and borough councils may divide their electoral areas into polling districts. Where this is done, the register of electors will be made up to correspond with those districts; otherwise it will correspond with the wards or parishes.

The register is published yearly, in February.

*Who is entitled to vote?* To be qualified for inclusion in the register of local government electors, a person must be a British subject of full age, and, at a 'qualifying date', be either resident in the electoral area, or occupy in the area, as owner or tenant, any rateable land or premises of an annual value of not less than £10.[9] The qualifying date, for elections held in the twelve months beginning on 16th February, is the preceding 10th October.

Persons who would ordinarily be resident in an area, but who are away on national service, may be registered in the area.

All these qualifications are applicable equally to men and to women.

A person is not, in any local government area, entitled to be registered more than once as an elector for the local council of that area; but he may, if he is qualified, be registered in more than one local government area so as to vote for the separate councils of those areas.[10]

*Legal incapacity.* Even if otherwise qualified, a person may not be registered as a voter if he or she is of unsound mind, or is serving a sentence of penal servitude, or of imprisonment with hard labour, or of imprisonment (without hard labour) for more than twelve months. A person may not be registered who has been convicted of certain corrupt practices at elections. The registration officer publishes, with the list of electors, a 'black list' of persons disqualified by reason of these practices.

A person who is on the register by virtue of a residence or property qualification retains the right to vote during the currency of the register, even though the qualification has, in fact, been lost.[11]

*Dates of general elections.* The Representation of the People

[9] The qualification by reason of the occupation of land or premises does not apply to parliamentary elections. This fact, and the fact that peers may vote at local government elections but not for parliamentary elections, makes the local government electorate generally much larger than the parliamentary electorate.

[10] Thus, for example, he may be registered in any county district in which he is qualified, and may vote as a district council elector in any district in which he is so registered; but he is entitled to only one registration in any county as county elector, and may vote only once for the county council of that county.

[11] The supervention of a legal incapacity such as a conviction, as mentioned in the text, will, however, affect the elector's right to vote even though he is in fact on the register.

Act, 1948, provides that general elections for county councils shall be held early in April, and for other councils early in May. The actual dates of election may be fixed within certain narrow limits as follows:

For county councils the general election must be held (subject to certain special variations to meet the incidence of Easter) in the week beginning on the Sunday which falls on or next before 9th April. The actual date for each general election may be fixed by the county council itself.

For all other councils[12] the general election must be held (subject to certain special variations to meet the incidence of Whitsun) in the week beginning on the Sunday which falls on or next before 9th May.

For all borough councils, the actual date is fixed (within the limits above-mentioned) by the Home Secretary each year.

The actual date for district council elections if fixed (within the prescribed limits) by the county council after consulting the district council. For parish councils the date is fixed by the county council, within the prescribed limits.[13]

*Year of election.* General elections for county councils and parish councils throughout the country are held in the same years, that is in 1952 and in every third subsequent year.

General elections for metropolitan borough councils fall in the year immediately following the general elections of county councillors.

For other boroughs an election is held every year for one-third of the councillors. In urban and rural districts there is no universal rule; for in some districts an election for one-third of the councillors is held every year, while in others (where the county council has made an order to that effect) an election for the whole council is held every three years.

*By-elections.* When a by-election is held to fill a casual vacancy in the council of a county, a borough or a county district, the election must be held within thirty days of the notification

[12] The annual general election for common councillors for the City of London is held on St. Thomas's Day (21st December).

[13] When elections for rural district and parish councils are held in the same area on the same day, as they frequently are, the elections are, as far as possible, to be taken together. This saves expense. Votes for both elections may be put into the same ballot box. They are sorted out afterwards.

of the vacancy. The actual date of election is fixed by the returning officer.

A casual vacancy among parish councillors is filled by the parish council itself, and the council must be convened forthwith for that purpose.

*Day of retirement.* County and borough councillors retire from office on the fourth day after the election, and the newly elected councillors come into office on that same day. In the case of district and parish councillors the date is 20th May. Councillors elected to fill casual vacancies enter into office forthwith.[14]

*Programme and procedure at an election.* The general conduct of an election of councillors follows the familiar lines of a parliamentary election. The relevant Acts and Rules lay down time limits for various stages in the procedure. The returning officer works out his programme for the various stages, issues public notice of the intended election, provides nomination papers for the use of candidates, looks over his stock of ballot boxes and polling booths, prepares the numerous necessary documents, and gets ready to engage the requisite staff.

*Nomination.* Each intending candidate must be nominated on a form containing the prescribed number of signatures of electors in support of the nomination.[15]

The candidate must formally consent to his own nomination; and his statement of consent must contain particulars of his qualification for election.[16]

There is no deposit to be paid (and consequently none to be forfeited) by a candidate, as in the case of a parliamentary election. If any candidate after nomination wishes to withdraw, he may do so not later than twelve days before the day fixed for the election.

*Uncontested election.* If the eventual number of candidates does not exceed the number of seats to be filled, the returning officer has a simple task. He publishes the list of nominated candidates and declares them duly returned, unopposed.

---

[14] In all cases the necessary declaration of acceptance of office must be made. See chapter 10.

[15] The number is, in an election for a county council, borough council outside London, or an urban district council, 10; for a metropolitan borough council or rural district council the number is 2.

[16] As to qualifications, see chapter 10.

*Contested election.* If the number of candidates exceeds the number of seats to be filled, then the election is on in earnest.

The candidates, with their supporters, get busy, if they have not already done so. It is possible for a candidate to get elected without cost to himself; for the work of the returning officer in arranging and conducting the election is paid for by the council, and not by the candidates.

*Candidate's expenses.* A candidate can, however, hardly avoid expense. He generally finds it necessary to issue an election address, display posters, hold public meetings, and generally advertise himself. This expense is his responsibility and is not met by the public authorities.

The law allows a candidate to incur expenditure of this kind, but imposes certain limitations and safeguards. Firstly, there are certain matters on which expenditure may not be incurred at all. A candidate may not, for instance, bribe electors nor treat them to drink, food or entertainment other than by way of normal hospitality. He may not hire conveyances to take electors to the poll, nor provide bands of music, torches, or banners. To incur expenditure on these matters is a corrupt or illegal practice.

Secondly, the amount he may spend on legitimate items such as public meetings and literature is limited according to the number of electors in the constituency, namely, £25 for the first 500 electors or less, and 2*d.* for each elector over 500, subject to a reduction in the case of joint candidates.

Thirdly, proper accounts must be kept of a candidate's election expenditure, and in due time after the election a return of expenditure must be made to the clerk of the local authority and be open to inspection by members of the public.

Commission of a corrupt or illegal practice, such as those mentioned above, or the offence of personation (pretending to be someone else when voting) or the exercise of undue influence, may render the candidate, and in some cases his supporters, liable to fines and imprisonment, and may result in the offender's being disqualified over a period of years from voting or seeking election. Moreover, interested parties may present an election petition to the court, and the court may set the whole election aside.

*The poll.* An elector must, in general, vote in person at the appropriate polling station, but special exceptions are made in respect of service voters, persons who are blind or physically incapable of attendance at a polling station, and persons whose employment on the day of election prevents their attendance at the proper polling station. Service voters, and certain other voters whose employment prevents their personal attendance, may vote by proxy. Other persons incapable of attendance by reason of physical incapacity, absence overseas, or the nature of their employments may apply to be put on the absent voters' list and may vote by post.

*Hours of poll.* The normal hours of poll are from 8 a.m. to 8 p.m. but may be extended in any constituency to 9 p.m. if a number of candidates, not being less than the number to be elected for that constituency, make written request for the extension.

*The count.* The excitement of an election reaches its culmination at the counting of the votes. To ensure that everything is fair, each candidate may appoint agents to attend the count on his behalf and keep an eye on the proceedings. The ballot papers are emptied from each ballot box and counted to ensure that the number in the box accords with the number issued to electors. The papers from all the boxes are then mixed up together and the counting of the individual votes takes place. Each elector has one vote for each seat contested and may not give more than one vote for each candidate. If there is only one seat, then the counting is easy; for each ballot paper should contain only one vote. All that needs to be done is to sort the papers into piles for each candidate and count the number in each pile.

But if there are several seats contested, the process becomes a little complicated. If there are, for instance, five seats contested, each elector has five votes. The number of candidates, of course, must exceed the number of seats. An elector may have ten candidates among whom to distribute his five votes. He may distribute them as he pleases; he may not wish to record all his five votes and may vote for only one or two candidates. The result is that the ballot papers are not always marked in the same way and it is not possible to sort them all out into similar piles. Two assistants usually work together in these cases, and one calls out from the ballot papers the names of the candidates voted for, and the other marks the votes on a list of all the candidates. The totals of each individual candidate's votes are then counted from the marked list.

Any ballot paper which is incorrectly marked, as, for instance, when too many votes have been recorded on the paper, or the mark is not clearly shown, is put aside and the returning officer decides as to its validity. A ballot paper is not to be rejected, however, if it is marked in the wrong place or otherwise than by means of a cross, if it is clear what the voter's intention was.

*Equality of votes—Recount.* If the numbers of votes cast for different candidates are exactly equal the returning officer must cast lots to determine which candidate shall be successful.

A candidate or his agent may, if present on the completion of the counting of the votes, demand a recount, and, on a recount, may demand a further recount; but the returning officer may refuse this request at his discretion.

When at last the counting is fully completed, and the returning officer has declared the result, no further recount can take place except by order of a competent court of law.

### ELECTIONS TO OTHER OFFICES

*The election of mayor or chairman.* Compared with the election of councillors the election of the mayor or chairman of a local council is a simple matter. It is the first business to be transacted at the annual meeting of the council or of a newly elected council and is not conducted in secret. The law does not specify any particular formality beyond that applicable to the ordinary business of the council. Nominations are invited by the person presiding, who is usually the outgoing mayor or chairman. The nominations are made orally by a proposer and seconder in each case, and the matter is put to the vote by show of hands. In the case of equality of votes the presiding member has a second or casting vote. Usually, however, there is only one nomination and accordingly no contest. No expense may be incurred by a candidate for election as mayor or chairman.

In the case of those councils which have aldermen (county and borough councils) an outgoing alderman, i.e. one whose term of office is due to expire on the day of the election of the mayor or chairman, may not vote in his capacity as alderman at that election. An alderman who has obtained election as a councillor may, however, vote in his capacity of newly elected councillor.

Upon election the mayor or chairman forthwith takes the chair and his term of office commences.

*Deputy mayor.* In boroughs outside London the mayor may appoint one of the aldermen or councillors to be deputy mayor. There is accordingly no election for this office. The appointment must be signified to the council in writing and be recorded in the minutes.

In metropolitan boroughs the council may appoint a member of the council to be deputy mayor. The election proceeds on the same lines as the election of the mayor.

*Vice-chairman.* A county council must appoint a vice-chairman. Urban and rural district councils may appoint. The London County Council may, in addition to a vice-chairman, appoint a deputy chairman. The elections proceed in the same way as the election of a chairman.

*Aldermen* both in counties and in boroughs are elected every third year at the annual meeting of the council. In counties their election takes place in the same year as the general election of the county councillors. They are elected immediately after the election of the chairman or mayor (or in boroughs where there is a sheriff after the appointment of the sheriff). Aldermen as such (whether outgoing or not) may not vote in the election of aldermen.

There are no nominations. Each person entitled to vote, i.e. each councillor and the mayor or chairman, fills up a form setting out the names and addresses of the persons he votes for. He has as many votes as there are vacancies to be filled. These papers are handed at the meeting to the presiding member, who, in the case of equality of votes, has a second or casting vote. The newly elected aldermen come into office forthwith and their predecessors immediately retire. No expenses may be incurred by a candidate for election as alderman.

A person cannot be both alderman and councillor. If a councillor is elected alderman, or *vice versa*, he must choose which office he will accept.

*General conclusion.* The object aimed at by all the various provisions of the law relating to public elections is to ensure that the choice of the electors may be freely made, without fear or fraud and without patronage or undue influence. Where voting is by ballot, the elector, alone in the polling booth, gives his vote without fear of detection. Except in the special cases where a person is allowed to vote by proxy, an elector's vote is a secret. If he does not disclose how he voted, no one else can discover it except the returning officer and his staff, and then only after considerable search.

When a ballot paper is issued to an elector, his registration number is written by the poll clerk on the counterfoil of the paper, so that, in a proper case, as where an elector is accused of voting twice, the manner in which any elector voted can be duly ascertained. It will, however, be remembered that after the papers are emptied out of the ballot boxes the papers from all the boxes are mixed up together. It would accordingly be a very tedious business to hunt through the ballot papers and find any particular one. Moreover, the returning officer and his staff are sworn to secrecy under heavy penalties. And the ballot papers are, after the counting of the votes, put away in sealed packets which may be opened only by order of the court.

These remarks do not, of course, apply in the case of an election of aldermen (where the two stages of nomination and voting are taken together), nor to the case of the election of a mayor or chairman, which takes place openly in council. But these elections are part of the proceedings of a council as a public representative body. It is accordingly appropriate that the transactions of such a body should bear public scrutiny, and that any elections it makes should be open and free from any suspicion of intrigue. Indeed, the secret ballot as a mode of deciding questions at council meetings is unknown in the English local government system.

All of which serves to illustrate and emphasize the cardinal principle mentioned at the outset of this chapter—that in English local government all members of a local council are chosen entirely by the people within the area administered by the council and by no one else.

# Members of Local Authorities

I T is obviously desirable that persons who are elected to membership of a public authority should be fit and proper persons to hold office and should, during the period of their membership, have a due sense of their public duties and responsibilities. The law therefore prescribes a number of requirements with which every member of a local authority must comply. The requirements are designed to ensure a member's suitability for election and for membership. The law does not concern itself with a member's capabilities. Those are matters for the judgment of the electors. The concern of the law is that public business shall be conducted without peculation or corruption, that members shall have a proper interest in the administration of their council's work, shall duly attend meetings, and avoid the temptation to take improper advantage of their position as members.

*Qualifications for being a member of a council.* To be a member of a local government authority a person must be of full age and a British subject, and have at least one of the following qualifications:

(i) Be on the register of local government electors for any place within the area administered by the authority in question;

(ii) own freehold or leasehold land in the area of the authority;

(iii) reside in the area of the authority during the whole of the twelve months preceding the election. In the case of a parish council, residence within three miles of the parish, since 25th March in the year preceding the election, is sufficient.

The proper qualification should be possessed by every member at the time of nomination for election. The member should also be duly qualified throughout the period of membership. Failure to be so qualified will involve forfeiture of the membership.

*Acceptance of office.* It was at one time the law that if a person, after being elected to a membership of a local government authority, refused to accept office, he was to be fined. Fines are not now payable in such cases, but the law requires that every person elected to membership, whether as chairman, mayor, alderman or councillor must, within two months after being elected, make and deliver to the clerk of the authority a formal declaration of acceptance of office.[1] If this declaration is not duly made the office is forfeited, and if the person attempts to act in that office severe penalties will be incurred.

*Disqualification for membership.* In addition to having the proper qualifications for membership, a member of a local government authority must, throughout the period of his membership, avoid certain disqualifications. These disqualifications fall into three main groups, (i) those arising from certain appointments or employment; (ii) those arising from financial incapacity; and (iii) those arising from the commission of an offence.

*Disqualification arising from employment.* Thus a person is disqualified from being a member of any local authority if he holds any paid office or other place of profit (other than that of mayor, chairman or sheriff) which is in the gift or disposal of the council or any of its committees.

A coroner or deputy-coroner for a county or a borough may not be a member of the council of that county or borough. A recorder of a borough may not sit on the borough council; nor may an elective auditor of a borough be a member of the borough council. And of course, officers and employees of a council may not, while being so employed, become members of the council.[2] Teachers or other persons employed in schools and/or educational institutions maintained or assisted by a council are ineligible for membership of the council.[3]

[1] A candidate for the office of councillor must formally consent to nomination before his election. This provides itself a safeguard of his seriousness in seeking office.

[2] A person who has been a member of a council may not accept an appointment under the council until he has ceased to be a member for twelve months.

[3] But not for membership of the education committee of the council.

The principle underlying all this is easy to appreciate. A person cannot be both servant and master. A person employed or appointed by a council ought not at the same time to be a member of the council and thus be in a position to take part in the control of his own employment, nor should members of a council be in a position to appoint each other to paid employment under the council. The law goes even further than this. It provides that where a local authority has a committee which contains representatives of other local authorities, the paid officers employed by that committee are disqualified from seeking election to any of the authorities represented on the committee. There is, however, nothing to prevent an officer in the local government service from becoming an elected member of an authority which is not concerned in his employment.

The London County Council is governed by provisions which go further than those applicable to other local authorities. A person is disqualified from being a member of the council if and so long as he has, directly or indirectly, by himself or his partner, any share or interest in any contract with the council. Thus a managing director, paid partly or wholly by commission on profits, would be unable to be a member of the London County Council during the currency of any contracts between his firm and the council. Shareholders in firms contracting with the council are not, however, disqualified, nor are persons renting houses from the council, nor are medical practitioners receiving certain fees from the council, and the disqualification does not apply to a share or interest in (i) sales, purchases and leases of land, (ii) newspapers in which the council advertises, and (iii) agreements for the loan or payment of money.

*Financial incapacity* arises from bankruptcy or the making of a composition with creditors.[4] The principle underlying these disqualifications is not quite clear. Is impecuniosity evidence that one is incapable of managing one's own affairs, and, in consequence, even more incapable for carrying on public affairs? Or is it that financial embarrassment exposes one to

---

[4] The receipt of national or local public assistance is (since the passing of the National Assistance Act, 1948) no longer a disqualification for membership of a local authority.

temptations from which more prosperous people are likely to be immune?

A person who is adjudged bankrupt, or who makes a composition with his creditors, immediately becomes disqualified for membership of a local government authority. The disqualification ceases if he pays his debts in full, or if he is discharged with a certificate that the bankruptcy was due to misfortune without any misconduct. If these mitigating circumstances are not present, then the disqualification continues for five years after the discharge from bankruptcy or from the date on which the terms of composition are fulfilled.

*Disqualification arising from the commission of an offence* is easier to appreciate. A person who has, within the five years previous to the day of election, or since his election, been convicted of an offence and ordered to be imprisoned for three months or more, without the option of a fine, is disqualified for election to or membership of a local government authority. It does not matter whether the offence was one of dishonesty, such as fraud, theft or embezzlement, or whether it was an offence which an honest person might commit, such as an assault, or the dangerous driving of a motor car. A person who is insufficiently law-abiding may be considered as unsuitable for taking part in public affairs.

The commission of certain corrupt and illegal practices in connection with elections has already been mentioned in chapter 9. Convictions for these offences involves not only disqualification from voting at elections, but from membership of a council as well.

Under the law relating to the audit of accounts a government auditor who discovers that the public funds of a local authority have been misapplied or improperly spent, may surcharge the members responsible. In other words, the auditor may order the responsible members to make good the misspent money out of their own pockets. If a member of a local government authority is surcharged in this way to an amount exceeding £500 he becomes disqualified for election and membership of any local authority for five years.

*Failure to attend meetings.* Members of a local authority are expected to give proper attention to the affairs of the authority. The law provides that if a member fails to attend any meetings of the authority over a period of six months, he shall cease to be a member of the authority, unless the reason for his absence was due to some reasons approved by the council, or was due to absence on government service during war or emergency.

*Proceedings in respect of qualification.* Legal proceedings may be taken against any person who acts as a member of a local authority while he is either unqualified or disqualified, or has resigned or has forfeited his membership through failure to attend meetings, or has failed to give the required declaration of acceptance of office. These proceedings may be commenced only by a local government elector for the area of the authority concerned, and must be started within six months of the commission of the offence. A fine not exceeding £50 may be imposed for each occasion on which the offence was committed.

*Resignation.* A member of a local authority may resign at any time by giving notice in writing to the clerk of the authority.

*Re-election.* A person who has been elected to membership of a council, or has been elected mayor, chairman or alderman, may, on the termination of his period of office, be duly re-elected so long as he is properly qualified, and is not disqualified.

*The Mayor, or Lord Mayor,* is in a special position, and has certain privileges which are not shared by the other members of the council. He is elected by the council and, although any alderman or councillor is eligible, the mayor, at the time of his election, need not be a member of the council at all. He (or she, since women are also eligible) must in any event have the same qualifications as a person must have for election as councillor. The mayor must also be free from the same disqualifications as are applicable to councillors. There is justification for this; for, on election, the mayor becomes the presiding member and legally entitled to take the chair at all meetings of the council and vote in its proceedings. In cases where he is elected from among the existing members of the council, his election does not cause any vacancy among the membership of the council, and there is no by-election. Where he is elected from outside the council he increases the membership of the council by one during his period of office, and no one has to resign from the council to make room for him.

His term of office is one year, but he holds office until his successor is appointed. On the expiry of his year of office he reverts to the status he had before election; if he was an alderman or councillor, he finishes out his term in that office; if he was elected from outside the council, he ceases to be a member of the council altogether.

A mayor will vote in the proceedings over which he presides, and, if the votes on any matter are equal, he has a second or casting vote. It is a convention in many boroughs, however, especially where the council is divided into political groups, for the mayor to take no part in the ordinary business of the council except to preside at its meetings. In those cases he does not vote, except on the rare occasions when he exercises his right to give a casting vote.

His ceremonial position is what gives particular prestige to his office. He is the first citizen of the borough, and is its chief representative. He takes social and official precedence over everyone else in the borough except the Sovereign and the lord lieutenant of the county within which the borough is situated.[5]

Apart from his official duties as a member of the council, he has the function of representing the borough as a whole. He is its personification, and this involves many calls upon his time and purse.

The borough council have power to pay him such remuneration as they think reasonable. Some borough councils in fact pay nothing. Others pay a salary, or mayoral purse, according to the wealth and importance of the borough. The larger county boroughs provide a mayoral salary of between £2,000 and £3,000 a year. In the smaller non-county boroughs it is correspondingly less, and £200 or £300 may suffice.

The mayoral robes of scarlet cloth and fur, the mayor's chain and badge of office cannot ordinarily be paid for out of the rates. The mayor provides his own robes, or takes over those of a predecessor. The badge and chain of office (provided in the first instance by gift or public subscription) are handed on from mayor to mayor.

The mayor provides a link between the system of local government and the system of administering justice. He is, by

[5] The mayors of Oxford and Cambridge do not take precedence over the vice-chancellors of the universities.

virtue of his office, a justice of the peace. In a borough outside London which has a separate commission of the peace,
he becomes a justice for the borough during his year of office.
In other boroughs, including metropolitan boroughs, he becomes during his mayoralty a justice for the county in which
the borough is situate.

In the cities of London and York the mayor uses the title
'Lord Mayor' by prescription or immemorial custom. In the
case of other cities it has been usual for the sovereign, by letters
patent, to authorize the use of the title.

At an election of councillors for a borough not divided into
wards, the mayor is (unless he himself is a candidate) the
returning officer, and has in consequence various duties in
relation to the conduct of the election.

*Deputy mayor.* In boroughs outside London the mayor appoints his own deputy mayor (if he wishes to have one). In
metropolitan boroughs the deputy mayor is appointed by the
borough council. In every case the appointment must be made
from among the aldermen or councillors, and not from outside the council. He is appointed for a year and holds office
until a new mayor is appointed. He does not become, by virtue
of his office, a justice of the peace. There is no power to pay
him any salary. The deputy mayor of a borough outside
London may only take the chair at any meeting if that meeting specially appoints him to do so. In a metropolitan borough,
the duties of the deputy mayor are generally the same as those
of the mayor, subject to any rules or directions given by the
council.

*The chairman of a county council* is, like the mayor of a borough,
elected by the council over which he is to preside, and he must
either be already a member of the council or be a person
qualified to be a member. And he must not suffer any of the
disqualifications applicable to members. His appointment from
outside the existing members of the council adds one more to
the membership for the year of his appointment. He may be
paid a salary by the county council, and becomes by virtue
of his office a justice of the peace. He wears no ceremonial
robes, but it is usual for him to be provided with a badge and
chain of office.

*A vice-chairman* of a county council must be appointed by

the county council. He must be already a member of the council. There is no power to pay him a salary and he does not become, by virtue of his office, a justice of the peace. The London County Council may, in addition, appoint, and pay, a deputy chairman from among the members of the council.

*The chairman of a district council* is elected by the council from among the members or persons qualified to be members. He is elected annually and holds office until his successor takes office. He is a justice of the peace by virtue of his office for the county in which his district is situated. There is power to pay him an allowance to meet the expenses of his office.

*A vice-chairman of a district council* may be appointed from among the members of the council. He receives no salary and does not become a justice of the peace *ex officio*.

*The chairman of a parish council* is elected annually by the council, and need not be already a member of the council, although he must, of course, be qualified to be a member. There is no salary.

A parish council may appoint a member of the council to be vice-chairman.

*Considerations affecting the choice of a mayor or chairman.* The power which a council has to elect to the mayoralty a person who is not already a member gives a wide freedom of choice. There are advantages in this. Although the mayor is in the position of chairman of the council and must be willing and competent to supervise the conduct of its proceedings, he has a leading position as a magistrate of the borough and a social and ceremonial status by virtue of his office.

The council, by being able to choose any qualified citizen (man or woman) to fill this important office, has the opportunity of offering the appointment to some personage who, although possessing the time, interest and capacity to fill the position, may not desire to involve himself in the chances of the troublesome process of a public election as councillor, or, while willing to serve as mayor for a year, may not wish to be a member of the council beyond that year of office. On the other hand, the council, not being restricted to members of the council in its choice of mayor, is in a position to re-elect the same person for a number of succeeding years.

The fact that the mayor need not be already a member of

the council emphasizes the dual nature of his position as head of the borough as a corporate entity, comprising the council and the citizens together, and as presiding member of the council itself. In so far as strict impartiality in the governance of the council's proceedings is regarded as a qualification desirable in a mayor, the possibility of electing a non-member of the council may be considered as giving the opportunity of choosing a person who is not too closely identified with local controversies or trends of opinion. On the other hand the opportunity of choosing the mayor from among the existing members of the council enables the council to select (especially in those boroughs where the mayor is expected to have a directing influence over the council's affairs) a member already familiar with and experienced in the council's work.

The considerations which apply to the choice of a mayor from outside the council are similar in many respects to those applicable to the choice of chairman. The first point of difference derives from that fact that the chairman of a county council, district council or parish council does not have the same ceremonial status and precedence within the area administered by his council as does a mayor within his borough. Therefore, in so far as considerations of that kind affect the appointment of a chairman, the comparison between his position and that of a mayor is not entirely exact. This is due to the peculiar nature of a borough as a corporate entity. The inhabitants of an administrative county, county district or administrative parish do not form corporate bodies. Accordingly the chairman of a council has the status, but no more than the status, of the leading member of a body elected to carry out certain necessary public functions in the area.

Every administrative county is part of or co-incident with a county at large. The ancient and royal offices of lord lieutenant and sheriff take ceremonial precedence over the chairman of the county council. The chairman of a district or parish council is even farther down the scale. Where an urban district consists (as is often the case) of a small town there is usually a civic life and a local social group consciousness which is to some extent unrelated to the affairs of the county of which the district forms part. Consequently, on a number of occasions, the chairman of the urban district council is called upon to occupy the role of first citizen of the town and take the lead in local functions. Indeed, there is probably no one else (unless it be the local member of Parliament) who can claim to represent the local civic life. That the office of chairman lacks the precedence, legal quality and traditional colour of that of a mayor is perhaps to be regretted especially by those who see a value in the formal expression of the civic sense and who consider that the existence of local government units can provide not only the organizations for the carrying out of certain mundane public services but also the opportunity for the maintenance and enhancement of local patriotism.

A council by being free to choose its chairman either from within or from outside the council has a greater opportunity than it otherwise would have to reflect these considerations in its choice.

*Aldermen* both in counties and in boroughs may be appointed either from among the councillors, or from persons qualified to be councillors. The number of aldermen on each council is fixed in relation to the number of councillors. Outside London the number of county and borough aldermen in each case is one-third of the number of councillors. London county aldermen and aldermen in metropolitan boroughs are, in each case, one-sixth of the number of councillors. This numerical relationship between the aldermen and councillors must be maintained. Accordingly, if an alderman is elected councillor or a councillor is elected alderman, a choice must be made by the person elected as to which of these offices he will accept. On accepting one office the other becomes vacant and a further election must be held to fill it.

Aldermen, whether of a borough or a county, are, in some respects, in a class apart from the councillors. This is not due so much to the possession by them of any particular powers, but rather to the mode of their election and to the length of their term of office.

In counties and metropolitan boroughs aldermen have no functions peculiar to their position. In boroughs outside London aldermen have occasional duties to perform as returning officers at elections of councillors. In all the proceedings of the council, however, whether of counties or of boroughs, aldermen speak and vote as councillors. They may, according to local practice, occupy special places reserved for them at council meetings, and may claim a ceremonial precedence over the councillors. In boroughs (but not in counties) they have robes of office.

But in no county or borough do the aldermen form a separate chamber or second house. The Court of Aldermen of the City of London provides a unique exception to this general rule.

What virtual difference there is between the position of an alderman and that of a councillor may perhaps be said to lie rather in the nature of the attitude and mental approach which these offices tend to create respectively towards the work of the council. Aldermen do not owe their position directly to the votes of the local public; and their normal term of office is double that of a councillor. These features are capable of providing the aldermen with a certain independence of outlook, or at least a certain detachment.

Aldermen form a link between successive councils and bring into the composition of a council the factors of continuity and stability. These notions were doubtless in the minds of those who framed the legislation governing the constitution of county and borough councils. Although the aldermen do not form, like the House of Lords in Parliament, a separate and distinct body meeting apart, they can be said to exercise in the affairs of a council (if only to a small degree) the same kind of influence as the House of Lords may be considered to exercise in the affairs of Parliament in contributing a second point of view, from an angle somewhat different from that of the popularly elected representatives. The position of aldermen is less dependent on changes of local feeling than is the position of a councillor, who is directly answerable to the electorate every three years.

Aldermen are of course by no means entirely independent of the electorate, especially in those areas where elections are conducted in an atmosphere of party politics, and where the council is organized on the basis of political parties. In those areas the choice of aldermen is made by the political party in power on the council, and persons are chosen of the political colour of the majority. There is no established rule or convention as to how the appointments of aldermen shall be allotted between the political parties on a council. The majority party may with full legal justification appoint only persons sympathetic to the political view of the majority. Indeed, deliberate use has been made of the appointment of aldermen to strengthen a political majority on a council. It is, however, a frequent practice so to arrange the appointments of aldermen that the proportion of aldermen of each political party on the council is similar to that of the councillors.

But whether politics enter into the appointments or not, the fact remains that aldermen are chosen, not from their capacity to appeal to or influence the electorate, but because of the value of their services to the council. It sometimes happens that a councillor with long experience of the council's work fails to secure re-election. The council can, by appointing him an alderman, obtain the continuance of his services.

Quite apart from any political considerations, the power which a borough or county council has to appoint aldermen provides a useful opportunity (as in the case of a mayor or chairman) of bringing into the council's membership persons who are capable, interested and experienced in public local affairs, who do not wish to enter into the excitement and risks of a public election as councillor, and who do not wish to be too closely identified with local controversies or political feeling.

*Expenses of members.* No member of a local government authority may make any personal financial profit out of his membership. This principle runs clearly through the English system. It is expressed in the provisions which disqualify a person for membership if he holds any paid office or place of profit in the disposal of the council. The payment of salaries to a chairman, mayor or sheriff are the only exceptions to the general rule, and even in those cases the salary is not meant to confer a personal financial profit, but is to be regarded as a reimbursement of the expense involved in carrying out the duties of the office. These expenses relate chiefly to official hospitality and ceremonies.

These are not the only expenses incurred by members of councils in carrying out public duties. The travelling expenses of a member in attending meetings of a council or its committees, in making official visits of inspection or in attending conferences, may be considerable. In addition, many members may have to sacrifice part of their earnings in order to obtain the time to attend to public business.

The Local Government Act, 1948, therefore makes provision for the making of payments to members of local government authorities (with the exception of the Common Council of the City of London), and other bodies. These payments are not salaries for public work, but take the form of (i) reimbursement of travelling expenses and subsistence incurred in attending meetings of a council or committee, and in carrying out other approved duties in the discharge of the functions of the council or committee, and (ii) financial loss allowance in cases where the member has lost earnings or incurred other expenses through carrying out public duties as a member.

The scales of travelling and subsistence expenses, and financial loss allowances, and the mode of making claims for reimbursement and allowances, are prescribed in regulations by the Minister of Housing and Local Government.

All local government authorities have power to pay the expenses of members in attending conferences of local authorities.

*Insurance of members.* Local authorities are empowered to take out policies of insurance to cover their members against accidents while engaged on the business of an authority.

*Disability from pecuniary interest.* A further illustration of the principle that members of local government authorities should make no profit out of their membership is provided by the various provisions of the law which prohibit a member from voting at a meeting of a council or committee on any matter in which he has any pecuniary interest. The law relating to London local authorities in this respect differs somewhat from that applicable to authorities outside London, but the general intention is the same. If a member has any personal interest in any contract which is being entered into, or in any matter which is being discussed in a council or committee, he must disclose the fact and refrain from voting on the matter or taking part in the discussion relating to it. If these provisions are not complied with, the offender may be fined £50 for each offence.[6]

[6] The provisions relating to the London County Council contain no penalty except in relation to matters arising under the Housing Acts.

The pecuniary interest creating the disability need not be a direct interest (such as a personal contract between the member and the council). It may be indirect. Thus a partner in a firm, or a managing director who receives commission on the firm's profits, would, if he were a member of the council, be disabled from voting on, or discussing, at a meeting of the council or a committee, any contract or matter arising between his firm and the council. In the case of married persons living together the pecuniary interest of one spouse is, if known to the other, deemed to be the interest of the other spouse.

To these rules there are a number of exceptions which have been made to cover cases where the pecuniary interest can be regarded as slight, or where the strict application of the rule would be a real hindrance to the council in its work. Thus, if the pecuniary interest of a member arises only by reason of his holding, in a company which contracts with the council, shares not exceeding £500 in nominal value, or one-hundredth of the total share capital, he is not debarred from voting, but he is under an obligation to disclose to the council his interest. And a member of the council who is also an employee of another public body (e.g. another council) is not debarred from voting on matters affecting the public body of which he is an employee. Nor does the disability arise merely because the member is interested as an ordinary ratepayer or member of the public in some service offered by the council to the public generally. So a member of the council is not disabled from voting on matters relating, for instance, to the council's education service, merely because his children get free education at the council's schools. And the disability will not arise in relation to the prices and charges for the public utility services provided by the council, merely because the member is a consumer or makes use of those services. Occupancy of a council house has been held by the courts to debar a member from voting on housing matters.[7]

If these various exceptions were not made it is probable that almost every member of the council would be debarred from

[7] The statutory provisions applicable to the London County Council are specific, and prohibit voting on any matter arising under the Housing Acts if it relates to any premises in which the member is beneficially interested.

taking part in a substantial portion of the council's business.[8]

How far these provisions achieve the anxious purpose that seems to lie behind them is a matter for speculation. That local government should be cleanly and honestly conducted, and that members should not be embarrassed by any conflict between their public duties and their private interests, is beyond dispute. As a statement of this essential public policy, or as a guide to members in their public conduct, the provisions serve a useful purpose. The penalty laid down in the provisions is an indication of the serious undesirability of mixing personal affairs with private business.

Prosecutions under the provisions are extremely few and seldom. The mere existence of the law may be sufficient deterrent to prospective offenders. It is probable, however, that a much more powerful deterrent is provided from sources outside the law, namely, from the force and weight of local public opinion. No body of electors would normally rest content to allow their public representatives to act corruptly in office. The basis of the relationship between the public representative and the elector is that the representative should be approved of by the elector and stand well in his regard. In areas where local government is organized on political lines the anxiety of the local politician to stand well in the eyes of the electorate is stimulated by the rivalry between the opposing parties. Any taint of scandal which attaches to any member or candidate reflects on the party as a whole. The parties are accordingly particularly desirous of ensuring that no suspicion of corruption in office shall mar their chances of re-election.

Besides this, it is questionable whether there is, in the daily functioning of local government, any great opportunities for peculation or misdealing. In the case of the smaller local authorities the amount of work done by the authority is not so great as to prevent individual members from getting aware of almost everything that goes on. Secrets are hard to keep in a small town. There is generally some busybody who sooner

[8] A county council, as respects a parish council, and the Minister of Housing and Local Government, as respects any other local authority, may remove a disability arising from pecuniary interest in special cases where the number of members so disabled would be an embarrassing proportion of the whole council or where the removal of the disability would be in the local public interest.

or later will ask awkward questions. In the case of large authorities the framework of the council's organization is usually so big and so departmentalized that a fraud on the public could only be committed to any substantial extent by implicating a sizeable group of persons. On the whole, local government in this country is cleanly and honourably conducted. The notion that persons seek election to local councils in order to line their own pockets is a lingering remnant of the public attitude to the unreformed borough corporations whose activities, in the days before the Municipal Corporations Act of 1835, were by no means prompted by zeal for the public welfare, and whose funds were often applied for the private advantage and entertainment of the members.[9]

The conflict between a member's public duty and his private interest may, however, arise in other directions than that of pecuniary advantage. A member is elected to serve the public. The public is composed of a number of individuals, among whom there may be a number who have complaints to be rectified, or who desire to urge a certain point of view. They accordingly approach a member and ask him to take action on their behalf. In a great number of cases it is quite justifiable for the member to respond to these requests. But there may come a point at which this private pressure upon a member may induce him to become the virtual tool of sectional interests, or to devote his efforts more to the serving of private demands than to the welfare of the public as a whole. It is difficult, if not impossible, to legislate against conditions of this kind.

Another difficulty arises from a member's personal bias, stimulated, it may be, by a religious, political or professional point of view, or even by personal jealousies. For instance, a shopkeeper who is a member of the council which has power to license street traders may deeply resent the competition presented to his business by local street markets. It is consequently a temptation for him to exercise his influence on the council against these street trading activities. A local builder who is a member of the committee which deals with the licensing of building work is perhaps the very person whose experience gives him a claim to serve on that committee and whose

[9] The use of the term 'corporation' in colloquial usage to denote large abdominal capacity is doubtless a survival from those days.

advice would probably be of great use. But might it not sometimes be a temptation to him, when an application from a rival firm for a building licence is before the committee, to allow his judgment to be coloured by his professional antipathies, even though there is no pecuniary interest whatever, direct or indirect?

The law does not, and probably cannot, deal with instances of this type. These do, however, represent the class of case about which public uneasiness may sometimes be felt rather than from any fear of financial corruption.

The local authorities have tried to meet the difficulty to some extent by provisions in their standing orders prohibiting members from attending meetings or from voting when they have any professional or family interest in the matters under consideration. The acquisition of a statesmanlike judgment by a member can, however, hardly be achieved by a legislative process. The principal safeguard to the public lies in their electing to local councils persons of various types and viewpoints so that from the interplay of opinion any individual bias of judgment may be counteracted.

As a profit-making career, local government offers meagre opportunities to the elected member. How then is it possible to account for the enthusiastic desire displayed by so many men and women to enter into local government, to take upon themselves the trouble and expense of seeking election, and to give their time and thought to public business? The staid common-sense British elector hesitates to believe that his representatives are inspired in their public work only by concern for the welfare of him and his fellow citizens, and that a desire for public service is all that prompts a candidate to seek the obligations of membership of a local authority.

The allegation is sometimes made that, even if local government offers the member no opportunity of making a direct profit out of his position, there are other advantages of an indirect kind to be obtained, such as the enlargement of one's business acquaintance, or the making of contacts which may be of professional use. It is doubtless probable that motives of this kind do actuate a number of candidates and members. But this cannot be true of all of them. A considerable proportion of the membership of local authorities is made up of persons of many varying types, married women, retired persons, trade union representatives, artisans, salaried employees, and other people who in fact have no business contacts to make, nor any professional advantage to obtain.

The truth is, whether the British public accepts it or not, that ulterior motives of the usual kind—monetary gain and professional advantage—are quite inapplicable and cannot explain what it is that prompts men and women to become involved in the work of local government.

The point remains that any study of British local democratic institutions cannot be fully understood without some realization of the motives which influence those who carry on this important branch of the national organization. The psychology of the local government representative deserves close and sensitive study. If local government is to function well, the members of local authorities must be keen to serve, alive to local needs, and willing to give time and thought to public affairs. If members lack these qualities, and become apathetic, self-sufficient and indifferent, and seek office only for the pride of position and such dubious advantages as they can find in their membership, local government becomes moribund and useless.

Since the motives of profit-seeking and pecuniary or professional advantages are inapplicable to explain the working of the system it can only be that the personnel of local councils is made up of people who are there because they like it, because it provides an outlet for their activities, a form of self-expression, a hobby, an interest, an opportunity for the exercise of reforming zeal, a means of having a say in how the locality should be administered, a sense of being in public life, of being participant, through local affairs, in the larger work of the country as a whole. Members of local authorities can, and indeed do, gain a deep sense of enrichment of the personality through their public work.

It is in this light that the motives and activities of local government representatives can best be explained.

The English local government system provides a number of safeguards against maladministration. Members lose their offices if they fail to attend meetings. Auditors may surcharge members the amount of any moneys misapplied. If a council fails to carry out its functions properly the central government may take action to remedy the default. And there are the various disqualifications and penalties which are designed to prevent a member from abusing his position. But all these will not make a council efficient. The threat of legal proceedings does not inspire a member to take an enthusiastic and live interest in the council's work, or make him anxious to serve the public well. The only safeguard which the elector has against lazy, insensitive, or apathetic administration is his right to turn the councillors out of office at the end of three years. If the councillors have nothing to gain by their membership, how can it be thought that they have anything to lose by not being re-elected? In the material sense they have, in fact, nothing to lose.

The threat of losing office gains its effectiveness because it impinges upon the member's pride, upon his social or political position, or his interest in the council's work, or his reputation as a public figure. The system of local government democracy is based on the assumption that the member of a local authority is susceptible to publicity. The method of seeking election by appeal to the electorate, the transaction of business in open council with the press and public admitted to the proceedings, the nature of the local government functions, carried out as they are for everyone to see and criticize, all serve to stimulate in a member a regard for public opinion, and, perhaps, a tendency to cultivate it. This regard may develop into a large-hearted and disinterested concern for the public weal. It may indeed degenerate into a petty anxiety for self-display. The broad result is the same. The member must seek and maintain the approbation of the public. If he ceases to retain their confidence, or fails to secure their support for the policy with which he has identified himself, or is unable to awaken or keep alive in them the interests which he has at heart, then he forfeits the right to represent them.

This it is which constitutes the main safeguard in the system of democratic local government. Where politics enter into the affairs of a local council the desire of the individual member for public support and approval is intensified by his association in a party group and by the rivalry between opposing parties.

169

Democratic local government in short means the administration of each local area by a body of persons willing to undertake that work upon condition that they shall secure in performing it the support and approval of the public.

In any modification of the local government system this elementary principle must be borne in mind.

# I I

# Committees

THE method of dealing with affairs through the medium of committees forms a special feature of the English local government system and has therein been developed to an unusual degree. The use of committees is, of course, utilized in all systems of government, both national and local. Its use arises from the universal experience of mankind that large assemblies are not appropriate for the discussion and settlement of matters of detail. Many local councils have fifty members or more; some have over a hundred. The work which the majority of councils have to do concerns a range of services, involving the management of staff and property, purchases of materials, and control of finance. If the details of all these matters were dealt with only at meetings of the full council the meetings would be of intolerable length. The tendency might be to skip over the detail and leave it to the council's officers.

In some foreign systems of local government, a great deal of authority is exercised by the mayor, burgomaster or other similar functionary. In many towns of the United States, and in some towns of Eire, the 'city manager system' has been adopted, by which the work of administration is left almost entirely to an appointed official, and the council (representative of the people) approves the budget, makes by-laws and decides general principles.

These methods do not accord with ideas underlying English local government. The British tradition is that power should rest in the hands of the elected representative. This being so, a busy council must find some way in which its members can manage to get through the council's business without having to delegate an undue amount of it to officers. The method adopted is to use the power, which all local government authorities have, to appoint committees.

A busy local authority usually appoints a committee to deal

with each main department of its work or with groups of departments. There will thus be a parks and museums committee, a works and highways committee, or a planning committee, for example. These committees are composed of a comparatively few members who in due course get familiar with that branch of the work dealt with by their particular committee. A council may delegate to its committees certain functions to exercise on the council's behalf. This in itself relieves the full council.

By the division of the council's work in this way among committees the tasks of individual members themselves are lightened; for each member need not attempt to familiarize himself with the details of that part of the council's work which is delegated to committees of which he is not a member.

The normal practice is that business relating to the functions of any committee goes first to the committee before any final decision by the council is arrived at.[1] Committees report their activities to the full council. Under these arrangements a member gets not only an insight into the details of those departments of the council's work which have been delegated to those committees on which he serves; he gets a conspectus of the activities of the council's work as a whole by means of the reports which come from committees to the full council.

Apart from the relief which this system gives to the council itself (by reducing the number of items that might otherwise figure on its agenda paper) and to the individual members (by enabling them to focus their close attention upon certain departments only of the council's work), the system has the advantage of giving the council the opportunity of dealing with the more important items of business in two stages, and from two viewpoints. An item will first go before a committee, and be considered by members who have, by their service on that committee, acquired particular experience; the item will then be reported by the committee to the full council with such advice and recommendations as the committee think appropriate. Thus the item is considered both from a particular and from a general viewpoint, and the council has, as it were, the opportunity of taking second thoughts on the item.

[1] In the case of statutory committees this practice is generally obligatory. See later, p. 173.

The holding of committee meetings in private enables the members of the committee to apply themselves to the business in hand without having regard to publicity.[2] It is in committee that qualities of sagacity, business acumen, and administrative skill are evoked and required, rather than oratorical accomplishments. Moreover, in committee, officers are given the opportunity of helping in the formulation of decisions. The officers present their reports, answer questions, give explanations, and at times intervene in the discussion to clarify a point or suggest a course of action. Committees are a council's workshop where technical knowledge of the officials, and the member's interpretation of public requirements, are brought together, blended and applied.

*Statutory Committees.* It is no doubt because of the various advantages of appointing committees that Parliament has not only allowed each local authority to appoint whatever committees it may think fit, but has for certain purposes made it a definite requirement that a committee shall be appointed.

Thus every borough with its own separate police force is required to appoint a watch committee for the purpose of administering the force; every local education authority must appoint one or more education committees.[3] Every county or county borough council must (unless the Home Secretary otherwise directs) appoint a children's committee.

To these statutory committees all business relating to the particular function or service for which the committee in each case is required to be set up stands referred, and the council may not (except in certain special cases) consider matters concerning those functions except after having received a report from the statutory committee concerned.

Apart from statutory restrictions of this kind, a council has complete discretion as to what committees it shall appoint.

*Constitution of Committees.* Besides making requirements for

[2] In the session of Parliament 1959-60 a Bill was introduced which when passed would require local authorities, except in certain special circumstances, to admit the Press to meetings of committees exercising delegated powers. A provision of this kind had already, under the Local Authorities (Admission of the Press to Meetings) Act, 1908, applied to an education committee.

[3] The Education Act, 1944, requires that Education Committees shall be established in accordance with arrangements approved by the Minister of Education.

the setting up of particular committees, Parliament has concerned itself with the constitution and personnel of a local authority's committees. For example, under the Fire Services Act, 1947, the constitution of a fire authority's fire brigade committee is to be provided for in a scheme of management to be approved by the Home Secretary, and the committee is to contain such representatives of county districts in the area of the fire authority as may be specified in the scheme.

There were at one time a number of statutory provisions dealing with the suitability of persons for membership of certain of a local authority's committees. It seems that Parliament was desirous not only to maintain a local government system with a series of authorities duly empowered to carry out functions, but that the membership of the committees concerned in those functions should be capable of fulfilling their tasks, and that the availability of suitable personnel for the committees should not depend on the mere chance that a council, brought into existence by popular election, would comprise persons of sufficient capacity and experience to form the membership of its committees. This was particularly the case where the service administered by the committees was of a personal character such as poor relief, the welfare of the blind, mental health or medical care. Provision was made that the committee concerned need not be composed entirely of members of the appointing council, but that the committee should include persons of suitable experience of the service administered. In some cases it was required that a committee should include one or more women. The services in question have for the most part now been transferred to national administration, and the local and regional arrangements for carrying on the nationalized services, and the personnel concerned, are directly controllable by the central government.

Important examples of this influence of the legislature over the composition of a committee of a local authority remain. The Education Act, 1944, requires that an education committee shall include persons of experience in education, and persons acquainted with the educational conditions prevailing in the area. The degree of experience or acquaintance is not specified.

The Children Act, 1948, provides that, if members are

co-opted to a children's committee they shall have appropriate training or experience, but the Act does not require a local authority to exercise the power of co-option.

With these important exceptions, the policy of the legislature in attempting to specify the qualities and experience which the members of any particular committee of a local authority shall possess has been abandoned.

Any anxiety that democratically elected local authorities might not always be appropriate for the discharge of functions of a specialized character may to some extent be assuaged by the reflection that when a local authority appoints its committees the common-sense course is to appoint to each committee persons who are already interested or show likelihood of becoming interested in the functions to be dealt with. Moreover, any lack of experience or special capacity in the membership can be adjusted, if need be, by the exercise of the general power which local authorities have to appoint to committees persons who are not already members of the council.

*Co-option.* A finance committee may not include in its membership any persons who are not members of the appointing council. With this exception a local authority may add to any of its committees persons who are not members of the council provided always that a majority of the members of the committee shall be members of the council. The appointment of these co-opted members provides, like the appointment of the mayor and aldermen, the opportunity of bringing into the work of the council persons of experience who have not secured, or do not wish to secure, membership by the normal process of public election.

*Sub-committees.* If the amount of work to be done by any committee is very large, a convenient course, frequently adopted, is to appoint sub-committees to deal with particular portions of the committee's work. Sub-committees may have certain functions delegated to them which they can carry out at their discretion; other matters may be referred to them for advice and report, so that the general relations between sub-committee and main committee is akin to that between the main committee and the full council.

Where the amount of work of a sub-committee is large enough to justify it, sections of sub-committees may be authorized to carry out minor and routine functions, such as the granting of applications for permissions and licences of a more or less formal kind, or the interviewing of applicants for minor appointments. Some local authorities find it convenient to provide each institution, school or clinic with a sub-committee or section. In other cases there may be a sub-committee for groups of institutions. Or if the authority divides up its area for the administration of certain services, sub-committes may be appointed for each division or area of administration.

*Parochial Committees.* A rural district council may appoint, for local areas within the rural district, parochial committees composed partly of members of the council and partly of other persons who are local government electors for the local area.[4] If the local area is a parish with its own parish council, the 'other persons' appointed to the parochial committee must be selected from members of the parish council, so that the committee becomes a joint committee representative of the rural district and parish councils. To these parochial committees may be delegated any functions of the rural district council which are exercisable in the local area, except the raising of a rate or the borrowing of money. If a rural district council refuse to appoint a parochial committee at the request of the parish council, the parish council may petition the Minister of Housing and Local Government, who may order a committee to be appointed.

Where a parish council has functions which are to be discharged in part only of the parish, the parish council may be required by a parish meeting of that part of the parish to appoint a committee for carrying out those functions. The committee is to consist partly of members of the parish council, and partly of persons representing the part of the parish in question.

A parish meeting, in a parish which has no separate parish council, may appoint committees, but all the acts of such a committee must be submitted to the parish meeting for approval.

*Qualifications and disqualifications.* To be able to serve on a

---

[4] The phrase used in the Local Government Act, 1933, is 'contributory place' —an area related to drainage districts under the Public Health Act, 1875. (Act of 1933, ss. 87 and 305.)

committee a person who is not already a member of the appointing committee must be free from any of the disqualifications as apply to members of the council,[5] with the exception
that a person employed as a teacher or in any other capacity
in a school or college maintained by the council is not disqualified, by reason of that employment, from being a member
of the council's education committee or any committee for
managing the council's public libraries. Co-opted members of
a children's committee must, in addition to the normal qualification, be specially qualified, by training or experience, in
matters relating to the committee's functions.

*Procedure of Committees.* The number of persons who shall
form a committee, the frequency of their meetings, the minimum number (quorum) to be present at a committee meeting,
the method of selecting the chairman, the functions to be performed, the frequency with which committees shall report their
actions to the council—all these and similar matters are usually
laid down by the council in its standing orders. The permanent
or standing committees are usually appointed annually. Special
committees for particular purposes may be appointed from
time to time as occasion requires.

*Delegation to Committees.* Although the law requires the appointment of certain 'statutory committees' to which matters
relating to particular functions stand referred, this does not
give the committee power to make final decisions, or to act
on the council's behalf. The delegation of duties to a committee (by which is meant the giving of power to a committee
to act on the council's behalf) is a matter for the discretion
of the council itself.

Local authorities have a general power to delegate to a
committee any functions exercisable by the council except the
power to levy, or issue a precept for, a rate, or the power to
borrow money.

It is impossible to describe in general terms the practices
of local authorities in regard to the delegation of function to
committees; for the practice varies with almost each local
authority. Some give wide latitude to their committees and
allow them to deal, within certain limits, with matters which
come before them, without further ratification or approval by

[5] As to qualifications and disqualifications, see chapter 10.

the council, and subject only to an obligation to report from time to time the action they have taken. It is found generally necessary to reserve for the council itself matters which are of importance either on account of their individual magnitude or by reason of their involving essential principles. On these important items, the function of the committee is to offer advice to the council and recommend a course of action. Other authorities, nervous of complete delegation, allow their committees no more than the right of framing provisional decisions, and require that the whole of the proceedings of the committees shall be reported to the council, and that no decision of a committee shall have effect until ratified by the council. In the first type of case the committee is virtually the agent of the council and competent to act in the council's name; in the second class of case the function of the committee is one of predigestion and presentation.

*Control of Committees—the Watch Committee.* A local authority has, with one exception, complete control over its own committees. It chooses the members, lays down rules as to the relations between committees, controls their spending, and may set what limits it likes upon the freedom of action of committees.

The one exception is the watch committee of a borough council which has its own police force. The Municipal Corporations Act, 1882, provides that this committee shall be appointed from among the members of the council, and that the mayor shall be *ex officio* a member. The committee must not be greater in number than one-third of the whole council. Three members form a quorum. Subject to these provisions, the borough council may make standing orders as to the place of meeting and general proceedings of the watch committee. The ordinary provisions as to pecuniary interest apply.

In order to carry out their functions of recruiting, regulating, paying and pensioning the borough police force, the committee may require from time to time payments out of the general rate fund of the borough. Orders for these payments may be made only by the full council. Accordingly the watch committee is obliged, when an order for such a payment is required, to report to the council to ask for an order and to explain why it is wanted. Otherwise the acts and proceedings of the watch committee are not required to be reported to or approved by the council. Apart from the financial link and the fact that the members of the watch committee are selected by and from the borough council, the committee is in a sense a separate entity.

A borough council may delegate to the watch committee functions other than those related to the borough police. When exercising these other delegated functions the committee is in the full control of the council, and must report its acts and obtain approval for them as may be required by the council.

*Co-ordination between Committees.* A local authority with many services, the council of a county borough, for instance, may have a wide range of committees, sub-committees and managing committees of institutions and schools. There may be a dozen or more main committees, several of which may have anything from one to five or more sub-committees. There may be as many as fifty different subsidiary bodies composed partly of members of the council, partly of other persons, all helping the council to carry on its work. Each of these subsidiary bodies has its own part to play, its own functions to perform within the general structure of the council's organization. How can the council keep all these bodies under control, make sure that their acts fit in with the general policy of the council, and ensure that no committee, sub-committee or section oversteps its proper duty or develops a separate policy at variance with that of the council?

Various methods are adopted to deal with this problem of co-ordination. The first is to define as clearly as possible the particular functions to be delegated. The standing orders of the council should describe in accurate terms the matters referred to each committee or sub-committee. The council should also lay down what is to happen if a matter arises which concerns more than one committee. In cases such as these a joint sub-committee may be provided for, or arrangements made for consultation between committees concerned.

Many councils appoint a general purposes committee to deal with matters of general policy affecting the council's services as a whole. To this committee may also be referred matters affecting more than one committee, so that the general purposes committee becomes a co-ordinating agency and obtains, and reconciles, the views of the other committees concerned. Upon the general purposes committee may be appointed the chairmen of the other committees of the council, to provide a link between this co-ordinating policy-forming committee and the other committees.

Few acts of a committee can take effect without money being involved. The council may allocate to each committee certain amounts for the purposes of the committees and allow each committee a discretion as to the way in which it spends the money allocated. A number of local authorities in their committee arrangements give to a finance committee the duty of co-ordinating the spending operations of the other committees by making that committee responsible for framing the annual budget of the authority, and also by providing that any substantial expenditure shall be incurred only with the concurrence of the finance committee.

Thus, by receiving periodical reports by committees as to their work, by reserving to itself the more important items of business, and allowing committees to offer advice and recommendations on them, and by the ultimate control of finance, and the use of one of the committees as a co-ordinating agency for the work of all the committees, the council may keep under review and control the operations of all its committees and secure the harmonious working of its organization as a whole.

In addition to the direct control which the council has over its committees, there are two other methods by which co-operation and co-ordination between committees can be secured. The first is through the medium of the chairmen, the second is by means of the officials.

*Co-ordination by the Chairmen of Committees.* The chairman of a committee is in a rather different position from the chairman of the council, or mayor. The chairman of a committee is deemed to have responsibility for its decisions. When the committee reports to the council the chairman is usually considered as answerable for the contents of the report. It is he who makes the proposal at the council meeting that the report shall be received, and its recommendations agreed to. It is he who explains its contents and replies to criticism of it. In committee, therefore, he is in the dual position of being both the presiding member responsible for the proper order of its proceedings, and also the guiding influence over its decisions. The chairman of a council or mayor, on the other hand, frequently regards himself as outside the arena of debates, and more in the position of umpire than of participant.

Since the chairmen of committees have a certain identity with the operations of their committees, an identity which in a number of councils is strengthened by giving the chairman of a committee power to act between meetings on behalf of the committee, the chairmen of committees may, in a sense, be regarded as Ministers in charge of departments of government. Consequently they can, by mutual consultation, establish mutually agreeable lines of action for their respective committees. Where the council's business is organized on a political party basis the chairman and the majority of the members of each committee are chosen from the party which has the majority on the council, the chairman's influence over his committee is thereby strengthened, and party discipline enables him to exercise a virtually complete control over his committee. At the same time the party discipline binds him and his fellow chairmen, and keeps them in line with the general policy of the party. In such a state of affairs it becomes inevitable that the chairmen should get together in order to co-ordinate the operations of their respective committees.

*Co-ordination by the Officials.* The officers of the council have a duty to advise the committees, and to carry out their instructions. If the education committee wished to buy a certain piece of land for a school, and it so happened that the parks committee were seeking land for an open space, it could never happen that the two committees became competitors in the market for the same piece of land; for the council's officer in charge of land purchases would, if he ever received instructions from two committees to buy the same piece of land, at once inform the committees of the position. It is indeed extremely unlikely that any committee would attempt to arrive at a decision without first obtaining the advice of its officers. And since the same set of officers, in relation to matters affecting their own duties, advise all committees, the officers can act as a co-ordinating agency throughout the local authority's business.[6]

[6] As to the co-ordination between departments, and the function of the clerk in this regard, see chapter 13.

It is through an examination of the working of the committee system in local government that the difference between central and local government can be easily appreciated. Each House of Parliament may appoint committees, and each House can join with the other in appointing a committee. The work given to these committees is either legislative or is advisory. A Bill introduced into either House goes first to the full House and the House decides, at the first reading stage, whether such a Bill is desirable, and, at the second reading stage, whether the general principles are acceptable. If the Bill passes successfully through these stages it may then, and only then, be referred to a committee.[7] The business of each House does not (as would be the normal practice in local government) stand referred to a committee in the first instance.

When a Bill reaches the committee stage it is discussed in detail, and, as the committee thinks fit, amended. The discussion in committee is conducted entirely by the members; officers have no voice and give no advice and are, indeed, not present for these purposes.[8] Whatever advice the officers may give is given outside the committee. Moreover, the various government departments are under the control of the Ministers. Accordingly, the assistance of the government departments in framing legislation is directed towards supporting the Minister, or, in other words, the party in power, whereas in local government the advice of the officers is given in open committee and is available to all members of the committee.

When a Bill has been amended in committee it is reported to the full House for approval of the amendments. The committees of Parliament have no power to make or amend laws on their own authority. In this respect there are no delegated powers which a committee may exercise.

Committees are often appointed in Parliament for other purposes as, for instance, to consider and inquire into special questions. Here the committees have only an advisory function, to report their conclusions to the House.

In local government, however, a council may use its com-

---

[7] The fact that the committee may consist of the whole House, sitting as a committee, does not alter what is said in the text.

[8] Except in committees dealing with private Bills.

mittees not only for the purpose of giving, after due consideration, advice to the council; a council may, and often does, use
its committees for the purpose of actually carrying on the services of the council, and may empower the committees to
engage staff, make purchases and expend money.

This difference between the committees of Parliament and
those of local authorities illustrates the fact that the work of
Parliament tends towards legislative action, whereas the work
of local government tends to be administrative and executive
in character.

Local authorities have no second chamber, as Parliament
has. With certain exceptions, Bills which go before one House
do not become law until the other House has also approved
them. The second viewpoint, the consideration of matters from
a different angle, is secured by reason of the fact that the two
Houses of Parliament are constituted differently. One is elected,
the other is not. In local government the second viewpoint,
the change of angle of consideration is obtainable by means
of the committee system, which enables each matter which is
not fully delegated to a committee to be considered twice, once
by the committee, and once by the council as a whole. In a
sense, therefore, the committee system of local government
plays somewhat the same part as is performed by operation of
the 'second house' principle in national government.

*Joint Committees.* Local authorities may concur with each
other in appointing a joint committee representative of the
appointing authorities, for the purpose of carrying out any of
the functions of those authorities other than the raising of a
rate or the borrowing of money. Where a joint committee is
appointed to carry out functions which would normally have
to be carried out by a 'statutory' committee, the constitution
of which is the subject of special provisions, then those provisions will apply, with suitable modifications, to the constitution of the joint committee.

The finances of joint committees are provided by the appointing authorities in such proportion as they may agree
upon. If the authorities cannot agree as to their respective
proportions the dispute is settled, in the case where the
appointing authorities are district or parish councils and are
all in the same county, by the county council; in other cases

the Minister of Housing and Local Government settles the matter.

The rules relating to pecuniary interest in contracts, and to qualifications and disqualifications, apply to joint committees in the same way as to committees.

# Meetings and Proceedings

SINCE local government authorities have important work to do which affects the welfare of the local public, it is very desirable that these authorities should not evade their duties nor act in so secretive a fashion as to keep the public entirely in ignorance of their proceedings.

It is useless to set up a series of corporate bodies for the performance of certain tasks, if the bodies never meet to perform their tasks. And if those bodies are publicly elected and are representative of the people, it is reasonable and just that the public to whom those bodies are responsible should have opportunity of seeing how the business of the elected bodies is carried on.

It was the clandestine mismanagement of corporate property, and the failure of the old borough corporations to face up to their civic responsibilities, which led to the Municipal Corporations Act of 1835 and the subsequent reforms in local government.

The Local Government Act, 1933, and the London Government Act, 1939, both contain schedules relating to the meetings and proceedings of local authorities. County and borough councils outside London, and all district and parish councils, must meet four times a year at least.[1] Parish meetings must be held at least once a year, and, if there is no local parish council, at least twice a year.

Local authorities may meet more often. In fact, many local authorities meet monthly, and even fortnightly or weekly, according to the amount of business to be done. Moreover, the law provides that a certain number of members of a council may themselves summon a meeting if the chairman, on being requested by them in writing, refuses to do so.[2]

---

[1] The London County Council and the metropolitan borough councils are legally obliged to meet only annually; they do in fact meet much more often.

[2] The requisite numbers are: London County Council—twenty members;

185

Having required local authorities to meet, the legislature went further and has made various provisions designed to ensure that the business transacted at the meetings shall be open and above board and not conducted in any hole and corner fashion. The law requires that prior public notice shall be given of every meeting of a local authority, and the notice must in each case specify the business to be transacted at the meeting. No business at all must be conducted unless there is a specified minimum number (quorum) of members present—one-third or one-fourth the total number according to the type of authority.

The law further provides that minutes shall be kept of the business transacted, and that these minutes shall be open to inspection by any local government elector for the area of the authority on payment of a fee not exceeding one shilling, and that the elector may take extracts.[3] Further, the accounts of local authorities are open to inspection free of charge by any local government elector.

Thus local authorities are all obliged to meet with a substantial number of members present, to publish what they intend to do, and to make available to the interested members of the public their accounts and the records of their proceedings.

The names of the members present at a meeting of a local authority must be recorded. All questions at a meeting must be decided by a majority of votes of the members.

At district and parish council meetings the voting is taken by show of hands, but on the requisition of any member the voting is to be recorded so as to show which way each member voted. A number of county and borough councils have voluntarily adopted a similar procedure. Normally a show of hands will suffice. The recording of the votes is usually called for on occasions when highly contentious issues are in question or

---

metropolitan borough councils—one-fourth of the whole number of the council; parish councils—two members; other county and borough and district councils —five members; parish meetings—the chairman of the parish council, or any two councillors, or (if there is no parish council) the chairman of the parish meeting, or one of the representatives of the parish on the rural district council, or any six local government electors.

[3] Similar provisions apply to minutes of education, health and welfare committees.

when political opinions are sharply divided on a matter of some import. The record of the actual votes cast and the manner in which each member voted being inserted in the minutes, become thereby open to public inspection. A demand for the recording of the votes ('taking a division' as it is sometimes called) may be considered therefore to enhance a member's sense of public responsibility when giving his vote on those occasions.

In order to give additional publicity to the transactions of local authorities, the law contains provisions to enable representatives of the press to be present at meetings. There is here, however, a certain difficulty which Parliament has duly recognized. Although it may be quite right that the final decisions of a local authority should be published, it may not be always desirable that the discussion and debate leading up to a decision should be conducted in public. The fact that each local authority is empowered to appoint committees, which can meet in private, is a recognition of the need for keeping some matters private during the formative stages. Questions as to the salary, appointment, or dismissal of officers provide examples of the type of matter that it is not always discreet or desirable to discuss in public. Members may in private feel freer to offer criticism on the council's work and services. Matters relating to litigation are in the same class—the council may not wish to disclose to its opponents its case or attitude.

The law therefore provides that although representatives of the press shall be entitled to be present at meetings of a local authority,[4] the authority may temporarily exclude the press as often as may be desirable at any meeting when, in the opinion of the majority of the members present, in view of the special nature of the business, such exclusion is advisable in the public interest. The intention of this provision is apparently that the exclusion of the press shall be the exception rather than the rule. The frequent use of the power of exclusion would be an abuse.

The meetings of parish councils must normally be open to

[4] Including an education committee when acting under delegated powers, and any joint committee or joint board to whom powers have been transferred or delegated. The law stated in the text was provided by the Local Authorities (Admission of the Press to Meetings) Act, 1908. See, however, footnote 2 on p. 173. *ante.*

the public, but, there again, the council may direct that the public be excluded.

As a matter of practice many local authorities allow the general public to be admitted to look on at the council meetings subject to the same limitations as to temporary exclusion as apply to the press.

For the regulation of their proceedings, local authorities are empowered to make standing orders to supplement, but not to contravene, the various legal provisions above referred to. In the standing orders the authority will define the terms of reference of its committees, and the degree of spending power or discretion allowed to them, the duties of chief officers and the authority delegated to each of them, the procedure for the presentation of reports, the frequency of meetings of the council and committees, the order of debate, the length of speeches, the form of motions and amendments, and numerous other points.

Every local authority must hold one of its meetings on a date prescribed by law.[5] At this annual or 'statutory' meeting, the first business to be transacted is the election of the chairman or mayor for the ensuing year. The next business in the case of a borough is the election of the sheriff, if there is one for the borough. Next follows, in counties and boroughs, in the years when aldermen are due to be elected, the election of any aldermen.

Thus at the annual meeting the first business is to get the council properly constituted. After that the vice-chairman or deputy mayor is elected. All these appointments may, of course, be accompanied by complimentary and valedictory speeches and votes of thanks, and the presentation of mementoes to

[5] The date is as follows:

*County Councils* in a year of election—the eighth day after the day of retirement of councillors, or such other day within twenty-one days after the day of retirement as the council may fix; in other years the annual meeting will be held on such day in March, April or May as the council may determine.

*Boroughs*—the eleventh day after the day of election, or such day within the following seven days as the borough council may fix. In the case of metropolitan boroughs, the 'day of election' for this purpose, in years when no elections are in fact held, will be the day of election fixed for boroughs outside London.

*Urban and Rural District Councils*—on, or as soon as conveniently may be after, 20th May.

*Parish Councils*—on or within fourteen days after 20th May.

*Parish Meetings*—on some day between 1st March and 1st April, both inclusive.

departing office-holders, and the formal investiture of those taking office. The formal signing of the acceptance of office may then be done.

These formalities over, the council then usually proceeds to deal with the appointment of committees. If it is a newly elected council, it may decide to set up a committee of selection to consider what committees to appoint, in addition to the obligatory 'statutory' committees, and what members shall serve on them. There is naturally a good deal of prior consultation between members as to their preferences. The committee structure being dealt with, the council proceeds to transact what other business there happens to be.

The ordinary business of a council consists of reports from committees, reports by officers, communications from other authorities and notices of motion by members of the council. The bulk of the business in an agenda paper of a council will be reports of committees. These reports take varying forms according to the practice of the particular authority. Some authorities require their committees to submit details of the proceedings in full, or present the committee minutes for confirmation by the council of the action proposed in the minutes. Other authorities require their committees to submit explanatory reports on those matters in relation to which committees have not been given powers of final decision. In those cases the reports of the committees will contain recommendations of the action to be taken by the council. Committees which have powers delegated to them will be required to submit periodical reports of the action they have taken in the exercise of those powers.

This prior reference to committees, especially when there are several committees to consult, and when the committees (as they generally do) defer their own consideration until they have received from the council's officers reports and advice, may tend to retard the operations of local authorities on important matters and may constitute a source of criticism of the democratic system of local government in this country. If, as in the United States of America, the mayor were directly elected by the people and were able to exercise administrative functions on his own without reference to his council other than on broad matters of policy, the speed of operations would be quicker. Representative government does involve delay in that important matters have to await the meetings of a committee or the council. The genius and justification of the British system is, however, that it enables the representatives of the people to take a real share in their own administration, and thereby learn the art of self-government, and that a council and its committees, being composed of a number of persons of both sexes, from different social classes, with varying occupations, and with individual points of view and experience, are perhaps able to express and represent public local feeling with a more sensitive understanding than a local authority composed of one person or very few. Most public work involves a reconciliation of conflicting claims and interests. Public authorities can hardly enter into competition with each other or take action which, while conferring a public benefit in one direction, involves serious public disadvantages in other directions. Two heads are better than one. And a council, elected by popular opinion, may have collective awareness which few individuals may have. The delay in procedure in the despatch of public business is the part of the price of British democratic local government.

*Meetings of Committees.* Apart from providing that minutes of all committees shall be kept, and shall be signed at the same or next ensuing meeting,[6] the law makes no provision about the conduct of meetings of committees.

The proceedings of committees, the number of members, the frequency of meetings, and the mode of conducting business are matters for the council to settle by standing orders.

The agenda of a committee will consist of correspondence, matters referred by the council to the committee for consideration, matters suggested by members for discussion, and reports by officers as to the state of work in their departments, or asking for action to be taken or to be authorized.

The proceedings are less formal than those in full council, members may speak more than once on any item, officers intervene, the chairman frequently does most of the talking, and (since he will be answerable in the full council for the reports presented by his committee) he acts not only as the

---

[6] In the case of the London local authorities the minutes must be signed at 'the same or a subsequent' meeting.

presiding member, but tries to influence the trend of the discussion.

On these various items the committee will, according to the authority delegated to them, issue instructions, or decide on the course they will recommend the council to take. If any other committees are concerned the necessary communications and consultations will ensue.

Where the spending of money is involved the finance committee will, in many cases, have to be consulted.

*Conferences and consultations.* Besides attending meetings of the council and its committees, members and officers spend a great deal of time in meetings and discussions affecting the business of the local authority. These preliminary and, to some extent, informal consultations form an important part of the administrative process. When two committees find or are likely to find themselves out of accord, or when two or more departments are concerned in the preparation of proposals, it is an obvious convenience that the people concerned should get together.

Similarly, when matters arise or action is proposed which may affect more than one public authority, it is highly convenient that, before any official action is taken by one authority, there should be unofficial preliminary conversations between the authorities concerned. It has accordingly become an increasing practice for local authorities, government departments, and other public bodies to arrange consultations either at 'officer level' or at 'member level', or both if need be, before any formal action is taken. Unofficial approaches are also often made as between a public authority and private persons or organizations, when a wage agreement, or the acquisition of buildings or land, or financial aid, or co-operation with voluntary agencies is desired. Officers and members spend a great deal of time upon negotiations of this type—in the lubrication of the official mechanism, as one might term it.

When a government department has the duty of drafting projected legislation affecting local authorities it is the general rule for the officers of the department, and even the Cabinet Ministers in person, to consult the local authorities. And in the running of those local services in which the central government has a concern (almost the whole range of local government activities) there is frequent informal contact between representatives of the departments and authorities concerned.

For the purpose of facilitating discussions of this kind, and for the better representation of the point of view of the local authorities, associations have been formed of various kinds, of which among the most prominent are the County Councils Association, the Association of Municipal Corporations (boroughs), the Urban District Councils Association, the Rural District Councils Association, the Association of Parish Councils and the Metropolitan Boroughs Standing Joint Committee. There are numerous others representing particular interests and services, and a number of associations of technical officers.

Negotiations between representative associations and bodies, akin to the negotiations between unions of employees and associations of employers, has become a feature of modern official life. Negotiations of this kind are always useful in the ventilation of ideas and in the expression of points of view. The effectiveness of any agreements arrived at thereby is dependent on their acceptance by the authorities represented. This acceptance may not be always easy to secure.

It is here that an advantage may be claimed for the organization of local authorities on political lines; for political organization imposes a certain discipline and does serve to canalize thought upon public questions into clearly defined channels. The introduction of socialism into local government affairs may be said to have lent special emphasis to the distinction (very relevant to the administration of local services) between those who favour state or municipal ownership and those who favour the system of private enterprise.

On many major issues, therefore, it is possible to estimate, according to current political trends, what will be the feeling of any particular local authority which is organized on party lines. Moreover, when negotiations are conducted by the political leader of the party in power on a local council, it is possible for him to speak with assurance, knowing that his party will support him, and that he can, like a foreign minister negotiating a treaty, virtually bind his administration in advance of a formal decision by it. A system of this kind does give representative negotiation greater force and clarity than when there is no political definition or discipline in the organization of the local authority concerned.

When negotiations take place between authorities among themselves or between authorities and Whitehall, and the political feeling is the same on both sides, the prospect of harmony is enhanced. When both sides do not share the same political faith, the differences in point of view are intensified. While, however, this may be broadly true in relation to certain matters, it must not be assumed that because there is political agreement between one authority and another, or between an authority and the central government, there will never be any disagreement between them. The political differences in local government are on some matters more apparent than real. On a number of important matters the political parties are in no vital disagreement. That there should be a public education service, sanitary services, municipal housing, clean and well-made roads, and care given to the poor and afflicted, all parties are agreed upon. What makes the main difference between them on these and other matters of local government are variations in points of view as to tone and approach, in emphasis and in modes of administration. And it is possible for there to be considerable conflict of opinion on these matters, even as between authorities sharing the same political creed.

The disadvantages of allowing politics to influence local government are claimed to be substantial. Since all public-spirited citizens accept the broad assumption that there should be local government services of the accepted types, would it not be more appropriate for members of local authorities to seek election and to be inspired more by an interest in those services rather than in the application to them of political principles? Many conscientious and able citizens, who would be capable of rendering great public service, fail to obtain election because they are of political colour not favoured in their localities, and their services are thereby lost, while a good party man may obtain election for his party affiliation rather than for his capability. Thus say the opponents of politics in local government.

There are other alleged disadvantages. Where the political organization is strong, there may be a tendency for the party machine to take the place of the authority itself. It is a common practice for members of political parties on a council or committee to meet together in private, in advance of the meetings, to settle their attitude towards the items on the agenda paper. Thus they arrive at the meetings with their minds more or less already made up, and, if they are of the party which holds the majority, the decisions of the council or committee are virtually made outside the council chamber or committee room. This does not mean to say that the opposition or the views of non-party members are ignored entirely, or that political parties are insensitive to the opinions of their opponents. But it does create a tendency to shift the centre of operations from the local authority's own structure to the party machine, with the result that a council or a committee may become little more than a forum for the exhibition of differing political views, rather than a creative assembly where, by the interplay of constructive debate, an authority's policy can be forged.

This tendency, it is true, becomes more apparent in a council chamber or a committee room where the press and public are admitted. People always tend to behave before an audience differently from when they are in private. And this shows itself in the conduct of business at public meetings of a local authority. Members of political parties are apt, in their public speeches, to have regard to future election prospects, and the debates assume the nature of a political contest. In committees which meet in private, however, the tendency is not so strong, and it may be found in many cases that discussions on those occasions are much more co-operative and display a concern on the part of members of all parties for the efficient working of the public services.

The statutory provisions relating to the constitution and operation of local authorities make no allowance for political groupings. The law does not provide for the management of local government affairs on the basis of there being a party in power with an official opposition, as in Parliament. There are still many local councils particularly in the rural areas where local government is run on non-party lines. In the areas where the influence of politics has penetrated into local government affairs, that influence will doubtless remain, and will extend to other areas.

Certain it is that, whatever may be the motives, political

or otherwise, which may prompt a person to seek election to a local authority, he (or she) will never maintain interest in local government work, and gain the moral and spiritual enrichment which comes with the performance of the arduous and unsalaried work which it entails, without gathering and maintaining a genuine interest in the work itself. It is by this interest and through the public-spirited endeavours of the thousands of members of local authorities that the democratic British system of local government is carried on. The part played by political considerations can easily be over-estimated. What politics certainly does is to provide a psychological stimulus and an enlivening effect in the conduct of local affairs. It provides both for the member and for the electorate an excitement that might otherwise be difficult to find. It provides the member of a party with a grouping from which he can obtain co-operation and strength, without necessarily diminishing his general interest in the public services, although it may at times (when political feeling is aroused) tend to bring into the conduct of local affairs considerations which the legislature, in framing the local government system, did not provide for.

# 13

## Officers of Local Authorities

A MODERN local authority would find it highly inconvenient, if not virtually impossible, to carry on its work without a staff of some kind, however small.

That it is not entirely impossible to do without a staff is illustrated by the fact that parish councils and meetings are in law under no obligation to appoint any staff, and a number of those authorities do operate without appointing any clerk or other officer. A parish council has power to appoint one of its own members to act as clerk without remuneration, or may, if it so wishes, appoint any other fit person to be clerk of the council at a reasonable remuneration. A parish council may also appoint one of the councillors, or some other fit person, to be treasurer without remuneration. A parish meeting has no direct power to appoint any officers at all, but the parish meeting may, if there is no parish council, ask the county council to confer on the meeting any powers of a parish council, and this conferment may include the power to appoint, for the parish meeting, the same officers as a parish council may appoint.

In parishes where no officers have been appointed, the duties of clerk and indeed any other duties necessary to carry on the work of the authority are performed by the chairman or by the members themselves.

Such an arrangement may be practicable in the case of these minor authorities where the functions to be performed are small and discontinuous. But it is difficult to conceive how any local authority with any substantial amount of work to do could carry on in this manner.

In medieval England, when local government was in its very early infancy, there was cast upon every man a vague and undefined obligation to maintain the King's highway. Highways were 'repairable by the inhabitants at large'. 'Let every man (as the saying was) sweep about his own door and the city shall be clean.' Such a method of carrying on a local service is obviously out of the question in modern times. Even Queen Mary I, as far back as 1555, found it necessary to require the appointment of Overseers of Highways to organize the local work of road repair. To-day neither the organized inhabitants nor their elected representatives could possibly undertake the range of public services which are carried on by local authorities. The work is too big, too technical and too complex.

Members of local authorities are, in the best sense of the term, amateurs. Many of them have great experience of local affairs, and many of them give a great deal of their waking hours to the business of their local council, but the fact remains that their work in the sphere of local government is largely periodical or occasional. Councils and committees meet at intervals. Between meetings, members may make inspections, pay visits, give advice and interim decisions, but few members are able to spend their continuous and uninterrupted time on the affairs of their authority. The public functions go on continuously. The children must be taught, the roads swept, the refuse collected, the institutions maintained. For this a staff of officials, administrative, technical and operative are needed.

Moreover, the elected representative is subject to periodical election. Democracy means that the electors are free to change their representatives from time to time. New members may not have the knowledge and experience of the old. It is an undoubted advantage for each local authority to be able to command a reserve of experience and technical capacity so that the functioning of the local services may be continuous and be maintained at a proper level of efficiency. This continuity, this experience, this technical capacity is provided by the officers.

*Compulsory appointments.* It is from considerations such as these that Parliament has imposed upon all local government authorities above the level of parish authorities the direct duty of appointing certain officers. Thus every county, borough and county district council must appoint a clerk, treasurer, medical officer of health, and surveyor. Borough and county district councils must each appoint at least one public health inspector. Deputies to the holders of these compulsory appointments may be appointed.

In addition there are a number of appointments which an authority must make according to the duties it has to carry out. Thus, a chief education officer, a coroner, a public analyst, a children's officer, inspectors of shops and of weights and measures, and registration and returning officers for election purposes must by various Acts of Parliament be appointed by every local authority having the duty of providing the services to which those appointments relate. Police and fire brigade authorities must establish forces of appropriate strength and composition.

It has in this way been recognized by law that, in respect of certain branches of local government work, the official is essential to the proper functioning of the public services. The law has, however, extended this recognition a stage further in respect of certain appointments by providing that the holders may not be dismissed without the prior consent of the central government. Thus the clerk of a county council outside London may not be dismissed from his office without the consent of the Minister of Housing and Local Government. Similar protection is given by statute to county medical officers of health, and, by regulations made by the Minister of Health, to certain medical officers and public health inspectors of other authorities. No statutory protection is accorded to the surveyor of a local authority, but when, as is commonly the practice, the Minister of Transport makes a contribution towards the salary of the surveyor, the contribution is made on condition that the holder of the office shall not be dismissed without the Minister's consent.

The holders of these important posts cannot therefore be dismissed at the mere caprice of the employing authority. It may be that on occasions one of these officers feels compelled to advise his authority to take a certain course which, although right according to the justice of the case or technically correct, is unpalatable to the members of the authority. In such a case it is undoubtedly to the public advantage that the officer should not be in danger of dismissal nor be forced, through the prospect of dismissal, to give advice which is not appropriate to the real needs of the situation.[1]

*Qualifications.* In respect of a number of local government appointments, requirements have been prescribed, either by statute or by regulations of the appropriate Ministers, that the appointees shall possess certain qualifications. This is particularly the case with appointments of medical officers of health, public health inspectors, health visitors, midwives and other medical staff. Inspectors of weights and measures must be certified by the Board of Trade as having proper qualifications. School teachers, firemen and policemen must undergo approved courses of training.

For some appointments, for example, the clerk, treasurer and surveyor, no special qualifications are prescribed other than that the appointee shall be a 'fit person'. The Education Act, 1944, and the Children Act, 1948, have unusual provisions which require that a local authority, before appointing a chief education officer or a children's officer, shall submit to the appropriate Minister the names of candidates from among whom the appointment will be made, with particulars of their qualifications and experience; and the Minister may prohibit the appointment of any candidate whom he considers to be not a 'fit person' for the appointment.

Where, as is usually the case, the Ministry of Transport makes a contribution towards the salary of a local authority's surveyor, it is normally made a condition of the contribution that the surveyor shall have appropriate professional qualifications.

*Staff generally.* In addition to the appointments which a local authority is required by law to make, there are a number of appointments which are necessary according to the work which the local authority has to do. Every local government authority above the level of parish authority has a general power to appoint such staff as the authority considers necessary for the efficient discharge of its functions.

*Remuneration and general conditions of service.* In respect of a considerable number of appointments the discretion of a local

---

[1] Under the former Poor Law, relieving officers, masters of workhouses and other senior officials could not be dismissed by their local authorities without the consent of the Minister of Health. The object apparently was to prevent a parsimonious and unsympathetic authority from unduly hampering the officers in the necessary administration of poor relief.

authority in the matter of remuneration of its staff has been limited by legal provision. Thus the salaries paid to the clerks of county councils outside London and to certain medical officers and sanitary inspectors must by statute be approved by the appropriate Minister. In a number of other cases the appropriate Minister is given power to make regulations or orders binding upon local authorities in respect of the salaries to be paid by them to their staff. Provisions of this kind exist in relation to staff engaged in the health and education services of local authorities.

In the case of staff which are not covered by any special legal provision, regulation or order, the law provides that an authority may pay its officers such reasonable remuneration as the authority may determine. A permissive provision of this kind would normally leave it open to an authority to employ, if it so desired, staff at no remuneration at all. At one time it was not unusual for fire brigades to be run on a voluntary basis; and certain minor appointments, such as home visitors, may have been made without remuneration. The practice of making unpaid appointments has, however, virtually disappeared.

Apart from those few special cases in which the dismissal of an officer requires the approval of a Minister, the staff of a local authority is, by law, engaged 'at the pleasure' of the authority. This, however, does not prevent agreements being made between the council and its officers as to the length of notice to be given on termination of services.

It is an important feature of the British system of local government that each local council is master of its own staff. The cases in which the central government can intervene in appointments by local authorities are limited to a very few, and even then, although the salary, qualifications and general duties may be laid down by a Minister, the actual choice of the appointee is with the local authority. Except in the few cases which have been mentioned, the local authority has full power to decide salaries, terms of service, and duties, and has full power of appointment and dismissal.

Local authorities are, however, affected, as are most other employers throughout the country, by the modern tendency to settle wages and terms of employment by negotiation through representative bodies. Employees who are members of a trade union look to their unions to represent their interests; and local authorities employing staff of this kind will have regard to the trade union rates and conditions. For certain types of local government staff there have been established a number of voluntary organizations or 'Whitley Councils'[2] representing both employers and employees for the purposes of negotiating agreements with regard to remuneration and terms of employment. Thus there are national and regional joint councils for manual workers engaged in local authorities' general services, councils for medical, nursing and subordinate staffs of hospitals and allied institutions, for county roadmen, and for administrative, professional, technical and clerical officers. These bodies issue from time to time standard conditions of service for adoption, with regional variations as may be appropriate, by all the local authorities concerned.[3]

For the most part these standard conditions are voluntarily accepted by the employing authorities and the employees. There is, moreover, a tendency on the part of the legislature to give legal recognition to settlements arrived at by bodies representative of employers and employees in the matter of wages and terms of service.[4] This is part of the general policy of the law for the avoidance and settlement of trade disputes. This policy has been expressed either in provisions which require employers to observe the agreed conditions, or by the practice of utilizing the agreed conditions as a criterion for the settlement of disputes between employers and employed by the process of arbitration, by the Industrial Court or by the Minister of Labour.

The Education Act, 1944, contains provisions which are illustrative of the general trend. Section 89 of the Act is to the effect that the Minister of Education shall secure that one or more committees are set up, consisting of representatives of local authorities and teachers for the purpose of settling

[2] So called after Mr. Whitley, a Speaker of the House of Commons, who in 1917-18 was Chairman of a government committee which suggested the appointment of these joint councils.

[3] These arrangements do not usually affect the appointments of principal officers, e.g. the clerk, surveyor or medical officer.

[4] See for example the Wages Councils Act, 1959.

scales of remuneration for teachers,[5] and that the Minister may by order require local authorities to pay their teachers in accordance with those scales.

By these various means there is being secured a great deal of uniformity as between one authority and another in the rates of pay and conditions of service of the respective types and grades of staff in their employ. There has accordingly grown up the conception of a local government service, or municipal civil service, nation-wide, employed by and subject to the direction of the individual local authorities, yet subject to broadly similar conditions of employment.

*Superannuation.* This conception received a great deal of strength from the statutory provisions relating to the superannuation of local government officers. Under the Local Government Superannuation Acts, 1937 to 1953, local government authorities are required to make provision for the superannuation of all their whole-time officers other than those, such as firemen, teachers and police officers, who are covered by other enactments relating to superannuation. Under certain circumstances an authority may also make provision for part-time officers and temporary employees with more than ten years' service.

The arrangements made by individual local authorities vary in detail according to local schemes made under the Act, and to some extent are affected by the schemes of national insurance and pensions. The broad effect of all local authorities' schemes is, however, the same, and provides for pensions after at least ten years' service. Employees must normally retire at the age of sixty-five; pensions are related in amount to the years of service and the employee's earnings; the maximum pension is based on forty years' service; pensions may be paid on earlier retirement on account of ill health or certain other reasons, and may be allocated in part to an employee's spouse or dependant. The important provision which gives strength to the conception of a nation-wide municipal civil service is that relating to the 'transfer value' of an employee's pension. The effect of this is that if a pensionable employee of one local

[5] This gives statutory support to the practice started in 1919 of appointing a standing joint committee of local authority associations and of teachers known as the Burnham Committee from its first chairman (Lord Burnham).

authority leaves his employment to enter the service of another local authority, arrangements must be made for this 'transfer value' to be paid by the former employing authority to the new employing authority.

The statutory provisions relating to the pensions of teachers, policemen and firemen also lay down broad national standards to be followed by local authorities in paying superannuation, and enable years of service with more than one local authority to be aggregated for the purpose of calculating the pensions.

In consequence of these various provisions, officers of local authorities may go from authority to authority, advancing their careers, and gaining experience in different localities and with authorities of different classes, without loss of pension rights, so that, on eventual retirement, an officer will receive a pension based on his total employment in local government. Thus the field of choice for employing authorities is improved, and the opportunities open to a local government officer are widened, with beneficial results to both authorities and officers and to the local government service as a whole.

*Permanency.* Although there are no legal provisions requiring appointments in the local government service to be permanent, and in fact any local government officer can, with proper notice and (in the few special cases) with the consent of the appropriate Minister be dismissed, the general practice is for local authorities to engage a staff of officials on a virtually permanent basis, and to divide this staff into grades according to duties and responsibilities, with scales of salary and regular increments within the grading. This body of permanent staff may be supplemented according to need by temporary employees.

*Part-time and joint appointments.* Permanent appointments are usually whole-time appointments, but part-time appointments may be made. A small authority may find it appropriate to appoint a part-time clerk of the council. Part-time consultants, teachers of special subjects, and chaplains for ministration in institutions are often appointed. A part-time medical officer of health may be appointed, but it is considered generally desirable that the holders of these appointments shall not engage in private practice, and accordingly local authorities are permitted, and in some cases may be definitely required, to combine for the purpose of appointment of a medical officer. This has the advantage of enabling an authority which has slender resources, or has only a relatively small amount of public health work, to obtain the services of a duly qualified officer engaged at a salary sufficient to attract applicants of sufficient standing and experience.

Part-time and joint appointments are, moreover, likely to prove embarrassing both to the holder and to the employing authorities and involve a conflict of interests.

One method of avoiding this difficulty is to employ an officer (in cases where it is practicable and legal) in more than one capacity so that his whole-time services may be exclusively given to one authority. The clerk of a council is frequently also that authority's solicitor; the surveyor may be the council's architect or housing manager; and inspectors of weights and measures may have the duties of inspectors under the legislation relating to shops. In some cases this fusion of appointments is not permissible. The clerk may not be also the treasurer. A county medical officer of health may hold no other appointment except with the consent of the Minister of Health. Moreover, it is impracticable to fuse two or more appointments in cases where the duties of the appointments demand special and differing technical qualifications or experience.

*Special obligations of the local government officer.* The local government officer, like any other employee, is bound by the rules of law implicit in the relationship of master and servant. He must render to his employing authority true and loyal service, obey their reasonable and lawful instructions, and avoid the temptations of bribery and corruption. By reason of his employment in a public service the law places upon him certain special obligations. Every local government officer has a statutory duty to account properly for all moneys and property committed to his charge. Every local authority is required to arrange for appropriate security to be given for the faithful execution of the duties of all their officers who are likely to be entrusted, in the course of their duties, with the custody or control of money.

If it comes to the knowledge of a local government officer that his employing authority has entered, or proposes to enter, upon a contract in which the officer has, directly or indirectly, any pecuniary interest, he must so inform the authority in writing. Thus, if he, or his wife, is a shareholder in a company which contracts with his council, he must inform the council, or be liable to heavy penalties.

No local government officer may, under colour of his office or employment, exact or accept any fee or reward other than his proper remuneration.

The fact that these particular requirements are imposed by Act of Parliament indicates that the proper conduct of local government officials is a matter of concern not only to their employing authorities, but also to the public at large. Local government officers stand in a special position. They owe a duty both to their employers and to the general public. It has been held by the courts that the position of a borough treasurer is that of a trustee, as custodian of the public funds of the borough, and is not merely that of a servant of the borough council; and that it is his duty to disobey orders which are unlawfully made upon him by the council.[6] The interesting part of this decision is not that it authorizes the treasurer to disobey an unlawful order; for, indeed, it is the general law that every employee of any master is entitled, if not obliged, to disregard orders which would involve the commission of an unlawful act. What is important is that the decision emphasizes the duty of the treasurer to act as a trustee of public funds; in other words, that the treasurer must, in the whole course of his duties, have regard to the public welfare and not resign all his discretion to his employing council.

Similar emphasis has been laid by the High Court upon the duty of a town clerk to assist in the proper conduct of public affairs by his advice and action. He ought not to withhold his advice if he sees that the actions of the council are likely to lead to improper or unlawful practice.[7]

The local government officer is employed to serve the public through the representative council which engages him. The council is itself a public corporate body and is not empowered to act other than in accordance with law. The officer's proper duty is to ensure that the operations of the council are such as accord with its proper functions.

[6] A.-G. v. De Winton (1906) 2 Ch. 106.
[7] In *re* Hurle Hobbs (James and Riley's appeals) 20th December, 1944 (unreported).

An anecdote which illustrates this principle is told of the late Sir Robert Blair when he was chief education officer of the London County Council. At one of the meetings of the Council's education committee he saw fit to intervene in the discussion. He rose and proceeded to give to the committee advice which they found to be unwelcome. The chairman told him to sit down. But Sir Robert replied, 'No, sir. I conceive it to be my duty to give the committee the advice which I think they ought to have when they ought to have it; and this is one of the occasions.' This attitude is typical of the best type of public servant.

All this does not make the position of the local government officer by any means easier than that of a servant of a private employer. The local government officer is the servant of his local authority, but the authority is composed of a body of elected members. The officer is not the servant of the individual members, and no member is entitled to give orders to an officer unless the member has been authorized to do so by the council either directly or through the medium of one of its committees. None the less, it is through the votes of individual members that an officer is appointed and can be dismissed. There are occasions when it becomes the duty of an officer to put himself in opposition to the wishes of the members. His position calls for the exercise of tact and firmness if he is to guide the council in a proper lawful course, without unduly endangering his career. The art of public administration consists, to a considerable extent, in reconciling and harmonizing conflicting interests. The local government officer must possess the qualities necessary to the exercise of that art.

However eminent the officer may be, however great his influence over the activities of his council, however deep the respect and confidence accorded him by his council, the fact remains that the officer is the servant of the council. The functions of member and officer do not overlap. No officer holding a place of profit in the disposal of the council can be at the same time a member. Conversely, no member can be a paid officer of the council of which he is a member. The law goes even further and provides that a member of a local authority is, for twelve months after he ceases to be a member, disqualified for appointment by that authority to any paid office other than chairman, mayor or sheriff.

The function of the officer is to advise, and to carry out the lawful instructions of his local authority, and to exercise on their behalf such functions as have been delegated to him. The authority is entitled to call for his advice, but not to tell him what that advice shall be. On the other hand, he must look to his employing authority on how to carry out his lawful duties.

In practice, especially in the case of the large authorities, a great deal of delegation is made to officers, and the council and committees reserve to themselves general policy and the more important items of business and of expenditure, leaving the day-to-day administration of the services to the officers.

*Departmental groupings.* Just as the members form themselves into committees for the more convenient exercise of the council's functions, so the officers of the council are normally grouped into departments. Since the clerk and treasurer cannot be the same person, and since the duties of the medical officer of health and the surveyor necessitate special technical skill, these various offices form the focal points for the main groupings of a local authority's staff and lead to the formation of departments concerned respectively with secretarial matters, financial business, health and public works. Where the local authority has functions which necessitate the appointment of a specialist chief officer with a supporting staff, an obvious course is to create separate departments for those functions, as for example the education and fire brigade services of counties and county boroughs. The formation of other departments, and the distribution of functions among the various departments, is arranged by each local authority according to its own functions, needs and preferences.

The following table gives an indication of the probable distribution of duties among a council's principal officers.

*Clerk*  Secretarial and committee work. General co-ordination. Is usually a solicitor and does legal work. Licensing of places of entertainment, etc.

In some authorities the licensing work may be given to a public control officer. There may also be a separate legal department. In those cases the clerk's duties will be mainly secretarial and co-ordination of all departments of the council.

*Treasurer*   Finance and accounts. In some authorities the treasurer is a local bank, and the council appoints a finance officer (who in smaller authorities is often the clerk) to advise on and conduct its financial business.

*Medical Officer*   Public health, clinical services, school medical service, notification of disease, reports on houses unfit for habitation, welfare services for the aged and blind. In some authorities these last-mentioned services may be given to a separate department. The public analyst and the public health inspector may be under the direction of the medical officer.

*Public Health Inspector*   Inspection of premises, nuisance to health, inspection of water supply, drainage, lodging-houses, dairies, workshops, etc.

*Surveyor*   Road construction and maintenance, refuse collection and disposal, sewerage and drainage works, housing, town planning, building by-laws, parks lay-out and maintenance.

In a small authority he will have all the functions involving the employment and supervision of manual labour.

In a large authority these duties may be distributed among an architect, engineer, housing manager and a parks manager.

*Education Officer*   The education services, museums, art galleries, libraries. In a large authority there may be separate departments for museums, etc.

*Chief Officer, Fire Brigade*   Fire brigade. Inspection of premises for fire protection and prevention.

To some extent the appointments made by a local authority and the grouping of the staff into departments will accord with the committee structure. Thus the education and finance committees will correspond with the chief education officer and the treasurer; the fire brigade committee will be related closely to the affairs of the fire brigade. But it is by no means the rule that each department should have its particular committee. It is not possible always to arrange it, nor is it always desirable. Indeed, it may be highly desirable to avoid creating a position in which each department or group of staff looks exclusively to a particular committee for instructions, and considers itself responsible to that committee only; for no matter how complex the organization of a local authority's work may be, and how great may be the number of departments and committees each with their particular duties, the fact remains that there is only one council, and that upon the council rests the ultimate responsibility for the activities of all its committees.

Just as it may be difficult to arrange the departmental grouping to accord exactly with the committee structure, so also it may be difficult, if not impossible, to divide up all the work of an authority among its officers in a way that will leave each officer a clear-cut range of duties that do not impinge upon the duties of other officers. The provision of housing, for example, involves the design of houses, the acquisition of land, the making of roads and drains, the provision of other sanitary services, and general considerations of town-planning, to say nothing of the work of rent-collecting and management after the houses are erected. The project will require the consideration of a number of officers. The surveyor and the medical officer of health may have something to say about roads and sanitary arrangements; the treasurer will have a say in the finance; and the clerk, besides having to present the necessary reports to the council, may have the legal work of arranging the land purchase.

Take another example. A local cinema is being erected by private enterprise. The plans will have to be submitted to the council for approval under the building by-laws; the town planning considerations will have to be looked at; the sanitary and fire protection arrangements approved, and in due course the necessary cinematograph licence will have to be issued subject to such conditions as the authority may impose relating to hours of performance, seating arrangements, safety precautions and the like. Several departments of the council will be concerned.

*The special position of the clerk.* Where in any working organization a number of separate groups of persons exist, it is always desirable that efforts should be made both to harmonize the activities of the different groups and to ensure that each group is given its proper share of the work of the whole.

Local government authorities are multi-purpose organizations each with several different types of function to carry out. It is accordingly desirable that the work of the various departments of an authority should be co-ordinated both to keep them in line with the council's general policy and legitimate functions, and to make sure that when any matter arises which affects the various departments, each department concerned is duly brought in to take its part in dealing with the matter.

Reference has already been made in chapter 11 to the co-ordination of the work of committees. This co-ordination is not secured without there being someone to watch the functioning of all committees and to see that the necessary steps are taken. Similarly it is necessary that there should be someone to have continuous oversight of the council's departmental organization to ensure that each department not only performs its proper duties but is duly informed on all matters in respect of which it has duties to do.

The officer who is in the best position to exercise the function of general co-ordination is the clerk of the local authority. Opportunity for carrying out this supervisory function can be afforded to him in various ways. If all important communications addressed to the council pass through his hands, if he signs all important communications sent out by the council, if he is clerk of the various committees of the council and supervises the agenda paper of the council itself, he is in a good position to keep an eye on the council's work generally. He can ensure that incoming communications are referred to the proper departments; he can, when a matter comes before a committee, see that every department concerned has been brought into the matter. When a decision has been reached by the council or a committee it will be his function to pass the requisite instructions to the departments concerned, and communicate the effect of any decisions to any other persons or authorities. By this means each department's responsibilities can be duly assigned, and the council, in communicating its decisions, speaks with one voice through the mouthpiece of the clerk.

If, besides being the chief secretarial officer of the authority, the clerk is given the status of chief administrative officer, with a position as head of the whole of the council's staff, and the duty to concern himself in the number, types and duties of the personnel employed by the council, his position will be greatly strengthened; for he will then have the right, if not the absolute duty, to interest himself in the working of each department and its organization and management.

Although the appointment of a clerk is required by statute, there are no statutory provisions prescribing his status and general position. The strength and importance of his position will vary according to the size of the authority and its internal arrangements. In a small authority, with functions which are small in scale and comparatively few in number, with a correspondingly small administrative staff and few departments, all working close together in the same suite of offices, the likelihood that each department may become entirely isolated from the others is perhaps less than in the case of the large local authority with very substantial functions and services. It is therefore more necesssary in the case of the larger authority that the status of the clerk and his co-ordinating functions should be clearly defined. This does not mean that in the case of the smaller authority co-ordination is not necessary. It is, indeed, essential always.

When different public services are administered without proper relation to each other, inconsistencies and anomalies arise which can be very bewildering to the public and may bring the responsible authorities into ridicule and contempt.

Co-ordination is necessary not only as between department and department; it is also necessary as between authority and authority. The field of local government is a complex patchwork. Public services are provided by different authorities, and the operations of one authority may have intimate effect on those of other authorities. Housing operations, for instance, necessitate co-ordination with the suppliers of water, gas and electricity. Where the housing is erected by one authority in the area of another authority, the latter authority will be responsible for the roads, drains and other local services.

The co-ordinating functions of the clerk of a local authority should therefore embrace the external relations of his authority. He should be aware of the respective functions of the different authorities and be able to advise his council accordingly. He may be called upon to represent his council in negotiations between his authority and other authorities and government departments.

Co-ordination between authority and authority may not be so easy of achievement, however, as it would be between the several departments of one authority. Herein lies one of the advantages of providing public services by means of multi-purpose bodies such as local government authorities rather than by separate bodies created for different services. This advantage may not always outweigh the technical advisability of having special *ad hoc* bodies in appropriate cases. The fact remains that when public services are administered in the same area by different authorities the policies of the various bodies can only be harmonized by collaboration between them. The unwillingness of any body to collaborate endangers the prospect of harmony. When, however, different services are provided by the one authority, the opportunity of harmonizing the administration of the various services is provided within the organization of the authority itself, by co-ordination between committees and departments, so that a consistent policy towards the general public may be followed. This capacity for resolving inconsistencies and anomalies within the one organization is an important feature of the administration of services by multi-purpose local government authorities.

*Associations of Officers.* In addition to the well-known professional organizations to which those officers with the appropriate qualifications, such as solicitor, architect, medical officer and engineer, can belong, there are a number of associations and institutes specially formed for local government officers of particular classes—treasurers and accountants, librarians and public health officers, for instance. The National Association of Local Government Officers commands a wide support among local government officers of all grades and types. In addition, there are trades unions or special branches of unions whose membership is open to particular groups of local government employees.

These bodies are active not only in promoting the welfare of the local government staffs who support them, but make it also their concern to interest themselves in their qualifications and in the improvement of technical equipment and methods.

# 14

# The Legal Position of Local Authorities

LOCAL authorities are the creation of the law. They are brought into existence by a legislative process, either by charter, by Act of Parliament or by statutory order.[1] They are artificial entities without natural rights or natural functions. They have no powers, rights or obligations except those conferred by law. They are accordingly governed throughout their creation, existence and dissolution by the operation of law.

*Local authorities as persons.* The fact that local authorities are artificially created does not entirely deprive them of certain rights possessed by ordinary persons, nor does it absolve them from certain normal obligations. A local authority has no natural body and cannot therefore be subjected to assault or imprisonment. But the fact that it is incorporated, or given a corporate (or bodily) status makes it at law a 'person' with such of the rights and duties of a private individual as are not inconsistent with its artificial nature.

Thus, a local authority can institute legal proceedings for the recovery of its property; it can sue for debt, take steps to enforce the payment of rates, to exact penalties, or to obtain damages for breach of contract. A local authority can also act as defendant in legal proceedings, it can be sued for failure to meet its obligations as employer, landowner, debtor, or purchaser. Action at law can be taken against it for breaches of the law committed in its name and under its sanction. Judgments given by the courts against local authorities can be enforced by the seizure of the authority's property.

This responsibility of a local authority as a legal person is separate from the individual responsibilities of the members and officers of the authority for acts done in the course of their duties.

*Judicial control.* A local authority may lawfully act only

---

[1] i.e. as in the case of metropolitan borough councils or joint boards.

within the limit of the powers given it by law. If an authority acts beyond its legal powers, the acts will be *ultra vires* and unlawful. Accordingly, if any litigation arises as to the acts done by a local authority, it will be for the courts to examine the powers and duties of the authority and ascertain whether the authority was acting within its legal powers.

The influence which the courts thus exercise, by decisions given in the course of litigation, over the operations of local authorities has given rise to the term 'judicial control'. Unlike the control exercised by the central government over local authorities, the control by the courts is discontinuous and spasmodic, and is directly exercisable over an authority only when proceedings are taken before the courts. A court's decisions are not, however, limited in their effect to the particular cases which arise. The decisions, published in reports of the proceedings, serve to build up a body of legal precedent and experience by which local authorities can obtain guidance as to the correct legal course to be followed in the carrying out of their functions.

*Injury to private persons by public activities.* In examining the legal position of a local authority, a distinction must be drawn between the authority's powers and its duties, or, in other words, between those things the authority may do, and those which it is legally obliged to do.

When the powers of the authority are permissive, the authority is not bound to exercise the powers. Its responsibility for what it does in carrying out those powers is therefore likely to be higher than in the case where the powers are obligatory or mandatory.

If a local authority exercises a permissive power negligently and in such a way as to cause injury to others, the authority may be sued by the persons adversely affected. If the power is mandatory, and injury is done to others, the authority may defend itself by pleading that the act performed was one which it was obliged by law to perform. In some Acts of Parliament, however, provision is expressly made for the payment by an authority of compensation for the injurious effects of an authority's lawful operations.

In a number of cases, Parliament, in conferring upon local authorities powers which may be likely to interfere with the rights of other persons, has expressly provided for an appeal to the courts against the acts of an authority. Thus orders made by a local authority for the demolition of insanitary dwellings or requiring the provision of drainage works may be appealed against by the persons affected. And certain refusals of permission, or refusals to grant licences, may be the subject of appeals to the courts.

*Injury caused through failure to perform duties.* The activities of local authorities have been classified by lawyers as either misfeasance (the doing of something in a wrongful manner) and non-feasance (or the omission to do something which ought to be done).

The general rule is that an authority is not liable for nonfeasance, as for example if a road gets out of repair and a road user is injured as a result; but an authority is liable for misfeasance as, for instance, where a local authority, in repairing a road, deposits heaps of materials and makes excavations, leaving them unlighted at night or unprotected by day.

This general rule has been a frequent subject of legal decision, and a number of exceptions have been made to it. Much may depend on the wording of the particular statute under which the local authority's duty arises. Some statutes specially provide a remedy for a private citizen who suffers loss or injury by the failure of a local authority to perform its duties properly. And the courts, in interpreting Acts of Parliament, have, in a number of instances, allowed private persons to obtain damages for personal loss occasioned by the neglectful or inefficient way in which an authority carries out its public functions.

*Responsibility to the general public.* If a local authority fails entirely to carry out some public duty, or performs some act *ultra vires*, legal proceedings may be taken by the Attorney-General, on behalf of the general public. He may be moved to act by some private person who has particularly suffered by the failure of the authority. Certain Acts of Parliament give Ministers of the central government specific power to apply to the courts for an order requiring a local authority to carry out its proper functions.

The form of the proceedings varies with the nature of the case. The procedure may be by way of *indictment* in the case of the commission of a wrongful act or in case of failure to do right. Or an application may be for an order of *mandamus* requiring the local authority to do its lawful duty. An application may be made for an *injunction* to restrain the authority from committing or continuing to commit a wrongful act. The court may be asked to give a *declaration* settling the rights of a particular point. An order of *prohibition* may be sought to prevent an authority from exceeding its proper functions when acting as a tribunal, as in the case of the grant of licences for cinemas and other matters. Or an order of *certiorari* may be applied for to bring before the court some matter which the local authority has power to decide but on which the judgment of a court of law would be desirable.

Although these various types of proceedings are based on the obligations of a local authority towards the public as a whole, a private person who has himself suffered special injury as a member of the public, or whose private rights have been affected, may be allowed to make use of these proceedings so as to obtain such redress as the court may award to him.

# 15

# Alteration of Areas and Status of
# Local Authorities

THE use of traditional areas for functional purposes for which
the areas were not originally designed has the advantage that,
as new purposes are evolved (as where new public services are
instituted), the areas in which the new purposes are to be
carried out are already publicly recognized and defined.

The disadvantage is that the old areas are not always those
best suited to the new purposes. The incidence of population
alters as industrial and social developments take place; unin-
habited areas become populated; towns which in medieval
times had importance lose for one reason or another their
influence; villages become busy towns and seek and obtain
charters of incorporation as boroughs; residential areas fall out
of fashion, become depressed and obsolescent and lose their
rateable value. Thus, for a number of reasons which have varied
according to local conditions, there has been a need, especially
in modern times by reason of the growth in the number and
technical development of the public services, for adjustments
of local government areas. For somewhat similar reasons it
has been found necessary to alter the status of local authorities.

Accordingly, Parliament has, from time to time, enacted
provisions by which changes in areas and status could be made,
either at the instance of local authorities themselves, or at the
instance of the appropriate Minister.

The main function of local government is the administration of services and areas. The area of each unit should be big
enough, yet not too big. There should be enough population
to justify setting up the establishments and equipment, such
as schools, libraries, sewage disposal works, public gardens and
the rest, for the services of the local authority. The authority
should command, by means of the rateable value of the area,

sufficient financial resources to carry on its services. The area should be geographically capable of convenient administration; detached portions, cut off by wide rivers or mountains from the main area, should be avoided where possible.

These considerations are easy to appreciate; but they are not all. Tradition is a strong influence in local government, especially where the ancient areas of county, borough and parish are concerned. Proposals for the variation of local areas often arouse considerable local interest and are often resisted on traditional grounds alone. The interest is much strengthened when, as is often the case, financial considerations arise.

Proposals for the creation and extension of county boroughs are a particularly fruitful source of controversy. Since 1888, when county boroughs were first constituted, there has been, throughout the country, considerable urban expansion, due to the increase in the population, the development of industry and other causes. Towns have grown larger, and the urban expansion has in many cases extended beyond the boundaries of the original boroughs into the area of adjoining administrative counties. This has two effects upon the counties. First, the rateable value of the county is increased since built-up land is more highly rated than land which is not built upon. The rate income from these built-up areas forms a useful contribution to the county fund. Second, the obligations of the county authorities are enlarged in that a demand arises for the provision, in the built-up areas surrounding the county borough, of urban services similar to those provided in the borough.

The measure of these effects varies in different areas. Whatever the situation may be, the extension of a county borough at the expense of an administrative county always presents acute problems of financial adjustments. It is not only the county council which is concerned; the county district council in the area proposed to be absorbed in the county borough is also intimately affected.

The suburban areas of county boroughs give rise to other special problems connected with planning and housing. Room cannot always be found, within the area of a county borough, for necessary re-housing according to modern standards. Many county borough councils whose areas are completely built-up cannot exercise their housing powers properly without utiliz-ing sites outside the borough. Moreover, slum clearance schemes and town planning proposals dictate a decongestion of areas which are overcrowded. The borough authorities find them-selves obliged to promote urban development outside the area of the borough. The outer areas are, however, under the con-trol of some other local authority, and any necessary local government services, such as public health and education, must be provided at the expense of those other authorities, who may be loath to expend money until the development is achieved, the newly constructed houses are occupied, and the rates start to come in. There may, therefore, be a time lag between the first occupation of the developed areas and the provision of the public services. And in addition the methods and standards of services provided by the authorities outside the borough may differ from those within the borough.

These difficulties can to a great extent be overcome by the willing co-operation of the local authorities concerned. This co-operation may not always be obtained, however. Each local authority has its own needs and its individual point of view and may not, quite justifiably, find itself able to comply with all the requirements of other authorities. The extension of the borough so as to bring the area of new development within the jurisdiction of the county borough council has therefore on a number of occasions been proposed as a solution.

Similar considerations arise when the creation of a new county borough is proposed. The county council will be re-lieved of the obligation to provide certain services in the borough, and will at the same time lose the rateable value of the borough. The corporation of the proposed new county borough will be faced with the duty of providing all local government services out of its own resources. Its population, the services which that population will require, and the re-sources which the borough council can command must be appropriate to justify county borough status. The Local Govern-ment Act, 1958, has laid it down that a population of 100,000 is to be a presumptive minimum for county borough status.

## I. ALTERATIONS AT THE INSTANCE OF LOCAL AUTHORITIES

*Charters of incorporation.* Any urban or rural district council may, after passing the appropriate resolution at a special meeting, petition the Crown for a charter of incorporation as a borough. The petition is deposited with the Privy Council, notices are given to the county council and the Minister of Housing and Local Government, a local inquiry is held, and, if all goes well, the promoting council will be asked to submit to the Privy Council a draft charter and a draft scheme to deal with any necessary adjustments of area, property, functions, liabilities and other such matters. Public notice is given so that any objections may be made, and, when any objections have been disposed of, the scheme is confirmed either by Order in Council (if the scheme is unopposed) or by a Bill promoted in Parliament.

The usual practice on presentation of a petition is to examine whether the area, population and rateable value of the district are sufficient to justify the higher status. The general shape of the area, whether the population is relatively compact forming a (more or less) self-contained social unit, whether there is a civic consciousness among the people, whether there is an administrative focal point, and a number of other similar considerations must be reviewed. The past record of the local authority in carrying out its public duties will also affect the prospect of obtaining the civic dignity of a borough.

*Boundaries of counties and county boroughs.* A county council (other than London) or a county borough council may make, to the Minister of Housing and Local Government, proposals for the alteration of their own areas by change of boundary, by union, or by division. The Minister, after holding any necessary local inquiry, may make an order to confirm or vary the proposals; the order requires approval by both Houses of Parliament.

*Boundaries within a county.* A county council (other than London), with or without receiving proposals from any other local authority, and after notice to the public and to all local authorities and government departments concerned, and after a public local inquiry, may make an order to alter or define the boundaries of any urban or rural district or parish within the county, to divide or amalgamate any such areas, to transfer part of an area to another area, to convert an urban district into a rural district and vice versa, and to create new urban or rural districts or parishes. The order requires confirmation by the Minister of Housing and Local Government.

*County reviews.* It is the duty of every county council (other than London) to review the circumstances of the county districts in the county and to make proposals to the Minister for effecting changes appearing to the county council to be desirable in the interests of effective and convenient local government. The changes proposed may include the alteration of the area of any county district (including a non-county borough), the amalgamation of areas, the abolition of an urban or rural district, the conversion of an urban into a rural district and vice versa, the creation, abolition and amalgamation of parishes, alterations of parish boundaries and the 'inclusion of a non-county borough in a rural district' (as to which, see below).

The county council must consult with the other authorities concerned, publish its proposals so as to allow objections to be made, and submit a report with any proposals to the Minister who may, after due consideration and consultation, make such order as seems fit to give effect to or modify the proposals.

After the expiration of ten years from the first review, the Minister may direct the holding of a further review.

*Inclusion of a non-county borough in a rural district.* There are, throughout the country, a number of small boroughs—some of them very ancient which, by modern standards, are not really large enough to provide the public services expected of a borough. Some have populations of under 2,000; and their rateable value is so low that a penny rate will yield under £50. Accordingly the Local Government Act, 1958, provides that a county council, when making its county review, may propose that a non-county borough may be included in a rural district. This would virtually reduce the non-county borough to the parish level. Because, however, of the dignity and civic tradition which is embodied in the status of a borough, the Act makes provision whereby a borough, when included in a rural district, may be relieved of much of its local government responsibility, and yet retain some of its dignity and title. A borough, after inclusion, will not lose its charter, nor its name, nor its title of borough. It will be known as a 'rural borough'. Its chairman will still be called the mayor, but there will be no aldermen, and although it will become in effect a parish council, its members will be called 'rural borough councillors'.

*Act of Parliament.* Before the passing of the Local Government Act, 1958, it was competent for any local authority above the parish level to promote a Bill in Parliament to change its area or status to create a new local area. That Act provides, however, that no such Bill may be promoted by any local authority before the expiration of fifteen years from the commencement of the Act, i.e. until July, 1973.

## II. ALTERATIONS AT THE INSTANCE OF THE CENTRAL GOVERNMENT

During the second world war many proposals put forward by local authorities for alterations of area and status, including claims for the creation and extension of county boroughs, had been held in suspense. In 1945 a Local Government Boundary Commission was created by statute with the duty of reviewing generally the boundaries of local authorities and in some cases their status.

The Commission published reports for 1946, 1947 and 1948 containing various suggestions for the re-organization of local government generally, and for far-reaching changes in the functions and status of authorities. The proposals of the Commission were not adopted, and in 1949 it was dissolved by statute.

In a White Paper (Cmd. 9831) issued in 1956, the government expressed the view that there was 'no convincing case for radically re-shaping the existing form of local government in England and Wales', and that what was needed was to overhaul it and make such improvements as were necessary to bring it up to date.

*The Local Government Commissions.* The Local Government Act, 1958, made provision for the establishment of two Local

Government Commissions, one for England and one for Wales, with the duties of reviewing the organization of local government and of making proposals 'for effecting changes desirable in the interests of effective and convenient local government'.

Certain 'special review areas' are defined in the Act. These are the large conurbations of Tyneside, West Yorkshire, South-East Lancashire, Merseyside, and the West Midlands. The 'metropolitan area' (as defined in the Act) of Greater London is excluded because for that area a separate Royal Commission had already been set up to consider the organization of local government.

In the 'special review areas' a Local Government Commission has two sets of powers: (i) It may make proposals for the alteration of the areas of counties or county boroughs, their division or amalgamation or abolition, the conversion of a non-county borough into a county borough, and vice versa, and the conversion of an urban district into a county borough.[1] (ii) In addition, in these areas the Commission may make proposals for the alteration of areas of county districts, including non-county boroughs, for the amalgamation or division of county districts, and for the conversion of an urban district into a rural district and vice versa.

Outside the 'special review areas' the Commission may not make proposals relating to these latter types of case (class (ii) above), because they are among the matters which would normally be dealt with in a county review undertaken by the county council. In the 'special review areas', however, the Commission and not the county council will deal with these items.

In the 'special review areas' the Commission may also make proposals for the re-arrangement of local government functions.

In no case is any alteration of boundary between England and Wales to be made.

*Functions of the Minister.* The Local Government Commissions act under the guidance of the Minister of Housing and Local Government, who directs the order in which the reviews shall be undertaken and issues general directions. The Commissions must give public notice before commencing a review, must publish their proposals in draft and consider representations

[1] Apparently without the grant of any charter.

on them, and consult fully with the local authorities and other bodies.

The proposals of each Commission are to be reported in due course to the Minister, who may make an order to give effect to the proposals with or without modifications. The orders of the Minister must be laid before Parliament together with the report of the Commission. The Minister may himself initiate changes without any proposals being put forward by a Commission, and may direct a Commission to undertake a county review instead of the appropriate county council. The Minister's orders may modify existing borough charters.

The establishment of these Commissions has not taken away the right of any urban or rural district council to petition for a Royal Charter, nor has it taken away the right of county councils and county borough councils to seek permission from the Minister (as indicated in part I of this chapter) for the alteration of areas and status of authorities; nor does it alter the obligation of a county council to make a county review.

County reviews may, however, be made only at a time when the county council or the Minister deems it to be opportune —and this consideration will doubtless apply to any other proposals which any local authority may have in contemplation for alterations of area and status. To that extent the activities of a Commission will overshadow and curtail the making of independent proposals by the local authorities themselves.

*Minister's Regulations.* The Minister of Housing and Local Government has issued, for the guidance of the Commissions, the Local Government Commission Regulations, 1958 (Statutory Instrument, No. 2115) in which it is laid down that a Commission, in reviewing an area, must examine the local government in the area as a whole, and not merely in each individual unit; a Commission must have reasonable regard to future circumstances; and in considering how far the local government organization in any area under review is effective, a Commission must take into account a number of special factors. The weight to be given to these and other factors will vary from case to case. The list is set out below (in italics), and the comment now added is by way of explanation and illustration.

(*a*) *Community of interest*. The regulations do not explain this term. Apparently two seaside resorts, or a borough and its suburbs, or two adjoining industrial areas, may each be considered as having community of interest. Two areas whose public services are run in the same way and are capable of being unified, two villages or two residential areas, may also have community of interest.

A busy manufacturing town may not appear to have much in common with the surrounding agricultural belt. The interests of an urban centre and the surrounding countryside should not, however, necessarily be regarded as diverse or as complementary. A blending of urban and rural territories may in some cases be desirable—the urban area may be able to give financial support to the rural area, and obtain, in return, room for expansion of urban development.

(b) *Development or anticipated development.* This point has already been alluded to in connection with extension of county boroughs. In planning future development, it is highly convenient if interrelated areas can be controlled by one local planning authority.

(c) *Economic and industrial characteristics.* A depressed area, consisting largely of working-class property, and where the local industries do not provide more than a low standard of living for the population, is likely to demand much in the way of public services. A high-class residential area on the other hand has less need of public services, since the inhabitants can afford to dispense with many of the services, such as public education, local welfare and public gardens, which local authorities provide. A commercial area containing highly rated offices has generally a small resident population; in other words, it can produce a high rate income yet few citizens requiring social services.

(d) *Financial resources measured in relation to financial need.* Financial need depends on the extent of the public services needed in the area. The rateable value of the area as a whole is no indication of the capacity of the area to provide its necessary services; for the total rateable value may be made up of very many lowly rated properties, and the population may be high and their standard of living low. In such an area the rateable value per head will be low, as will be the rates raised per head. In a highly rated area, where the population is small, these figures will be correspondingly high. The total rateable value of both the areas may be the same. The total rateable value may, therefore, taken alone, be misleading.

The estimated product of a given rate poundage, e.g. a penny rate, is not merely a multiple of the rateable value of the area. There are losses and costs in collection. Some ratepayers default. Discounts may be allowed for prompt payment. Allowances may be made to landlords who collect the rates from their tenants. The estimated receipts from a rate should take items such as these into account.

(e) *Physical features, including suitable boundaries, means of communications, and accessibility to administrative centres and centres of business and social life.* Local government is concerned particularly with services which are administered 'on the ground', for example, roads, drainage and the erection and inspection of buildings of many kinds. The area is a cardinal factor. Administrative boundaries are invisible to the citizen. He wants his services provided in the way most suitable to him. He may prefer to patronize the most convenient park, library, swimming bath or school, irrespective of whether it is in his own local government area. He may thus get services for which he does not pay; and the local authorities may find themselves catering for citizens who are not ratepayers of the area. Local areas should be of convenient shape, without odd pockets, detached portions and deep indentations, unless these are justified by the geographical configuration of the area, or there are other special reasons for it. The county town, city hall or other administrative centre should be easily accessible to members, and be a suitable control point for the management of the public services. Accessibility to centres of business and social life is not, in itself, essential to the efficient running of local services. A local government area should, however, not be a purely artificial area devised on the basis of technical considerations alone. Local government, since it affects the citizens in many intimate ways, is closely related to his (and her) life and work. The centres of business and social life will in practice usually be those places where local government services are most needed or can be most conveniently provided, and from which they can most appropriately be administered. Moreover, those who have business in local government, either as members, officers or citizens, will find it more convenient to

227

find their town hall, shire hall, and even parish hall, in the centre which would be usually visited for business or social purposes.

(*f*) *Population—size, distribution and characteristics.* The size of the population of a local area has for many years been a major consideration. A population of 20,000 was at one time regarded as the minimum for a newly created borough.[2] A borough with a population much smaller than this may be regarded as too small for the efficient discharge of modern borough functions. The Minister's regulations state that the existence or early prospect of a population of 100,000 shall not be regarded as an indispensable requirement for the constitution of a new county borough, but the Commission shall not propose such a change for an area having, or expected to have, a smaller population unless they are satisfied that there are special circumstances which make it desirable to consider such a change in that case.

The size of the population is one factor to be considered in estimating the extent of local government services required in an area. The distribution of the population is another important factor. A compact grouping makes easier the provision of local services, a dispersed population (as in the case of 'ribbon development' or scattered groups) makes it difficult and more expensive.

Among the characteristics to be considered an important one is the economic condition of the people, their financial capacity to pay rates, and the prospective demand they will make upon the public services. A high floating population of tourists or daily workers for whose temporary requirements local services must be provided at the expense of the permanent population is another factor.

(*g*) *Record of administration by the local authorities concerned.* Obviously a bad local authority should not be perpetuated. A good local authority may deserve extension of area and powers.

(*h*) *Size and shape of the areas.* The necessity for taking into account these factors is alluded to in paragraph (*e*) above.

(*i*) *Wishes of the inhabitants.* The phrase 'wishes of the inhabitants' in the regulations is doubtless intended to mean what it

[2] This was a recommendation of the Royal Commission on Local Government, 1925 (Cmd. 2506).

says, namely, the wishes of the body of local citizens themselves, and not the wishes of the elected council. The contention that a local council should be considered to be fully representative of the inhabitants at large may in some senses be valid; in other senses it is not. For not every inhabitant votes; nor does every voter cast his vote for the councillors who get elected. Moreover, there is a tendency for a council as a body, together with its associated officials, to develop a special 'council' consciousness and view-point. And a council may at times be tempted to regard the public interest in its widest sense as being identical with the council's particular interests as an organization. A council may accordingly resist or encourage proposals to suit its own purposes without necessarily suiting the interests of the public generally.

The keen interest which councillors and officers quite properly take in the affairs of their councils has, it is said, a tendency to develop into a very strong 'vested interest'. And a council, in approaching any question of local government reform, may utilize its representative position to urge its own point of view on a matter to which the inhabitants at large are quite indifferent or on which their views as a body of citizens may be quite out of accord with those of the council.

In circumstances such as these, to accept the wishes of the council (or of the leading members who influence its policy) as the 'wishes of the inhabitants' would involve a likelihood of error. It is doubtless with such considerations in mind that the Minister's regulations were drafted.

It is always easier for any type of government to function if it has the good will and support of the governed. While it is true that public opinion can be influenced and altered, and a local civic consciousness can be created, modified and destroyed, and while it is also true that what is called local patriotism may to some extent arise from sentimental considerations which have nothing to do with efficient local government administration, it would be impolitic to ignore any strong local feeling which may be aroused when proposals are put forward for the alteration of areas and status of authorities. It would be unfortunate if the adoption of proposals created a situation in which the new local government arrangements were viewed with disfavour, or even contempt, by the citizens for whose service those arrangements had been specially devised. When local group consciousness and local administration are in alliance, local government becomes healthy and well-accepted, and a strong influence towards social order and social improvement. If this alliance is destroyed or hindered, local government suffers. Tradition, social habit, and popular sentiment can be a great nuisance to the innovator. If he can get them on his side, his arm is much strengthened.

*County boroughs and conurbations.* The regulations further require a Commission, when proposing the creation or extension of a county borough, to have regard not only to the circumstances of the proposed borough area, but also the circumstances of the remaining parts of the county affected; and the question must also be considered whether any present or future adjoining town areas will not only form a continuation of the existing borough area, but have or will have closer and more special links with the existing borough than arise from mere proximity.

In the 'special review areas' (the great conurbations) a Commission is required to look at the suitability of the existing local government arrangements for the purposes of the area as a whole; whether in such an area county boroughs and counties should operate side by side; whether the number of authorities in the area should be reduced; whether the discharge of any function throughout the area is hampered by lack of unified or co-ordinated control (in which case the Commission may propose the establishment of a joint board or boards). A Commission must, moreover, in a 'special review area' have regard to the need for avoiding a multiplicity of autonomous local authorities.

The duties of the Commissions are accordingly not limited to the consideration of areas alone. The question of functions in relation to areas is important; for as has been seen in connection with such public services as the provision of hospitals, electricity, gas and water, the pre-existing areas have been found inappropriate, and special arrangements for these services has had to be made, and a number of services (e.g. fire brigades and town planning) formerly administered in county districts have been transferred to county councils. Each public service has apparently its own optimum area. It will always be matter for consideration how far the technical demands for special areas, with special authorities, making a complex pattern of public administration, should be acceded to at the expense of breaking down still further the ordinary pattern of local government.

*Change of name.* Any local authority can propose a change of the name of its area. The change can be effected only with the consent of a higher authority. This higher authority is, in the case of counties and boroughs, the Minister, and in the case of urban district, rural district, and parish councils, and parish meetings, is the county council.

# 16

## Conclusion

COMPARED with the national government, with its massive but simple structure of Crown, Lords and Commons, its Cabinet of Ministers and its range of government departments, the structure of local government in England and Wales may seem unduly complex. The authorities concerned are numerous and of diverse character; the areas of administration vary considerably in size, in shape, and in social and geographical characteristics, and form a confusing patchwork in which the boundaries coincide for some purposes and overlap for others.

The complexities of the structure are derived from the varied purposes which it is expected to achieve, and from the advantages and safeguards which it is intended to provide. It is not a system given or imposed by any purely logical or ideal concept. It has developed to meet human needs, susceptibilities and anxieties, as they have been seen and measured from time to time according to social, economic and political trends. The effect of these trends in recent times especially since the second world war have been so profound that the question has become pertinent whether the local government structure remains any longer suitable for modern requirements.

The appropriateness of creating local subsidiary units to assist in and supplement the activities of large-scale organizations which operate over wide territories has been well authenticated by human experience. Thus the army has its several local commands, the churches have their dioceses and parishes, and commercial concerns have their local offices and branches.

The local government system occupies in relation to the organization of the nation's public affairs a somewhat similar position. Although it can in some respects be regarded as separate from the system of national government, it is, none the less, an integral part of the administration of the country.

There are a certain number of public services, for example, the postal service, and the distribution of monetary benefits under the schemes of national insurance, national assistance and pensions, which are carried on in every locality and managed directly by the central government. In the administration of these services a high degree of uniformity is possible and necessary, both in the scales of benefits and in the rates of charge or contribution for the services provided. It is accepted, moreover, that the burden of cost of these services should be borne by the nation as a whole and not be related to local resources.

But even in the case of these particular services local organizations have been found convenient. Although there is, for instance, in the work of the Post Office a high degree of uniformity in that the forms and methods used and the rates of postage are the same everywhere in the country, and the staffing and equipment of post offices has everywhere great similarities, all of which make the whole organization suitable for central management, none the less the local conditions under which the work of the Post Office has to be carried on are extremely variable. The standard and type of service required in a great commercial city, in the countryside, in a group of scattered islands and in a large residential suburb are dissimilar. Someone somewhere must make decisions to deal with the local position. It is in practice convenient that some officer in the locality, who has knowledge of the local conditions, should be able to deal, within the general framework of the organization as a whole, with the local position. Some sort of local organization becomes almost inevitable.

Accordingly the Post Office and, for somewhat similar reasons, a number of other departments of the central government, such as the Ministry of Labour and the War Damage Commission, have regional organizations, or regional officers, with delegated functions in areas defined to suit the needs of the particular services to be performed. Although the discretion allowed to these local organizations, their answerability and the method by which they are controlled from the centre vary considerably, similar broad features are present in every case. The central body lays down general lines to be followed and limits to be observed by the local organizations which in their turn make reports and returns of action taken, appeal in necessary cases for assistance and advice from the centre, and are subject to the criticism and approval of the central body.

A similar outline is discernible in the local government system. Parliament defines the general powers of the government departments and of the local councils, allows the local authorities a certain freedom of discretion, and gives the central departments powers of supervision and control.

Whenever there are dissimilarities in the local conditions, whether due to geographical features, industrial activities, the incidence of population, the type of development (whether urban or rural), or other causes which affect the social needs of a locality, special local problems arise. The ancient historic market town, the seaside resort, the industrial and commercial area in the heart of a great city, and a residential suburb of the same city each provide vastly different conditions for the performance of local services and have widely differing needs.

In the historic market town, with its ancient memorials, its periodic sales of cattle and produce, and its residential population whose work is mainly within the area of the town itself, the street plan and the traffic requirements, the by-laws, the system of refuse collection and the other public services must be matched to the trade and amenities of the town. The historic buildings and the streets surrounding them need to be kept quiet, the market requires management and control, and the traffic arrangements should take into account the periodical influx of buyers and sellers with their goods and transport, as well as the sightseers and tourists. Moreover, the provision of schools and health services must be suited to a residential population which is more or less constant.

In a seaside resort, the regular population is generally small compared with the holiday population. Thus the school provision may be quite small, whereas the sanitary arrangements may have to be large enough to cope with an expanded seasonal holiday population. The amenities of the town must be suitably cared for and the local authority must concern itself with the protection of the foreshore, and the provision of gardens and facilities for entertainment on a scale that would be beyond the needs of the normal permanent population.

In the area forming the heart of a great commercial and

industrial city there is, as with the seaside resort, a vast difference between the normal resident population and the temporary population. The night population may number some thousands, but the day population, composed of those who come into the city on business, may number hundreds of thousands. Accordingly, the standards of street paving and lighting, and the general traffic arrangements, must be related to the enormous influx and efflux of daily travellers. Amenities such as public parks are difficult and expensive to provide in such an area, and may not be called for; since the day-time population has little occasion to make use of them. Similarly, mother and baby clinics, primary schools, and the provision of housing accommodation will be required on a scale comparatively small in relation to the wealth and importance of the area.

The residential suburbs of that city, however, will require provision for all these facilities on a scale which is probably quite the reverse. The streets need only be of a standard for light traffic, the need for parks, schools, clinics and housing will be relatively high.

The services mentioned form only a small part of the work of local government, but they illustrate the inescapable fact that localities differ very greatly in their needs in relation to public services.

In cases where the total area of national administration is small, as in the case of such states as Liechtenstein or the Vatican City, local organization need not exist. In a tiny country, the central government may have the time and intimate knowledge of every part of the country to enable every aspect of the country's affairs, legislative and administrative, national and local, to be dealt with from the centre.

Central administration of every type of governmental activity is theoretically feasible in any country, however large. It would, however, involve the danger of delays and congestion at the centre. And, what is probably most important, there would be a serious prospect that the over-centralized administration would get out of touch with local conditions and would be carried on with a lack of awareness of local problems.

The question how far the local units can and should be allowed freedom of discretion is important. In some services such as education, main roads, police and fire brigades, the maintenance of minimum national standards is desirable, and in the general activities of local authorities some safeguards should exist against default or misuse of powers. The imposition of requirements by the central government to some extent serves to apply necessary controls and prevent negligence and bad management. A negative or preventive effect is, however, not enough. A public authority should be active, not passive, its duty is to be diligent and responsive to public demands, and at times to anticipate them, to be anxious and assiduous for the public good. Moreover, the imposition of national standards will be ineffective if the local authorities have not adequate means to observe those standards. Efficiency in the public services can only be achieved if the authorities have the necessary funds. And the public good can be properly served only if the authorities show a proper sense of financial and governmental responsibility.

All these considerations are reflected in the English system of local government which provides local authorities with revenue derived both from national sources (by way of government grants) and from local sources by way of rates levied upon those persons who (broadly speaking) have power to elect the authorities by whom the rates are spent.

The rating system has its defects, not the least of which is the great disparity in some areas between the rate income and the financial needs. The payment of government grants, by way of percentage contributions towards approved expenditure, provides a useful mode of supplementing local resources and of applying, at the same time, central control, while leaving with the local authority the initiative in making proposals for the development of its services.

The system of assisting local finances by the payment of general grants and rate-deficiency grants, which are unrelated to any particular branches or items of expenditure, helps to bridge the gap between local needs and local resources without imposing on the local authorities any direct limits on their discretion. No system of government grants has, however, been yet devised which can bridge the gap completely in every case, and which at the same time is sufficiently attractive and economical for the central government to adopt and is equitable to all concerned.

Although the formulae for the fixation and distribution of rate-deficiency grants are in a number of respects arbitrary and artificial, the capability of each local authority to raise local revenue is a principal factor in the calculations. This capability forms an important element in creating and maintaining a local authority's sense of responsibility towards its elector-ratepayers.

The rating system has therefore the advantage that it provides opportunities for combining local financial responsibility with local discretion. This combination is particularly desirable in the administration of those public services, common in local government, which do not produce a revenue commensurate with the expenditure.

There are a number of public services which can be so managed as to require no financial assistance from rates or taxes—services in which the income from charges made for the service can equal or outbalance the cost of provision. Services such as public transport, entertainments, and water supply are in this class. They can, in fact, be run commercially and made to pay a profit and are often referred to as trading services.

There are other types of service which cannot be self-supporting, and which provide no income at all, or very little. Services such as education, maternity and child welfare, and the local welfare service for the disabled can hardly be made to produce an income equal to their expenditure without destroying the purpose and value of the service. Local government services of this kind are intended for the benefit of those who need them irrespective of whether the recipient of the service can afford to pay for it. Somewhat similar considerations apply to the housing service, which is provided mainly to ensure a sufficient supply of dwelling accommodation irrespective of whether the rents will be economic.

The truly governmental functions of local government, such as the licensing of places of entertainment, the inspection of weights and measures, food and drugs, town-planning and the making of by-laws, are also 'profitless' services, in that the fees or fines which arise from them are outweighed by the cost of administration.

There are other public services the expense of which is borne wholly or mainly out of public funds because no other method is suitable. Police and fire services, and the sanitary services, are in this class. The purpose of these services is largely preventive. The benefits are shared by all. The citizen can be offered no choice whether he will accept and pay for the service or dispense with it. The burning building, the insanitary premises, the commission of crime, are matters affecting others besides those whose property is immediately concerned.

The maintenance and improvement of highways is another important service highly necessary to the public welfare but which does not provide an income.

The member of a local authority administering these various services has a responsibility of a dual kind towards the public. He is responsible to them in their capacity as ratepayers who will have to contribute to the expense of the services (irrespective of what use they as individuals may make of them), and he is responsible to the public in their capacity as actual or potential users of the services (irrespective of whether they as individuals in fact make any contribution towards the cost). Here becomes apparent another advantage of the elective principle in local affairs—the representation of the consumer interest.

Representation of the consumer by means of consultative councils and committees representative of various local interests has been provided for in the statutes relating to the transfer of the gas and electricity services out of the sphere of local government into national control. These consultative bodies have power to offer advice and to make representations, but have no executive functions.

Whether these consultative bodies can be of real use (and whether the lack of them in the national hospital services is a public loss) depends upon the validity of such advice as they may give, and the respect accorded to them by the executive body concerned. They are not, as a local government authority is in respect of its own services, able to be both a channel for complaints and an effective instrument for providing a remedy.

But even when it is granted that (since local public services exist to serve the public) opportunity should be given for the expression of local public demand, is it to be assumed that the elected members of a local authority are alone qualified, or best qualified, to exercise a determining influence over the policy to be followed in running the services? In matters of technical efficiency, for instance, might not management be left entirely to technicians? Elected representatives are not the only persons with knowledge of local conditions capable of assessing local needs.

One method of obtaining local advice and assistance is provided in the National Assistance Act, 1948, under which the National Assistance Board is required to set up local advisory committees composed of persons having local knowledge and experience of matters affecting the functions of the Board.

In some foreign systems of local government the management of local services is in the hands of city managers, or county managers, who are expert professional officers, appointed by the local elected council, given a budget of expenditure and general directions as to the lines of policy to be followed, and then left to appoint their own staffs and carry on the actual administration while the elected council remains in the background. This system has been proved to be successful in Eire and the U.S.A.

These foreign systems differ from the modern practice in this country of appointing area boards for certain public services in that under the foreign systems the administration of a service is in the hands of one person, whereas in this country the area boards are composed of a number of persons. This accords with the long-standing British tradition of government by a group, a council or a committee, rather than by a single head. One-man government, even when conducted by an elected administrator, such as the Mayor of New York City (who has wide executive powers and is in some respects independent of the elected City Council), is not acceptable in the British way of life. The appointment by the central government, during the second world war, of commissioners in local areas for such purposes as air-raid precautions, housing of the homeless and other similar purposes was accepted in the special conditions of war, but was not popular and was abandoned as soon as the war ended.

The English method of administration by elected local government authorities has features which are not always present in foreign systems. In the English system the local government officer provides the technical knowledge and continuity of experience, and is not without awareness of local needs. The virtual permanence of his position and his non-political character give him a certain independence of judgment.

Although in practice it often happens that elected members of long standing acquire considerable knowledge of the services administered by their authorities, the fact remains that, speaking generally, the elected member is, in the best sense of the word, an amateur. Herein lies a certain virtue. Members of local government authorities include both men and women, drawn from diverse types, trades, professions, and social levels, with varied experience and political opinions.

The allegation is sometimes made, perhaps not without justification, that administration by experts alone has a tendency to become unrealistic, unenterprising, impersonal, 'bureaucratic' and influenced solely by technical considerations. Against such a danger as this the presence of the inexpert member is capable of introducing a safeguard and a corrective. He brings to the administration his common sense, a variety of opinion, and the point of view of the ordinary citizen. The expert may be prone to disregard any criticism or suggestion made by members of the lay public, regarding them as uninformed and unqualified to express opinion. He may feel entitled to rely exclusively upon his own judgment. But in the local government structure the expert local government officer, although he may have a valid answer to all criticism, cannot ignore criticism if his elected members press it upon him; for he is their servant, directly controllable by them, and must give to them as plain men an answer which is intelligible to them.

A major problem in any system of local government is that of areas. The determination of areas is governed by many factors among which local history and tradition have, in the English system, been particularly influential. The ancient units of the county, the borough and the parish have persisted for centuries, and have been adapted for many modern purposes, not always with success.

Among the most important influences which have had effect upon local government areas are the technical developments in public services.

Before the advent of heavy motor traffic, road administration was entirely in the hands of local authorities. The development of motor transport and the corresponding demand for specially large main roads—the trunk roads—for fast long-distance traffic imposed a burden of expense upon the local authorities which they felt to be inequitable because those roads served a relatively slight local need. The trunk roads in fact served a national purpose. The responsibility for these roads was accordingly assumed by the central government. It was the technical development in motor transport and in road construction which promoted and necessitated this transfer from local to the larger national sphere of control.

Similarly, advances in the technique of education and medical treatment have led to the adoption of wider areas of administration. For the purposes of primary education alone a comparatively small area was for a long time found to be suitable enough. But when primary education had to be integrated more closely with secondary and technical education wider areas were adopted. For the provision of a polytechnic or a series of colleges for special trades the area must necessarily be wider than that of the small town. Accordingly, the education service in which urban district and non-county borough councils formerly had a substantial share, is now subject to the general administration of the county councils and the councils of the county boroughs.

In the field of hospital services the impact of technical advance has also been felt. There are general hospitals for the ordinary type of patient, other hospitals for infectious diseases, and special hospitals with equipment for dealing with certain unusual types of case. In the nineteenth century one hospital could do the whole; medical science had not then sufficiently advanced to make possible or desirable the setting up of special hospitals for special cases.

The modern progress in medical science and the development of specialized forms of treatment were prominent among the influences which led to the widening of the areas for the administration of hospital services so as to make possible the economical and efficient grouping of the various types of medical units.

The technical advances in electricity supply and transmission, in water engineering, in the gas industry and in the development of public transport systems have made the traditional areas of local government out-of-date for the administration of public utility services.

In addition to the technical achievements in the provision of services, improvements in communications and transport have made it possible for public administration to be carried on over areas wider than would have been convenient before the invention of the motor car and the telephone. Motor coaches bring children to school from distant places; councillors and officials find it easier than in the nineteenth century to journey to and from the administrative offices and to tour and inspect their areas.

The improvement in public services and facilities has also led to a general desire that the benefit of modern public services, together with the cost of them, should be shared more equally throughout the country.

As a result of these influences, areas of administration have for a number of services been widened either by the transfer of functions from county district to county administration, or by schemes of nationalization. The pattern of local areas has in consequence become more complex and the principle of administration by locally elected bodies has, in relation to the nationalized services, been abandoned. The areas for those services do not coincide either with each other or with any local government area. Direct control by the local electorate could only be applied by setting up elected bodies for each service. This would have been a reversion to the state of affairs of the late nineteenth century when separate elected bodies for different services existed, and the citizen, confused by the numerous elections, lost interest.

The local government system can serve, however, to minister to other social requirements than the administration of public services. The existence of locally elected bodies provides an outlet for the desire, strong in the British people, for self-government, and provides a training ground for those who would practise the art of governing their fellow citizens. It can also furnish a pivot for local civic interest, can embody the community spirit, and foster, through historical associations, a sense of social organization. It can provide a channel for public sentiment and the opportunity for the organizing of public action at times of celebration, emergency or distress.

The local government council, representative of the public, can in this regard meet a social need which it would be entirely inappropriate for the purely functional area boards and consultative councils to attempt to meet.

From this review of the general features of the local government system in England and Wales it will be appreciated that the system offers advantages which may not always be obtained by other methods of administering local services.

The system, besides relieving the national government of much that would otherwise overburden a central administration, allows, by the variety of authorities and of local functions, the opportunity of adjusting public services to the peculiar needs of each locality; it combines freedom of local discretion with local responsibility and with central control; it provides, through the elective principle, means whereby those who make use of local services (the consumers) and those who contribute locally towards the cost of services (the ratepayers) can effectively voice their demands; it allows expert technical capacity and common-sense opinion to be allied with and tempered by each other; it gains strength from its traditional associations and can bring governmental functions into association with local patriotism and social self-expression.

The fact that the local government system cannot always be conveniently made use of for the provision of particular public services, due to the unsuitability of its areas and to the difficulty of equating local resources with local needs, does not diminish those advantages in relation to such services as can properly be provided within the system.

What is desirable is that those advantages, or their equivalent, should, where possible, be obtained in other systems of local administration.

The existence of numerous local bodies of various types, all engaged in providing for the needs of the citizen, raises the problem of co-ordination between the activities of the different authorities.

Over the general activities of local authorities the Ministry of Housing and Local Government has powers of supervision, but in respect of certain services other departments exercise central control. Thus the Home Office is concerned with police and fire services, the Ministry of Transport with highways and bridges, and the Ministry of Education with the education service. Co-ordination at ministerial level on matters of the highest policy affecting more than one department is provided by the Cabinet which settles the general lines of government policy. The need for co-ordination at departmental level between the various Ministries concerned with daily affairs of local government has long been appreciated; it is in practice obtained by voluntary liaison, mutual consultation and meetings of officers.

At a still lower level, in the actual field of local affairs, in the regions and in the overlapping areas within which local services are provided, it is desirable that some means of harmonizing the activities of the various bodies should exist.

In some foreign countries the central government appoints, in each appropriate local area, an official representative, who has the duty of supervising the local bodies so as to ensure that their activities are harmonized in consonance with general government policy. The adoption of this practice in England and Wales would (to judge from the experience of the appointment of war-time commissioners) not be acceptable.

Before the nationalization of hospitals and public utility services, one suggestion that was frequently made was that multipurpose regional bodies should be created, either by direct election or by other means. The intention was that these regional bodies, or regional parliaments, should operate certain large-scale services, and co-ordinate the operation of other public services.

Had the attempt been made to bring these regional bodies into existence, difficulties in delimiting the areas of the regions would doubtless have been encountered; for, as has in fact been found, the area best suited for the regional operation of one service is by no means co-incident with that appropriate for any other service. The introduction of regional bodies would have imposed a third tier in the urban county districts, and a fourth tier in the rural districts to the existing structure of local government, unless some reduction in the types of local authority had also been made. Although much canvassed, the suggestion for these multi-purpose regional authorities gained little practical support, largely because of the opposition of the existing local authorities who saw in the suggestion a threat to their status, powers and existence.

One advantage of these regional bodies would have been that co-ordination of the large-scale services operated by them could have been obtained (as is the case with existing local government authorities) within the domestic organization of the authority itself, its committees and departments.

Co-ordination between the various boards and other local bodies whose services are in practice brought into inter-relation can doubtless be secured by voluntary co-operation, by consultation between officers and members of the various bodies, or perhaps by the appointment of representative co-ordinating committees.

It is obvious that a co-ordinating agency which has no executive powers of enforcement can function effectively only with the good-will of the authorities concerned. Moreover, a co-ordinating body that is not elected by the people might lack the stimulus from local opinion which the elective principle can provide.

This illustrates the difficulty (well known to those engaged in local government) of devising an ideal system which will have the advantages of all systems. Co-ordination is but one important element in general efficiency. How best to achieve efficiency is a question that can never be permanently answered; for technical developments and social and other changes will continually alter the considerations to be taken into account.

Although the democratic system of administration is well established in this country, the assumption should not be made as a matter of course that an elected body is the only type of body that can serve the public well. What is essential in any public authority is that it should operate with a sensitive anxiety for the public welfare. The presence of this quality depends primarily on the personality of the individual members and officers. The problem in creating a public body is to provide means whereby this essential quality shall not be stifled, but shall be encouraged and expressed.

The democratic system provides for the interplay of opinion, and provides the citizen with the opportunity of sharing in his own government. The system implies that the citizen will accept the duty of expressing his opinion. If public opinion is not expressed; if the citizen does not take sufficient interest in public matters, and neglects to vote, an election becomes a formality or a farce, and the public body may become self-sufficient, moribund or corrupt. The citizen must not only take an interest and record his vote; the interest he takes and the opinions he, as his own self-governor, expresses should be informed and responsible.

If both elector and representative fail to maintain a responsible and responsive relationship between each other, the value of democracy is lost. This relationship need not, however, be displayed in democracy alone. Other systems of administration may allow for it.

The modern development of what is called 'public relations' is therefore to be welcomed, not as a means of providing public bodies with opportunity for self-advertisement, but as a method by which a public body can explain itself to the citizen and seek his confidence and understanding, and can, at the same time, ascertain public opinion in relation to the services which the body provides.

Local government, public administration, and the management of public services are not ends in themselves; they have one ultimate purpose in common, the highest welfare of the people. Those engaged in public service, however important their positions or however obscure, must, to do their duty, keep this constantly in mind.

# Index

# Index

249